D0984030

BAIL REFORM IN AMERICA

BAIL REFORM
IN AMERICA

WAYNE H. THOMAS, JR.

Foreword by Floyd Feeney

UNIVERSITY OF CALIFORNIA PRESS

BERKELEY   LOS ANGELES   LONDON

University of California Press
Berkeley and Los Angeles, California
University of California Press, Ltd.
London, England
Copyright © 1976 by
The Regents of the University of California
ISBN O-520-03131-8
Library of Congress Catalog Card Number: 75-27936
Printed in the United States of America

CONTENTS

LIST OF TABLES

FOREWORD

JAIL. The very name is used to strike fear in the minds of children. And the reality is at least as bad as the thought. Not just for murderers and robbers, but for thousands of others who have done nothing more serious than argue or fight a little too vigorously with their wives or friends or succumb to a moment's temptation to take something that did not belong to them. Or maybe they have done nothing at all. One does not have to be guilty of anything to land in jail. Only to be accused.

You step out of the patrol car into the light of a busy but sterile room. You are ordered here, then there. Your clothes may be taken and the innermost parts of your body subjected to searching hands. Despite the people all around, there is no one to talk to or to tell you what is going to happen next.

Then, as quickly as you came in, you go out. The door clangs to, and you are alone. Or crowded into a tiny room full of foul-smelling strangers who are at best not friendly and at worst physically or sexually threatening. Either way you feel helpless, ashamed, and afraid. Even if you've been there before, the fear may be overpowering. You don't know what's going to happen—to you, to your family, or to your job. Maybe if you had a dime, were able to collect your thoughts together enough, and the right people were home, you were able to use your one phone call to tell someone that you are in jail and to please come get you out. Maybe if you're lucky, they will. If they care enough and either they or you have enough money to pay for a bail bond. If you are poor, however, you don't get out.

That is the way it was in 1961 when New York businessman Louis Schweitzer visited the Brooklyn House of Detention. That is the way it still is today in far too many places and for far too many defendants.

For many other defendants, however, Louis Schweitzer's

visit proved to be a very significant event. For Louis Schweitzer was not of the view that everything was somebody else's business and that individual citizens lacked the power to change things. More than judges, lawyers, policemen, jailors, defendants, anybody, he believed that, when the Constitution said that a person was innocent until proven guilty, the system owed that person no less than to treat him as if he were innocent until he was proven guilty.

With his own money and a lot of encouragement from a far-seeing judge, he hired a young social worker named Herbert Sturz and began to attack the problem. The result was the Manhattan Bail Project, and the beginning of one of the most revolutionary periods in the annals of American criminal justice. Within a short while Schweitzer and Sturz had not only brought the problem of bail and the poor defendant who could not afford bail to the attention of the public but had also developed impressive new ways of doing something about the problem. Through an imaginative experiment they adapted the release on one's own promise to appear to widespread use and invented an administrative mechanism, the O.R. (own recognizance) project, to make that use a reality.

The excitement and the hope for change they brought into the system was a force so potent and so needed that it soon spilled out of New York and across the land. While the movement thus started has had its downs as well as its ups since then, it has changed the face of American justice and continues to do so today.

This book is a chronicling of the history of this movement and an attempt to measure its effects in some quantitative way. It traces the development of release on own recognizance programs to cities other than New York, the passage of the Federal Bail Reform Act and other legislative reforms, the eruption of the controversy over preventive detention, and the transformations that have taken place as the ideas involved have moved from a position at the forward edge of reform toward that of a more established view.

Even more importantly, the book succeeds in measuring the effects of all this effort, showing that the bail reform movement has been a huge success and that a much greater percentage of defendants is now released prior to trial than before.

It also shows how far there still is to go. The old French saying that "the more things change the more they are the same" was never more true than in the bail system. Things have changed tremendously. But in addition to the many defendants still held under very high bail or some other kind of preventive detention because they are feared to be dangerous, literally thousands of largely harmless defendants continue to remain in jail prior to trial because the changes have not reached them. How the reforms can be extended to these defendants and how the system should now evolve remain major unanswered questions.

As one solution, the book suggests what nearly every current observer of the bail scene already knows: At a minimum, the present system of commercial surety bail should be simply and totally abolished. Whatever it may have accomplished in the past, it is now an anachronism. It is not so much that bondsmen are evil—although they sometimes are—but rather that they serve no useful purpose. The only benefit which they seriously claim to confer—that of catching persons who jump bail—is largely illusory. In reality, bail jumpers are far more often caught by the police than by the bailbondsman, and society's reliance on a private bounty system for such a serious purpose seems unwarranted in any event. Commercial bonds in fact protect neither the state nor the defendant. They do, however, exact a heavy economic toll on one of the country's most deprived populations.

This does not necessarily mean that all money bail should be ended. That, as the book shows, is a more complicated question. To the extent that money bail is necessary or desirable, however, the Illinois, Oregon and Kentucky systems, which operate successfully without commercial bondsmen and which have the enormous advantage of returning all or the majority of the bond amount to the defendant who appears in court, are far superior to the commercial bond system which returns nothing to the defendant even if he appears.

The book also documents the need to integrate and refine the topsy-turvy systems of pretrial release that have grown up in the course of the reform movement, arguing basically for earlier and more automatic methods of dealing with the problems involved. In such a system the police would exercise much greater responsibility for the initial release decision. In addition, if there was any delay at all in appearing before a magistrate, the bail amount would be established by a preset schedule so that the defendant could seek to meet it immediately rather than having to wait for appearance in court. O.R. projects, with their apparatus of interviews and checks, would be brought into play only as a system monitor and for cases left in custody by the other cheaper, faster methods of release.

The book does not offer answers to every pretrial release problem. In particular, the question of the dangerous defendant is left unresolved. While the Nixon act authorizing the preventive detention of dangerous defendants in the District of Columbia is subject to serious constitutional challenge, has been used sparingly, and is not widely emulated, many defendants throughout the country remain incarcerated as a result of high bail amounts that are only thinly disguised versions of the same urge. In this situation the author clearly favors liberal release, but also recognizes the problems involved—including the lack of any clear resolution of the legal issues by the courts and the failure thus far to solve the problem of crime on pretrial release.

While not attempting to resolve all bail questions, the book clearly adds importantly to our knowledge of both the bail reform movement and the ways in which change is brought about. This latter is particularly interesting. Whether one favors the changes which have occurred or not, one can hardly fail to be impressed with the tall oaks that have grown from the acorns sown by Schweitzer and Sturz.

Written by a lawyer and a law teacher who has seen and been involved at first hand in many of the problems and programs about which he writes, the book is an ambitious

undertaking. It involves the all too rare attempt to measure the effects of legal developments quantitatively as well
as by opinion evidence. As in all such studies, the data
generated raise as well as answer questions. The contribution the book makes is substantial, however, and should
enable future thinking and action in this important area to
go forward on a much surer footing.

FLOYD FEENEY

Davis, California

ACKNOWLEDGMENTS

THE IDEA of writing the story of bail reform in America—how it progressed and what it has accomplished—originated with Floyd Feeney, Executive Director of the Center on Administration of Criminal Justice at the School of Law of the University of California at Davis, and a Professor of Law at that school. Floyd was actively involved in every phase of this book from the selection of cities and methodology for the National Bail Study to long hours of extensive editing of the final manuscript. His influence on this book as well as on the author is extensive, and both are considerably better for it.

Also involved in the early planning of this book were Edward L. Barrett, Jr., and Lloyd Musolf, Co-Directors of the Center on Administration of Criminal Justice, and Roger Baron, a criminal justice consultant on the Center's staff. Roger, formerly with the Vera Institute of Justice and an early director of the Manhattan Bail Project, provided considerable information on the early years of O.R. projects and helped arrange the first series of program site visits in 1970.

This book was financed by the Center on Administration of Criminal Justice through a grant from the Ford Foundation.

One of the rewards in writing this book has been the number of interesting and talented people whom I met and who have since become close friends. The most important has been Barry Mahoney of the National Center for State Courts. In making the long step from first draft to final manuscript over the past year, Barry has contributed immensely with pertinent editorial suggestions. I am also indebted to Bruce Beaudin, Director of the D.C. Bail Agency, and Tony Partridge of the Federal Judicial Center, who edited early drafts and offered their suggestions.

To the people in the field—the pretrial release program

directors—who took the time to meet and discuss bail reform, I am particularly indebted. The progress that has been made in bail reform is due in large part to these persons who have accepted the responsibility to make tough and sometimes controversial decisions concerning pretrial release. In particular, I would like to acknowledge the contributions of the following directors: Bruce Beaudin, Washington D.C.; Dewaine Gedney, Philadelphia; Dick Scherman, Minneapolis; Ken Babb, San Francisco; Ron Obert, San Jose; Jim Toomey, Los Angeles; Susan Bookman, Berkeley; and Jim Droege, Indianapolis. I would also like to acknowledge the contributions of Judge Peter Bakakos of the Circuit Court of Cook County, who provided considerable data and personal insight on the operation of the deposit bail system in that state, and Judge Richard F. X. Hayden of the Los Angeles County Superior Court, who also reviewed drafts of this book and offered numerous welcomed suggestions in meetings with me.

Two major figures in the early years of bail reform, Herbert Sturz, Director of the Vera Institute of Justice, and Professor Dan Freed of Yale University Law School, reviewed early drafts of this book and gave me their personal observations. The contributions of these two men to the bail reform effort are unequaled.

In the National Bail Study we attempted to do something which had not been tried before—the collection of comprehensive, standardized data on the processing of criminal cases in twenty jurisdictions throughout the country. Literally scores of persons were involved in this effort. To the clerks and assistant clerks of courts who provided us access to court records and assistance in interpreting them, I am gratefully indebted. To the forty law students— now lawyers—who so diligently and accurately collected the data, a special thank you.

Kevin Corrington assisted me in supervising the data collection efforts in the various jurisdictions, and I am grateful to him. Coding of the data for computer analysis was done by law students at the University of California at Davis and Judy Campos and Tom Greene deserve special recognition for doing the bulk of this work. Mike Spedick of the Center on Administration of Criminal Justice handled all of the computer programming for the National Bail Study.

Lainda Boosembark has for the past two years typed and retyped draft after draft of this book. It is a pleasure to recognize her contribution and tell her it's finally done.

Finally, a special thank you to my wife, Meta, who persevered through my several long road trips and long nights of writing and editing. She was an invaluable source of support, encouragement and ideas. While I managed to be home for the birth of two sons during the course of this study, the task of raising the boys has fallen unfairly to her. To Meta, Roger, and Mark, I dedicate this book.

WAYNE H. THOMAS, JR.

Davis, California
April, 1976

PART I

Beginnings of Bail Reform

1

The Bail Reform Movement

FEW legal practices comport more closely with the American legal principles of equal justice and innocence until proven guilty than that of releasing a criminal defendant on his own recognizance, his personal promise to appear. The plethora of material written on the subject attests to the extreme interest in bail reform in the United States during the decade of the 1960s. It was fifteen years ago, in October of 1961, that the Vera Foundation, now the Vera Institute of Justice, launched a three-year pretrial release experiment called the Manhattan Bail Project. The success of this New York City experiment and the reaction it generated were truly overwhelming. Indeed, the response was so great that within three years, before the Manhattan experiment had even run its course, a national conference was held on the problem of bail and criminal justice. The interim report of this May 1964 conference, which was cosponsored by the Department of Justice, under the leadership of Attorney General Robert F. Kennedy, and the Vera Foundation, was able to boast that, "In sheer volume, probably never before in our legal history has so substantial a movement for reform in the law taken place in so short a time."[1]

In the fall of 1960 criminal justice was not a topic of major national concern. The Supreme Court had yet to begin issuing the series of landmark decisions that were to revolutionalize criminal law before the decade was out.

1. *National Conference on Bail and Criminal Jusice* (Washington, D.C.: U.S. Department of Justice and the Vera Foundation, Inc., April, 1975), p. xxv.

Poverty law was virtually unheard of, and the plight of the indigent accused was far from the national mind. Nonetheless, Louis Schweitzer, a wealthy New York chemical industrialist, agreed to visit the Brooklyn House of Detention, one of the city's largest jails, when he was invited to do so by a friend. "Appalled" by the many youthful defendants in jail pending trial because they could not afford bail, Schweitzer, "who had never been in a criminal court, and hardly knew anybody who had," recognized a fact to which those in the jail every day had become immune: "The youngsters were treated like already convicted criminals, despite our treasured principle that people are presumed innocent until proven guilty."[2]

Learning later that most of the detainees "were eventually given suspended sentences or acquitted—after an average wait in jail of more than a month,"[3] Schweitzer decided to do something about the problem. With $25,000 of his own money, he created the Vera Foundation with the mission of assisting the defendants who were too poor to post bail. Herbert Sturz, a young social worker, was selected as director of the Foundation and began to work on the problem.

Within six months the Manhattan Bail Project was launched. The idea behind the project proved as powerful in practice as it was simple in concept. The project was to provide information to the court about the defendant's ties to the community and thereby hope that the court would release the defendant without requiring a bail bond. In the words of Sturz:

Months of study preceded our first day in court. Our early thought was to provide a revolving bail fund which would be available to indigents. But helping the poor to buy their freedom is no solution; it merely perpetuates reliance upon money as the criterion for release. We wanted to break the pattern and stimulate a more basic change in bail thinking. The release of greater numbers on their own recognizance appeared the broadest and most potentially valuable approach. We decided to test

2. Don Oberdorfer, "The Bail Bond Scandal," *Saturday Evening Post,* June 20, 1964, p. 66.
3. Ibid.

the hypothesis that a greater number of defendants could be successfully released in this way if verified information about their stability and community roots could be presented in court. This was the goal of Vera Foundation's first undertaking: The Manhattan Bail Project.[4]

The project achieved immediate success. Within a year over 250 defendants had been released and the project had begun to attract considerable interest. After only nine months of operation, in June of 1962, the *New York Times* deemed the project important enough to warrant strong editorial endorsement:

The bail system as practiced in New York City has been working unjustly against the poor. While the man of means can post bail in almost any amount, the poor person often finds difficulty in meeting even modest bail at the price of a bond asked by a professional bondsman. . . .

The role that poverty assumes in the administration of criminal justice in this city is being explored by the newly created Vera Foundation, which has been working with students of the New York University Law School in an experiment that questions the worth of bail in the search for justice. The experiment already shows that the incidence of defendants who are released upon recommendation of the Vera staff and then fail to show up for trial is smaller than that of those who furnish and then later "jump" bail. It is clear that many defendants could be safely released to the community on pre-trial parole, thus obviating weeks or months of corroding 'detention' while awaiting trial.[5]

Two months later the *Times* followed with a full-length feature article on the Manhattan Bail Project in its Sunday magazine section and then in November, after the project had completed its first year, praised it in a second editorial:

In the past year, a quiet experiment in human trust in Criminal Court has been gaining the respectful support of judges, district attorneys, prison officials, and, not the least, persons accused of crime. This is the Manhattan Bail Project, initiated by the Vera Foundation in cooperation with New York University Law School.[6]

4. *National Conference,* supra n. 1, p. 43.
5. *New York Times,* June 19, 1962, p. 34.
6. *New York Times,* November 21, 1962, p. 32.

With over 2,000 releases in just two and one-half years of operation, the project had succeeded in generating national interest in bail reform. The spread of programs modeled after the Manhattan Bail Project actually started in 1963 with the development of projects in St. Louis, Chicago, Tulsa, and Nassau County, New York.[7] In the first three months of 1964, projects were launched in Washington, D.C., Des Moines, and Los Angeles.[8]

The Manhattan Bail Project also attracted the attention of Robert Kennedy, the Attorney General of the United States. Impressed with the results which had been achieved in so short a time, Kennedy agreed to co-sponsor with Vera a national conference to consider the problem of bail on a wider scale. In May of 1964 the National Conference on Bail and Criminal Justice was convened. Addressed by both Attorney General Kennedy and Chief Justice Earl Warren, the conference was attended by over 400 judges, attorneys, law enforcement personnel, and court officials representing nearly every major jurisdiction in the country. The interest in bail reform generated by this conference led to the rapid proliferation of own recognizance release programs in the last half of 1964 and 1965 and to the convening of a second national conference in New York City in 1965. The conference also attracted the interest of several national magazines with wide general readership. The *Saturday Evening Post, Time,* and *Readers Digest* all carried articles in 1964 praising the accomplishments of the Manhattan Bail Project.

Also in 1964, on the eve of the National Bail Conference, Senator Sam J. Ervin, Jr., who had been following with close interest the progress of the Manhattan Bail Project, introduced a series of bills designed to reform bail practices in the federal courts.[9] In 1964 and 1965 the Subcommittee on Constitutional Rights of the Senate Judiciary Committee, chaired by Senator Ervin, held hearings on

7. *Bail and Summons: 1965* (New York: U.S. Department of Justice and the Vera Foundation, Inc., August, 1966), p. 8.
8. Ibid.
9. Hon. Sam J. Ervin, Jr., "The Legislative Role in Bail Reform," *George Washington Law Review,* vol. 35 (1966-67), pp. 429, 434.

these bills which eventually culminated in passage of the Federal Bail Reform Act of 1966.[10] This Act, the first major change in national bail policy since the Judiciary Act of 1789, created a presumption in favor of releasing defendants on their personal recognizance and also set forth a series of conditions that were to be used to structure pretrial release to the needs of the individual defendant. Money bail was to be used only if nonfinancial conditional release would not adequately assure the defendant's appearance in court. The Federal Bail Reform Act of 1966 led to the revision of bail laws in at least a dozen states within five years of its passage.

Earlier, in 1963, spurred by a dissatisfaction with the commercial bail system in Chicago, the state of Illinois had adopted a somewhat different approach to bail reform. Known as the Illinois Ten Percent Deposit Plan, this legislation retained the use of money bail as the predominant form of release but eliminated the commercial bail bondsman. Under this legislation, the 10 percent bonding fee that had previously been paid to the bondsman was to be paid to the court, which was now required to release the defendant on less than full bond.[11] Moreover, the fee paid to the court, unlike the fee paid to a bondsman, is refunded to the defendant upon completion of the case, less a small service fee.

The year 1964 also saw an important change in the operation of the Manhattan Bail Project and further innovation by the Vera Foundation. Having proved so remarkably successful as a demonstration program, the Manhattan Bail Project was fully institutionalized and made a part of routine court procedure through transfering the operation of the program from Vera to the New York City Office of Probation. Vera, meanwhile, had begun in the spring of 1964, in conjunction with the New York City Police Department, a program designed to release minor offenders at the police station on personal promises to appear and thereby eliminate the need for custody until arraignment. Started in a few select police

10. Bail Reform Act of 1966, 18 U.S.C. §3146 *et seq.*
11. Ill. Ann. Stats., Ch. 38 § 110-7 (1970).

precincts, the Manhattan Summons Project also achieved rapid success and was extended to all of Manhattan in 1966 and adopted throughout the entire city in 1967.

It is difficult now to reconstruct the full impact that the Manhattan Bail Project had during its first several years. The enthusiasm and excitement which it generated grew by leaps and bounds—first in New York City and later throughout the country. The project touched a nerve that ran deep. Later came poverty programs and poverty law and the expansion of criminal defense services following the *Gideon* decision.[12] In a sense the project helped to create these developments, and as they occurred, they in turn gave new life and new impetus to the bail reform movement.

Despite its impressive beginning, however, the bail reform movement waned considerably in the late 1960s. Many of the early own recognizance release programs ceased operating, and those that remained often had tenuous financial and official support.

While the problem of defendants unable to post bail largely passed from the public consciousness, the "law and order" philosophy of the Nixon administration sparked a new debate. Crime rather than poverty was its focus, and it came from those who felt that the bail reform movement had gone too far. The bail problem as they saw it was how to keep allegedly dangerous defendants in jail and off the streets. It was not surprising therefore when the Nixon administration in 1969 proposed a program of preventive detention as a major part of its legislative program against crime.

In the Senate hearings before Senator Ervin's Subcommittee on Constitutional Rights which followed, the sharply different views that had developed about bail reform emerged more clearly than ever before. Ultimately, owing to the opposition of the subcommittee, the Nixon bill was not passed in regard to the entire federal court system. Through a legislative end run in another committee, however, it was passed as to the District of Columbia and

12. *Gideon* v. *Wainwright,* 372 U.S. 335 (1963).

became law in February, 1971.[13] Thus, the bail reform movement came to the end of its first decade with something of a counterrevolution in progress.

The 1970s, however, brought a new impetus to the movement. A number of factors combined to bring about this reawakening. The availability of federal funds through Law Enforcement Assistance Administration grants enabled a number of new programs to start and also provided additional monies to existing programs.[14] The interchange of information among the bail programs and a national concern for the status of the programs which Vera had provided in the early 1960s was reasserted in 1972 with the formation of the National Association of Pretrial Services Agencies.[15] National scope research studies in 1973 by the Office of Planning, Research and Evaluation of the U.S. Office of Economic Opportunity[16] and in 1975 by the National Center for State Courts[17] also served to heighten interest in the current status and future of pretrial release programs.

The bail reform movement of the 1970s is, however, considerably different from the movement of the 1960s. While the dominant concern of the 1960s was with own

13. District of Columbia Court Reform and Criminal Procedure Act of 1970, Pub. L. No. 91-358, 84 Stat. 473.

14. A 1973 national study of pretrial release programs by the Office of Economic Opportunity reported that over half of the responding programs had started in the 1970s, and that of these forty-six programs, twenty-four were funded primarily by LEAA and that others received partial support from this source. Hank Goldman, Devra Bloom, and Carolyn Worrell, *The Pretrial Release Program* (Washington, D.C.: Office of Economic Opportunity, Office of Planning, Research and Evaluation, 1973) pp. 9-10.

15. The directors of pretrial release programs in Philadelphia, Washington, D.C., and San Francisco organized a national conference of pretrial release program directors in May of 1972 in San Francisco. The organization created at this conference, the National Association of Pretrial Services Agencies, has held annual meetings in each of the succeeding years.

16. Goldman et al., supra n. 14.

17. National Center for State Courts, *An Evaluation of Policy Related Research on the Effectiveness of Pretrial Release Programs* (Denver, Colo.: National Center for State Courts, August, 1975).

recognizance release, the movement today is largely focused upon conditional releases, 10 percent deposit bail plans, and police citation releases. While the seeds of each of these forms of release were planted in legislation adopted in the 1960s, it was not until the 1970s that they attracted widespread national attention. Preventive detention also remains an important question for the movement of the 1970s.

This book is an analysis of the bail reform movement from the Manhattan Bail Project to the present day. It seeks to describe the process by which the bail reform movement progressed, to show how its early reported successes held up over the period of a decade, and to make some suggestions as to the future. Because the issues which touched Louis Schweitzer go to the heart of society and the criminal justice system, it should not be surprising that the drama involved is not yet complete and that this report must of necessity be a partial one.

2

The American System of Bail

THE American system of bail allows a person arrested for a criminal offense the right to purchase his release pending trial. Those who can afford the price are released; those who cannot remain in jail. Innocence, the likelihood that the person will appear at trial, reputation in the community—all are essentially irrelevant. Money is the key to the jail, and it is the bondsman who owns the key.

The American system of bail is derived from practices that originated in medieval England when magistrates traveled from county to county and were often present in a particular locality for only a few months each year. In order to prevent prolonged detention in the primitive jails, defendants were released by the sheriff into the custody of a friend or neighbor who was responsible for assuring that the defendant would return at the appropriate time. Initially, if the defendant absconded, the third party custodian was required to surrender himself in the defendant's place. In time, however, the system evolved to permit the custodian to forfeit a promised sum of money if the defendant failed to appear.

The system operating in the United States today is vastly different. Most bonds are posted by commercial bondsmen who have never previously met the defendant and who perform their service solely for the fee involved, normally 10 percent of the bond amount. This change from a personal to a commercial system of pretrial release apparently came about early in the annals of American justice. There were several reasons for the adoption of a commercial bail system in early America. First, unlike English

11

law, the Judiciary Act of 1789 and the constitutions of most states provided for an absolute right to have bail set except in capital cases. Second, the absence of close friends and neighbors in frontier America would have made it very difficult for the court to find an acceptable personal custodian for many defendants, and, third, the vast unsettled American frontier provided a ready sanctuary for any defendant wanting to flee. Commercial bonds, never permitted in England, were thus a useful device in America.

Bail is the mechanism by which the defendant's right to freedom prior to trial is squared with society's interest in the smooth administration of criminal justice. The traditional practice of routinely conditioning pretrial release upon the posting of bail rests on an assumption that this money, subject to forfeiture if the defendant absconds, will serve to ensure his appearance in court. The belief is that the defendant will be motivated to appear as required and not risk forfeiture of the money which has been posted. Reasoning that the likelihood of a defendant failing to appear increases with the severity of the charge and the consequent sentence which can be imposed upon conviction, judges generally increase the amount of bail in relation to the seriousness of the alleged charges. The single most important factor in the setting of bail is therefore the alleged present offense.

The flaw in this logic, however, is its failure to take account of the fact that in most instances the bond to ensure the defendant's appearance is posted not by the defendant but by a commercial bondsman. The fee that a defendant pays to a bondsman to post the bond in his case is never returned to the defendant regardless of whether he appears or not or whether he is convicted or acquitted. The risk of the bond forfeiture is therefore on the bondsman and not the defendant. The real risk placed on the defendant for failure to appear is the collateral requirements imposed by the bondsman. If the bondsman requires no collateral, there is no pecuniary risk for the defendant regardless of the amount of bond that has been set by the court. This system undermines the whole purpose of bail:

It is frequently urged that eligibility for release and the amount of the bond are intimately related, because the higher the bail the less 'likelihood (there is) of appellant fleeing or going into hiding.' This argument presupposes that an appellant with higher bail has a more substantial stake and therefore a greater incentive not to flee. This may be true if no professional bondsman is involved. But if one is, it is he and not the court who determines appellant's real stake. Under present practice the bondsman ordinarily makes the decision whether or not to require collateral for the bond. If he does, then appellant's stake may be related to the amount of the bond. If he does not, then appellant has no real financial stake in complying with the conditions of the bond, regardless of the amount, since the fee paid for the bond is not refundable under any circumstances. Hence the court does not decide—or even know—whether a higher bond for a particular applicant means that he has a greater stake.[1]

Even more serious than the irrationality of the American system of surety bail are the inequities which flow from such a system. Concern for the American system of bail dates back at least fifty years. Arthur L. Beeley in 1927 published his landmark study *The Bail System in Chicago* which publicized the inequities of the bail system and explored the possibility of using alternatives to surety bail to effectuate pretrial release.[2] Based on his study of the records of the Municipal and Criminal Court of Cook County, Beeley found that bail amounts were based soley on the alleged offense and that about 20 percent of the defendants were unable to post bail. He also noted that professional bondsmen played too important a role in the administration of the criminal justice system and reported a number of abuses by bondsmen, including their failure to pay off on forfeited bonds. Beeley concluded that "in

1. *Pannell* v. *United States,* 320 F. 2d 698, 701-702 (D.C. Cir., 1963) (concurring opinion of Bazelon, Chief Judge).
2. Arthur L. Beeley, *The Bail System in Chicago* (Chicago: University of Chicago Press, 1927; reprinted 1966).

too many instances, the present system . . . neither guarantees security to society nor safeguards the right of the accused." It is "lax with those with whom it should be stringent and stringent with those with whom it could safely be less severe." Among Beeley's recommendations were a greater use of summons to avoid unnecessary arrests and the inauguration of fact-finding investigations so that bail determinations could be tailored to the individual.

Little happened as a result of the Beeley study, but his ideas remained as a beacon for later workers in the field. Among the most important of these were Professor Caleb Foote and a group of University of Pennsylvania law students who investigated the administration of bail in Philadelphia in 1954.[3] Their study showed that in minor offenses bail was generally based solely on police evidence, and that in serious cases bail recommendations by the District Attorney were followed 95 percent of the time. Foote estimated that 75 percent of the defendants charged with serious crimes were never released prior to trial and noted that the city's jail system was severely overcrowded with pretrial detainees. This was also the first study which documented the tremendous discrepancy in disposition and sentencing of bailed versus jailed defendants. Foote found that only 18 percent of the jailed sample were not convicted, compared with 48 percent of the bailed sample, and that jailed defendants who were convicted received prison terms over two and one-half times as often as those who had been free.

In 1957 another group of students under Professor Foote's guidance undertook a study of the administration of bail in New York City.[4] As in the earlier two studies, the results in New York indicated that the nature of the alleged offense, more than any other factor, determined

3. Caleb Foote, "Compelling Appearance in Court: Administration of Bail in Philadelphia," *University of Pennsylvania Law Review,* vol. 102 (1954), pp. 1031-1079.
4. John W. Roberts and James S. Palermo, "The Administration of Bail in New York City," *University of Pennsylvania Law Review,* vol. 106 (1958), pp. 693-730.

the amount of bail which was set. Not surprisingly, the study showed that as the amount of bail increased, the ability of the defendants to post bail decreased. The study also showed, however, that even bail in low amounts was beyond the reach of many defendants, but that no inquiry as to how much bail the defendant could afford was made at the time bail was set.

These studies of the administration of bail in Chicago, Philadelphia, and New York laid the foundation for the bail reform movement of the 1960s. The studies had shown the dominating role played by bondsmen in the administration of bail, the lack of any meaningful consideration to the issue of bail by the courts, and the detention of large numbers of defendants who could and should have been released but were not because bail, even in modest amounts, was beyond their means. The studies also revealed that bail was often used to "punish" defendants prior to a determination of guilt or to "protect" society from anticipated future conduct, neither of which is a permissible purpose of bail; that defendants detained prior to trial often spent months in jail only to be acquitted or to receive a suspended sentence after conviction; and that jails were severely overcrowded with pretrial detainees housed in conditions far worse than those of convicted criminals. Commenting in a 1970 letter to Mayor John Lindsay on the harsh conditions under which pretrial detainees were housed in New York City, William vanden Heuvel, chairman of the New York City Board of Corrections, stated: "If we keep our animals in the Central Park Zoo in the same way we cage fellow human beings in the Tombs and other city detention institutions, a citizen's committee would be organized and prominent community leaders would be protesting the inhumanity of our society."[5] The need for reform was obvious.

The activities of bail bondsmen themselves were an equally compelling reason to seek bail reform. It is not altogether clear when the bail system began to grow

5. "Pre-Trial Detention in the New York City Jails," *Columbia Journal of Law and Social Problems,* vol. 7 (1971), pp. 350, 351.

corrupt. Perhaps it always was.[6] In any event, by the middle of the twentieth century, bondsmen had become a permanent and often seamy side of courtroom life. In city after city investigations by grand juries, bar associations, the press, and other local groups disclosed evidence of payoffs and corruption in the activities of commercial bail bondsmen. In the New York City area alone there were four full-scale grand jury investigations of bondsmen between 1939 and 1960.[7]

A common finding of these investigations was the infiltration of criminals and organized crime into the bonding business. The *Indianapolis Star* disclosed in a series of articles in 1959 and 1960 several instances of this, including the fact that in Cleveland racketeers had organized a twenty-three state bail bond syndicate that wrote eight million dollars worth of bail in an eight-month period; that in a Louisiana city two racket-related characters operated a highly profitable bonding business through close alliances with police, judges, and public officials; that in a midwestern city the bail bonding business was controlled by an ex-convict with a forty-year police recrod; and that in a southern city the man running the bail bond business had been convicted for accepting bribes while in state office.[8]

Investigations of bondsmen also disclosed payoffs to policemen and court officials. In 1961 a grand jury in Jackson County, Missouri, reported that most bondsmen were quasi-partners of certain policemen. Some police, in return for steering defendants to certain bondsmen, would receive a kickback of 20 percent of the bond fee.[9] In Brooklyn a local bail bond investigation led to the removal

6. In his illuminating book on the bail bond business, Ronald Goldfarb offers a characterization of bondsmen from Charles Dickens's *Pickwick Papers:* "Curious trade . . . these men earn a livelihood by waiting about here, to perjure themselves before the judges of the land, at the rate of half-a-crown a crime!" Ronald Goldfarb, *Ransom* (New York: Harper & Row, 1965), p. 92.
7. Daniel J. Freed and Patricia M. Wald, *Bail in the United States: 1964* (Washington, D.C.: U.S. Department of Justice and the Vera Foundation, Inc., 1964), p. 34.
8. Goldfarb, supra n. 6, pp. 103-104.
9. Ibid., p. 110.

of one magistrate and twenty-eight police captains, the disciplining of a number of lieutenants and sergeants, and the conviction of others for bail bond frauds.[10] In Cincinnati it was discovered that some municipal court clerks were receiving referral kickbacks of up to 30 percent.[11] Bondsmen have also been investigated for bribing process servers to avoid immediate arrests of indicted clients.[12]

Many other instances of corruption and collusion between bondsmen and court officials, police, judges, and attorneys have been uncovered. The failure of bondsmen to pay off on forfeited bonds has been a major problem. Such a practice undermines the whole purpose of the bail bond by defeating whatever incentive the bondsman might have to fulfill his commitment to produce the defendant in court. Concern over collusion and bribery of judges and court officials which allowed bondsmen to escape payment on bonds that had been forfeited was a major factor in Illinois' decision to replace bondsmen with the innovative Ten Percent Deposit Bail Plan. It was discovered that in a three-year period from 1956 to 1959 the Municipal Court of Chicago recorded only one forfeiture payment.[13] A 1960 investigation further revealed that $300,000 in forfeitures had been set aside by one judge. Their reinstatement caused five bonding companies to go out of business.[14]

By 1960 there was ample evidence that the present system of bail was intolerable. More than this, however, the study of Beeley and the studies by Foote suggested that this system of money bail might in fact be unconstitutional, at least insofar as it involved amounts beyond the ability of a defendant to pay.[15]

The United States Constitution's only mention of bail is the Eighth Amendment's proviso that "excessive bail shall not be required." The extent to which this means that bail

10. Ibid.
11. Ibid.
12. Freed and Wald, supra n. 7, p. 34.
13. Ibid., p. 30.
14. Ibid.
15. See Caleb Foote, "The Coming Constitutional Crisis in Bail," *University of Pennsylvania Law Review,* vol. 113 (1965), p. 959.

must be set has never been definitively interpreted by the Supreme Court of the United States. Even more important, since as a practical matter bail is generally set except in death penalty cases and a few other situations, is what is meant by *excessive*. Does this term mean "more than the defendant can pay" or does it refer to "what is customary or reasonable in the situation without regard to the defendant's financial situation"? Justice William O. Douglas in 1960 discussed the problem:

> The fundamental tradition in the country is that one charged with a crime is not, in ordinary circumstances, imprisoned until after a judgment of guilt. . . . This traditional right to freedom during trial . . . has to be squared with the possibility that the defendant may flee or hide himself. Bail is the device which we have borrowed to reconcile these conflicting interests. . . . It is assumed that the threat of forfeiture of one's goods will be an effective deterrent to the temptation to break the conditions of one's release. . . .
> But this theory is based on the assumption that a defendant has property. To continue to demand a substantial bond which the defendant is unable to secure raises considerable problems for the equal administration of the law. We have held that an indigent defendant is denied equal protection of the law if he is denied an appeal on equal terms with other defendants solely because of his indigence. Can an indigent be denied freedom, where a wealthy man would not, because he does not happen to have enough property to pledge for his freedom?

He concluded:

> It would be unconstitutional to fix excessive bail to assure that a defendant will not gain his freedom. Yet in the case of an indigent defendant, the fixing of bail in even a modest amount may have the practical effect of denying him release . . .[16]

Summarizing the defects in the American system of bail, an advisory committee of the American Bar Association's Project on Minimum Standards for Criminal Justice commented:

> The bail system as it now generally exists is unsatisfactory from either the public's or the defendant's point of view. Its very

16. *Bandy* v. *United States* 7 L. Ed. 9, 11 (opinion in chambers, Justice Douglas).

nature requires the practically impossible task of translating risk of flight into dollars and cents and even its basic premise—that risk of financial loss is necessary to prevent defendants from fleeing prosecution—is itself of doubtful validity. The requirement that virtually every defendant must post bail causes discrimination against defendants who are poor and on the public which must bear the cost of their detention and frequently support their dependents on welfare. Moreover, bail is generally set in such a routinely haphazard fashion that what should be an informed, individualized decision is in fact a largely mechanical one in which the name of the charge, rather than all the facts about the defendant, dictates the amount of bail.[17]

17. American Bar Association Project on Minimum Standards for Criminal Justice, *Standards Relating to Pretrial Release* (New York: Institute of Judicial Administration, September 1968), p. 1.

3

The Bail Reform Movement:
1961–1965

THE challenge to reform the bail system was accepted by
Louis Schweitzer. The concern of Schweitzer and his
associate, Herbert Sturz, was not to replace the money bail
system but rather to eliminate the discriminatory aspects
of that system. Vera's first thought, in fact, was merely to
create a bail fund for indigent, primarily youthful offenders. This idea was forsaken, however, when it was realized
that helping the poor to buy their release would only
perpetuate the court's reliance on money. The approach
that Vera finally settled on had been suggested in the
earlier studies by Beeley and Foote. The plan that evolved
was to expand the use of personal recognizance by identifying for the court those indigent defendants, who, based
on certain established guidelines, could be safely released
without money bail. The reform effort that was generated
by the Manhattan Bail Project was not a direct challenge
to the use of money bail but rather an effort to adapt and
reform the present bail system to the needs of the poor.

The Manhattan Bail Project was designed to fit into the
existing court structure. Arrestees were interviewed by
New York University law students in holding cells in the
Manhattan Criminal Courts building prior to their arraignment. Questionnaires used by the law students were
designed to elicit information about the defendant's ties in
the New York area—with whom does the defendant live;
are there other relatives with whom he is in contact; where
does he live and how long has he lived there; is he employed or a student and, if so, where and for what length

of time—and about his prior criminal record. The information given by the defendant was then verified by contacting references by phone. Based on the verified information, a decision was made either to recommend or not recommend the defendant for "pretrial parole." (The terminology is often confusing. "Pretrial parole" meant release on one's promise to appear without any requirement of money bond. Own recognizance means the same thing.)

Initially this decision was made subjectively by the law students. However, in order to relieve the students from the pressure of making this decision and to standardize the project's policy on recommendations, a quantitative scale was quickly devised. In order to qualify for a release recommendation, a defendant needed to be a New York area resident and achieve a minimum of five points on the following scale:

Prior Record
1   No convictions.
0   One misdemeanor conviction.
-1   Two misdemeanor convictions or one felony conviction.
-2   Three or more misdemeanor or two or more felony convictions.

Family Ties
3   Lives in established family home and visits other family members. (immediate family only)
2   Lives in established family home. (immediate family)

Employment or School
3   Present job one year or more, steadily.
2   Present job four months or present and prior six months.
1   Has present job which is still available.
    OR Unemployed three months or less and nine months or more steady prior job.
    OR Unemployment Compensation OR Welfare.
3   Presently in school, attending regularly.
2   Out of school less than six months but employed or in training.
1   Out of school three months or less, unemployed and not in training.

Residence (in New York area steadily)
3   One year at present residence.

2   One year at present or last prior residence or six months at
    present residence.
1   Six months at present and last prior residence or in New
    York City five years or more.

Discretion
1   Positive, over 65, attending hospital, appeared on some
    previous case.
-1 Negative, intoxicated, intention to leave jurisdiction.

Favorable release recommendations were then presented
in court at the defendant's arraignment. The decision to
release on pretrial parole was, of course, the sole province
of the judge in each case. Vera's program, however, did
not end with the release decision. At the time of his
release, each defendant was interviewed again by Vera and
made aware of his obligation to appear as scheduled.
Follow-up procedures, including mailed reminders of court
dates, telephone calls, and even personal visits at home or
work, continued after the defendant's release.

The Manhattan Bail Project started cautiously. In the
first months, defendants were screened very closely; only
27 percent of those interviewed were favorably recommended for own recognizance release.[1] Furthermore, at
the outset, Vera excluded defendants charged with serious
felonies—homicide, forcible rape, sodomy involving a
minor, corrupting the morals of a child, carnal abuse,
narcotics offenses, and assault on a police officer—from
being interviewed.[2] During the project's first eleven
months (from October 16, 1961, to September 20, 1962),
Vera presented 363 release recommendations and 215 of
these were accepted and the defendant released by the
court.[3]

The number of releases during Vera's first year might
well have been twice this number, however, if not for a
control group experiment undertaken by the project. The
control group was created to answer a number of questions. Most importantly, Vera wanted to know what effect

1. Charles E. Ares, Anne Rankin, and Herbert Sturz, "The Manhattan
Bail Project: An Interim Report on the Use of Pre-Trial Parole," *New
York University Law Review,* vol. 38 (1963), pp. 67, 86.
2. Ibid., p. 72.
3. Ibid., p. 86.

its recommendations had on a defendant's chances of being released without bond. A law student was stationed in the court room with a chart on which each questionnaire was randomly placed in either the experimental or control group. This student would then check each recommendation which came into court to see whether it was an experimental or control case. If the case was in the control group, the recommendation was withheld; if the case was experimental, the recommendation was presented to the court. The results of the control group experiment vividly demonstrated the impact of the Vera recommendation on the defendant's chances of pretrial parole. Sixty percent of those defendants recommended by Vera secured release without bond, while only 14 percent of the defendants for whom the recommendation was withheld were similarly released.[4]

As Vera's confidence in the program grew, the Manhattan Bail Project expanded. During its first year the project eliminated most of the exclusions for serious offenses which kept many defendants from consideration. Under the new procedures only defendants charged with homicide and narcotic offenses were not interviewed. The original requirement that the defendant be indigent was also dropped. The project also expanded to include women. On May 24, 1962, 327 women were held in the Women's House of Detention; six months later the number had dropped to 194.[5]

The percentage of defendants interviewed that the project recommended for pretrial release steadily increased. While in the beginning just 27 percent of those defendants interviewed were favorably recommended for parole, by the end of the first year about 45 percent of those interviewed were being recommended.[6] By the beginning of 1964, 65 percent of those interviewed were favorably recommended.[7]

While during its first year of operation only 250 defendants were released through Vera's efforts, by the beginning of the program's third year an average of 65 defend-

4. Ibid.   5. Ibid., p. 88.   6. Ibid., pp. 86-87.
7. Daniel J. Freed and Patricia M. Wald, *Bail in the United States: 1964* (Washington, D.C.: U.S. Department of Justice and the Vera Foundation, Inc., 1964), p. 62.

ants per week were being released on pretrial parole based on its recommendations.[8] Over all, in the period from October 16, 1961, to April 8, 1964, the Manhattan Bail Project interviewed 13,000 defendants and 2,195 were paroled.[9]

Triggered by Vera's success, bail projects were created in many other communities. By 1965 programs were reported operational in the following jurisdictions:[10]

Anaheim, California
Berkeley, California
Contra Costa, California
Los Angeles, California
Oakland, California
San Francisco, California
Sunnyvale, California
Tulare County, California
West Covina, California
Denver, Colorado
District of Columbia
Duval County, Florida
Miami, Florida
Atlanta, Georgia
Chicago, Illinois
Gary, Indiana
Des Moines, Iowa
Lexington, Kentucky
Louisville, Kentucky
Baltimore, Maryland
Montgomery County,
    Maryland
Prince George County,
    Maryland
Albuquerque, New Mexico
Nassau County, New York
New York City, New York

Onondaga County, New
    York
Orange County, New York
Plattsburgh, New York
Rochester, New York
Suffolk County, New York
Syracuse, New York
Cleveland, Ohio
Toledo, Ohio
Willoughby, Ohio
Oklahoma County,
    Oklahoma
Tulsa, Oklahoma
Bucks County, Pennsylvania
Philadelphia, Pennsylvania
Pittsburgh, Pennsylvania
Westmoreland County,
    Pennsylvania
Providence, Rhode Island
Houston, Texas
Bountiful, Utah
Seattle, Washington
Boston, Massachusetts
Kalamazoo, Michigan
Lansing, Michigan
Minneapolis-St. Paul,
    Minnesota

8. Ibid., p. 63.
9. Ibid., p. 62.
10. Included in this list are all programs which were reported as being in operation at the time of the 1964 Conference on Bail and Criminal Justice or the 1965 Institute on the Operation of Pretrial Release Programs.

Kansas City, Missouri   Charleston, West Virginia
St. Louis, Missouri   Huntington, West Virginia
Madison, Wisconsin   Toronto, Canada
Milwaukee, Wisconsin   Bayamón, Puerto Rico

In addition, statewide projects were reported to be operating in the Municipal Courts of New Jersey and the Circuit Courts of Connecticut.

The procedure adopted for the release of defendants prior to trial in each of these jurisdictions was the written promise to appear. No money was required to secure such release. Although in limited use prior to the Vera experiment, written promises to appear became much more widely used as a result of the Manhattan Bail Project. The terminology varied from one jurisdiction to another, but whether it was known as own recognizance (O.R.), personal recognizance, pretrial parole, nominal bond, personal bond, or unsecured appearance bond, the result was the same. The defendant was released without posting money bail. In theory, the mechanisms differed; for example, nominal bond required the defendant to post one dollar. In practice, however, this was usually never posted. Also, unsecured appearance bonds, in theory, required the defendant to pay the full bond amount should he fail to appear, but this was rarely more than an idle threat. Likewise, most own recognizance releases involved criminal penalties for failure to appear, but these too were rarely enforced. The result was that defendants were released on their personal promises to appear, and this alone proved a sufficient guarantee of their appearance in court. Defendants released on O.R. appeared as well as or better than those on money bail. The Manhattan Bail Project reported a failure to appear rate of less than seven-tenths of 1 percent.[11]

By the mid-1960s own recognizance was recognized as a very workable solution to the most obvious inequities of the money bail system. Aside from the fact that persons released on O.R. consistently made their scheduled court appearances, the most obvious virtue of own recognizance was the ease with which it could be integrated into existing

11. Freed and Wald, supra n. 7, p. 62.

court procedures. Existing bail practices and the use of money as the criterion for release were not directly challenged. The purpose of own recognizance release programs was simply to provide the court with information so that decisions regarding bail would be more rational. Own recognizance release programs did not seek the release of all defendants as a matter of right but they did provide a mechanism for releasing the most obvious victims of the inequity of the money bail system—those who were too poor to afford modest bails set in relatively minor offenses. The momentum of the bail reform movement from 1961 to 1965 must be partly attributable to the fact that it was such a noncontroversial solution to a very serious problem.

In the rapid proliferation of O.R. projects, the bail reform movement was truly sweeping the country. Articles in law reviews, as well as in magazines and newspapers of general circulation, sparked even more interest in the subject of bail reform. Following quickly on the heels of O.R. projects was important bail reform legislation. Influenced by the success of O.R. and prodded by the need to reform a corrupt system of surety bail, the state of Illinois in 1965 totally eliminated professional bondsmen and replaced them with a court-operated system of money bail. Today a number of jurisdictions have passed or are considering deposit bail legislation. The Illinois statute and its operation are discussed fully in Chapter 16.

An even more dramatic legislative success of the bail reform movement was passage by the Congress of the United States of the Bail Reform Act of 1966.[12] This Act, applicable in all federal courts, for the first time designated personal recognizance as the preferred method of pretrial release. Judicial officers setting bail were instructed by this Act to release all defendants on personal recognizance or an unsecured appearance bond, "unless the officer determines, in the exercise of his discretion, that such a release will not reasonably assure the appearance of the person as required."[13] However, even when such a determination is made, the officer setting bail shall

12. Bail Reform Act of 1966, 18 U.S.C. § 3146 *et seq.*
13. Ibid., § 3146.

still give first priority to creating an acceptable method of nonfinancial release by imposing conditions or restrictions on the defendant's release. Only if nonfinancial conditions will not reasonably assure the appearance of the person at trial is the officer permitted to require the execution of a bail bond.[14] The Federal Bail Reform Act has since led to the revision of state bail laws to authorize the use of own recognizance,[15] and at least eighteen states have followed the federal law in creating a presumption in favor of own recognizance.[16]

14. Ibid.

15. By 1971 at least thirty-six states had enacted statutes authorizing the release of defendants on their own recognizance. John J. Murphy, "Revision of State Bail Laws," *Ohio State Law Journal,* vol. 32 (1971), pp. 451, 485.

16. The following states have created by either statute or court rule a presumption in favor of the release of defendants on their own personal recognizance: Alaska, Arizona, Connecticut, Delaware, Iowa, Maryland, Massachusetts, Minnesota, Missouri, Nebraska, New Mexico, North Dakota, Ohio, Oregon, South Carolina, Vermont, Virginia, and Wyoming.

PART II

The Results of the First Decade

4

National Bail Study

AFTER the national bail conferences of 1964 and 1965, bail reform received very little national attention. What interest there was in bail reform in the late 1960s generally focused on preventive detention legislation designed to restrict the use of pretrial releases. By 1970 efforts to expand the use of own recognizance and to create O.R. projects did not appear high on the national agenda. Apparently the tremendous accomplishments of the early 1960s and the continued favorable reports on individual bail projects led many people to believe that the bail problem had been solved.

A look at 1970 jail populations would have shown, however, that this was clearly not the case. According to the 1970 National Jail Census, as of March 15, 1970, local jails that confine inmates for forty-eight hours or more held a total of 160,863 persons. Of those incarcerated, 52 percent were awaiting trial and an additional 5 percent were awaiting further legal action such as sentencing or appeal.[1] Despite the Federal Bail Reform Act of 1966 and the efforts of the D.C. Bail Agency, in 1971 over 1,000 men were reportedly detained prior to trial in the Washington, D.C., jail, a greater number than before bail reform efforts began.[2] In New York City, where the bail

1. U.S. Department of Justice, *1970 National Jail Census* (Washington D.C.: U.S. Department of Justice, Law Enforcement Assistance Administration, 1971), p. 1.
2. Patricia M. Wald, "The Right to Bail Revisited: A Decade of Promise without Fulfillment," chap. 6 in Stuart S. Nagel (ed.), *The Rights of the Accused,* Sage Criminal Justice System Annuals, vol. 1 (Beverly Hills, Calif.: Sage Publications, 1972), p. 184.

reform movement started, riots in August of 1970 by inmates in the Tombs made it abundantly clear that the overcrowded condition had not been alleviated. An investigation by a New York City Council subcommittee estimated that 7,000 men and women were in city jails awaiting trial.[3] At the time of the riots the city jails were at almost 200 percent of capacity.[4]

In order to answer the question of what, in fact, had been accomplished by the bail reform movement, a study of bail practices in several major cities both before and after the bail movement seemed appropriate. In the following several chapters, the results of that study are set forth.

Twenty cities across the United States were selected for study.[5] Most were major metropolitan areas in which an O.R. project was operating. In a few of the cities O.R. projects which were once operational had been discontinued, and a few cities which had never had a project were also included. In order to measure the impact of the bail reform movement in each of these cities, a sampling of criminal defendants was taken from each of two years, 1962 and 1971. The year 1962 was selected as the base year for this study since it was the last year prior to the beginning of the spread of the bail reform movement.[6] The first O.R. programs following the Manhattan Bail Project started in 1963. A second virtue in selecting 1962 as the base year was that the only previous national study of bail practices—that done by the American Bar Foundation—also concerned the year 1962. This afforded an opportunity to verify the information that was being

3. Ibid., p. 185.
4. "Pre-Trial Detention in the New York City Jails," *Columbia Journal of Law and Social Problems,* vol. 7 (1971), pp. 350, 355.
5. The National Bail Study included the following cities: Boston, Champaign-Urbana, Chicago, Denver, Des Moines, Detroit, Washington D.C., Hartford, Houston, Kansas City, Los Angeles, Minneapolis, Oakland, Peoria, Philadelphia, Sacramento, San Diego, San Francisco, San Jose, and Wilmington.
6. The base year for the study was 1962 in all cities with these exceptions: Oakland, 1963; Champaign-Urbana, 1964; and Peoria, 1964. In these three cities, 1962 court records were either unavailable or too incomplete for our purposes.

gathered. The year 1971 was selected since it represented the most recent time period in which the cases chosen for study could be expected to be closed. The data on which this study is based were collected in late 1972 and the early part of 1973.

The number of persons processed annually through the criminal justice system on charges ranging from violations to misdemeanors to felonies is tremendous. The necessity for limiting any sampling of criminal defendants to a manageable size is obvious. Because of the number of cities involved in this study, the number of defendants that could be effectively handled in each city was necessarily quite limited. The details on how the sampling was conducted are set forth in the appendix. Suffice it here to say that the sample in each city consisted of 200 felony and 200 misdemeanor defendants from each year. Eliminated were persons charged with traffic violations (other than drunk driving and vehicular manslaughter) and public intoxication offenses.

Each defendant whose case number fell within the sample was traced through the court records from the time of his initial appearance until disposition. All facts bearing on his or her pretrial release status were noted. A copy of the data sheet that was completed for each defendant can be found in the appendix. Information recorded included the number of times bail was set and the amount at which it was set; whether the defendant was released or not and, if released, the date of such release; whether the release was by citation, O.R. or bond and, if by bond, whether the bond was full cash, surety, deposit, or property; the number of days from first court appearance to disposition; the number of days the defendant was on pretrial release; and the number of times the defendant failed to appear and the length of time he was lost to the system, as well as how the failure to appear affected his pretrial release status after his return to court.

The purposes of this study were several. First, it was intended to reflect what changes, if any, had occurred from 1962 to 1971 in the percentage of defendants securing pretrial release. Conversely, the study was intended to show the effect of the bail reform movement on the rate of pretrial detention. Were in fact a higher percentage of defendants free on pretrial release in 1971 than in 1962? Second, the study was designed to show the impact, if any, of the various types of bail reform, such as O.R., conditional releases, citations, and deposit bail. If changes were observed in the rate of pretrial detention from 1962 to 1971, what role did the use of these alternative methods of release play in bringing about the change? Third, the study was intended to address the question of how well the alternative methods of pretrial release were ensuring the appearance of defendants at trial. By using a standardized definition of failure to appear, a realistic comparison of the failure to appear rates for defendants on O.R. and bail could be made. Fourth, the study was intended to show the effect of any change in the rate of pretrial release on the problem of court delay. Does increasing the number of defendants on pretrial release negatively affect the court's ability to bring cases to disposition? And fifth, in addressing the previous questions, the study will hopefully answer the question of what has been accomplished by the bail reform movement and give some insight as to where the bail reform effort should go from here.

Prior to discussing the results of this study, a brief comment on the problems of studies such as this is appropriate. First, and most obviously, the very limited sample size in each city in relation to the total volume of criminal cases must be recognized. The results of this study are not offered as conclusive proof but rather only as an indication of what has been the apparent effect of the bail reform movement. The results are also, quite obviously, limited to the cities studied.

Second, the information that could be collected was limited to that which was available in court records. The first problem raised by this fact is that a large number of persons are arrested and detained on charges which are never filed in court. What happens to these arrestees—how long they are detained; how often they make bail; how often they are O.R.'d—is not reflected in this study. Secondly, the completeness and readability of court records was a problem in itself. While in most cities the court records were quite complete and very readable, in several cities the court records were handwritten and very sketchy accounts of what had transpired. This was more of a problem with the 1962 than the 1971 records. Information which would have been very basic to this study was often not available. For example, the date of arrest was rarely given in court records and thus the amount of time from arrest to first court appearance is not reflected in this study. In several cities the date that the defendant actually made bail was not indicated in the court records. The only information available was whether the defendant was in custody or out on bail at the time of his court appearance. The sketchiness of court records also made it difficult to identify failures to appear by the defendants and almost impossible to learn what happened to the defendant after a failure to appear. These are only examples of the problems that were incurred in collecting the data for this study. These difficulties, as well as others, will be explained in further detail as they become appropriate to the discussion of the study's findings.

One of this study's major purposes was to collect standardized data which would permit a comparison of pretrial release rates from one jurisdiction to another. Since the steps involved in bringing criminal cases to disposition vary widely from one jurisdiction to another, this proved very difficult. While comparing the experiences of one jurisdiction to that of another is very difficult, it is, at the same time, very necessary if we are to learn from the experiences of others.

In the course of analyzing the data that were collected, efforts were made to standardize the results so as to account for major inconsistencies that were found in the court procedures. A major problem that developed at the outset was in the classification of felony and misdemeanor offenses. The basic outline for this study was to discuss pretrial release figures in terms of felony and misdemeanor offenses. It became quickly obvious, however, that these categories of offenses were not consistent from one jurisdiction to another. An offense that was a misdemeanor in one jurisdiction might well be a felony in another, and several jurisdictions had a middle category of "high" or "indictable" misdemeanors, which, for the purposes of the study, were included in the felony samples. In order to account for differences in the classification of a criminal act as either felony or misdemeanor, this study will analyze pretrial release rates for specific criminal acts such as robbery, burglary, narcotic and drug offenses, felony assault, and grand theft. This does not, of course, resolve the problem completely, since the decision as to what offense to charge will still vary from one jurisdiction to another.

5

Felony Detention Rates

BETWEEN 1962 and 1971, in the cities studied, the percentage of felony defendants detained from the time of their arrest to disposition dropped by one-third. In 1962, 52 percent of the felony defendants studied never secured pretrial release. By 1971 this number had dropped to 33 percent.

The extent of detention in 1962 varied greatly by city—from a low of 24 percent in Philadelphia[1] to a high of 78 percent in Kansas City,[2] as shown in Table 1. Two-thirds of the cities studied, however, were in the 40 to 60 percent range. The 52 percent average compares with average detention rates in the American Bar Foundation study for the same year of 53, 51, and 61 percent in large, medium, and small counties.[3]

By 1971 all of the cities studied, except Kansas City and Boston, had reduced their custody rates to below 50 percent, as shown in Table 1. Only three additional

1. Because of the unavailability of 1962 lower court records in Philadelphia, the felony sample was limited to those defendants who reached the trial court level. The data for Philadelphia are, therefore, not strictly comparable to that obtained in the other cities where our sampling did include felony cases terminated in the lower courts. The overall felony detention rate in Philadelphia in 1962 may, in fact, be lower than the 24 percent we report. The American Bar Foundation study disclosed a detention rate of just 14 percent in Philadelphia 1962 felony cases. See Lee Silverstein, "Bail in the State Courts—A Study and Report," *Minnesota Law Review,* vol. 50 (1965-66), p. 621, Table 2.
2. The high rate of pretrial detention in Kansas City is confirmed by the American Bar Foundation study which indicated a 1962 detention rate of 70 percent. See Silverstein, supra n. 1, Table 2.
3. Silverstein, supra n. 1, Tables 2, 3, and 4.

TABLE 1
Percentage of Felony Defendants
Detained through Disposition—1962, 1971

	Percent detained 1962	Percent detained 1971	Change
Boston	61	62	+ 1
Champaign-Urbana[1]	45	19	—26
Chicago	72	42	—30
Denver	48	23	—25
Des Moines	39	21	—18
Detroit	50	30	—20
Hartford	43	37	— 6
Houston	33	34	+ 1
Kansas City	78	63	—15
Los Angeles	60	38	—22
Minneapolis	54	13	—41
Oakland[2]	51	49	— 2
Peoria[1]	39	28	—11
Philadelphia	24	20	— 4
Sacramento	73	36	—37
San Diego	67	26	—41
San Francisco	54	44	—10
San Jose	57	33	—24
Washington, D.C.	62	31	—31
Wilmington	56	39	—17

[1]Base year is 1964.
[2]Base year is 1963.

cities—Oakland, San Francisco, and Chicago—had rates above 40 percent, and most were close to the average of 33 percent. In five cities—Boston, Hartford, Houston, Oakland, and Philadelphia—there was little change in the detention rate from 1962 to 1971. In the remaining cities, however, the decrease was substantial. By far the largest decreases—over 40 percentage points—were those in Minneapolis and San Diego. In Minneapolis the decrease was particularly striking—from 54 to 13 percent.

THE CAUSES OF CHANGE

An enormous increase in the use of nonfinancial releases was the major reason for the decrease in the percentage of defendants held in custody from arrest to disposition. Available to less than 5 percent of the defendants in 1962, nonfinancial releases spread to over 23 percent of the felony defendant population by 1971—an increase in use of over 450 percent. In the base year only four cities—Boston, Detroit, Oakland, and Peoria—were using nonfinancial releases in at least 10 percent of the felony cases. (See Table 2.) In 1971, on the other hand, only two cities— Houston and Kansas City—failed to release at least 10 percent of the defendants on nonfinancial releases. (See Table 3).

Generally, own recognizance releases in 1962 were limited to a very select group of felony defendants. The five San Francisco O.R. releases, for example, included codefendants in a forgery case who were released so that they could enter the hospital for treatment; a robbery defendant who wanted to enlist in the army; and two other defendants who had been in custody a month and a half each. In other cities, particularly Chicago, O.R. in 1962 served the purpose of giving the defendant a period of pretrial probation, which if successfully completed resulted in the charges being dismissed.

In 1971 nonfinancial releases were available for a sizable percentage of felony defendants. In the District of Columbia over 50 percent of the felony defendants achieved some form of nonfinancial release. Two cities—Des Moines and San Diego—released better than 40 percent of the felony defendants without money bail; three cities—Champaign-Urbana, Detroit, and Philadelphia—released between 30 and 40 percent; and two cities—Sacramento and San Jose—had rates between 25 and 30 percent. In the majority of cities, nonfinancial release rates ranged from 10 to 20 percent.

Despite this increase in the use of nonfinancial releases, however, money bail remained the predominant form of pretrial release. Bail bonds were responsible for the release

TABLE 2
Percentage of Felony Defendants
Released and Detained—1962

	Percent released O.R.	Percent released Bail	Percent not released	Number of cases
Boston	12.4	26.7	60.9	(202)
Champaign-Urbana[1]	3.9	51.2	44.9	(205)
Chicago	2.1	25.7	72.2	(187)
Denver	6.8	45.6	47.7	(237)
Des Moines	2.8	58.1	39.2	(217)
Detroit	14.4	35.3	50.3	(201)
Hartford	1.5	55.1	43.4	(196)
Houston	0.0	66.9	33.1	(181)
Kansas City	1.2	21.1	77.6	(161)
Los Angeles	2.1	37.7	60.2	(191)
Minneapolis	7.1	38.9	54.0	(198)
Oakland[2]	10.1	38.7	51.3	(199)
Peoria[1]	10.8	50.0	39.2	(130)
Philadelphia	0.0	76.2	23.8	(202)
Sacramento	8.5	18.6	72.9	(188)
San Diego	4.7	27.8	67.4	(212)
San Francisco	2.5	43.7	53.8	(199)
San Jose	6.3	37.0	56.8	(192)
Washington, D.C.	0.0	38.5	61.5	(200)
Wilmington	6.1	38.1	55.8	(147)

[1]Base year is 1964.
[2]Base year is 1963.

of 44 percent of the felony defendants in 1971, about the same percentage as in 1962 when money bail was virtually the only method of release.

In five cities, in fact, reduction of the custody rate from 1962 to 1971 was primarily due to the increased use of money bail. Thus, the percentage of defendants released on money bail increased in Minneapolis 34 percentage points; in Peoria, 26; in Chicago, 21; Denver, 18; and Kansas City, 15 points. Two of the three cities with the

TABLE 3
Percentage of Felony Defendants
Released and Detained—1971

	Percent released O.R.	Percent released Bail	Percent not released	Number of cases
Boston	12.8	25.5	61.8	(196)
Champaign-Urbana	36.9	44.6	18.5	(195)
Chicago	10.5	47.4	42.1	(285)
Denver	13.2	64.2	22.6	(190)
Des Moines	46.6	32.4	20.9	(253)
Detroit	36.5	34.0	29.5	(200)
Hartford	17.6	45.4	37.0	(216)
Houston	1.8	63.8	34.3	(163)
Kansas City	3.0	33.5	63.4	(164)
Los Angeles	17.2	44.4	38.4	(198)
Minneapolis	14.0	73.0	13.0	(200)
Oakland	18.0	33.0	49.0	(200)
Peoria	19.0	52.8	28.2	(195)
Philadelphia	33.5	46.1	20.4	(191)
Sacramento	29.5	34.7	35.8	(190)
San Diego	44.6	29.6	25.8	(213)
San Francisco	16.7	38.9	44.4	(198)
San Jose	26.4	40.8	32.8	(201)
Washington, D.C.	55.5	13.2	31.3	(243)
Wilmington	14.1	46.6	39.2	(191)

largest increase in the use of money bail were Chicago and Peoria, both Illinois cities, operating in 1971 under that state's deposit bail law. In the third Illinois city, Champaign-Urbana, the number of felony defendants released on bail decreased by 6 percentage points. The use of O.R. however, increased by 33 percentage points, and overall the percentage of defendants held in custody declined.

In 1971 Washington, D.C., Des Moines, San Diego, and Detroit were the only cities in which nonfinancial releases outnumbered bail bonds. Washington, D.C., and Des Moines were also the only cities studied to witness a large decrease in the use of money bail. In each city the bail release rate dropped over 25 percentage points. Not surprisingly, these two cities also showed the largest increase in the use of nonfinancial releases: in the District from zero in 1962 to 55 percent in 1971, and in Des Moines from 2 to 47 percent. Washington, D.C., and Des Moines developed O.R. release programs quite early, and both have been widely recognized for their effectiveness.

BAIL AMOUNTS

Except for the increase in the use of own recognizance, there was little change between 1962 and 1971 in the amounts of bail required for felony defendants, as shown in Table 4. In both years the number of defendants for whom no bail was set was low, about 2 percent. In both years the percentage of bails set in amounts above $3,000 was about the same, a little over 20 percent. Likewise, the number of low bail settings—between $100 and $999—was unchanged between the two years, remaining at about 18 percent. The major change that did occur as a result of the increased use of own recognizance was in the number of

TABLE 4

Bail Amounts Set in
Felony Cases—1962, 1971

(Percentage of final bail settings
in each range)

Bail amount	1962	1971
O.R.	5.9	23.0
$100-499	5.6	6.1
$500-999	13.7	10.8
$1,000-2,999	50.1	33.7
$3,000-4,999	6.2	7.5
$5,000-9,999	9.4	8.3
$10,000-14,999	3.5	3.6
$15,000 and up	1.6	1.8
No bail	2.1	2.2

bail settings in the $1,000 to $2,999 range. The increased use of O.R. was almost wholly reflected in the decrease from 50 to 34 percent in the number of bail settings in this medium range.

Similarly, the bail setting practices in the individual cities remained largely unchanged. The cities setting the lowest bails in 1962—Philadelphia, Hartford, and Des Moines—also had the highest frequency of low bail settings in 1971. High bail cities in 1962, such as Oakland, Kansas City, and Boston, remained high bail cities in 1971.

Although bail amounts were largely unchanged between 1962 and 1971, this study does indicate that felony defendants were much more able to post bail in 1971 than in the earlier year. The increased ability of defendants to post bail was observed in each of the bail ranges but it is most readily seen in the percentage of bails posted in the medium range of $1,000-2,999, which accounted for the bulk of bail settings in both years. The percentage of bails in this range which were met increased in all but six cities, as shown in Table 5. In most cities the increase was substantial. As a result of the increased percentage of defendants posting bail in each range, the overall percentage of defendants released on money bail remained about the same from 1962 to 1971 in most cities, despite the large increase in the use of O.R.

If it were clear that the increased number of nonfinancial releases were going to defendants who previously had been unable to meet money bail requirements, it could be argued that the change in ability to meet the bond amount was due to this factor. There is nothing to indicate that this is true, however, and Table 6 is some support for the opposite conclusion that the increased use of nonfinancial releases has cut into the number of defendants who would have posted bail. With some exceptions, Table 6 shows a pattern of bail releases decreasing as the use of O.R. increases. It thus seems likely that other factors are also involved in the increased ability of defendants to post bail in 1971.

TABLE 5
Percentage of Bail Settings
in the $1,000-2,999 Range
in Which Defendants Posted Bail—1962, 1971

	Percent posted 1962	Percent posted 1971	Change
Boston	67	54	—13
Champaign-Urbana[1]	53	82	+29
Chicago	40	74	+34
Denver	53	87	+34
Des Moines	63	52	—11
Detroit	31	61	+30
Hartford	56	51	— 5
Houston	66	74	+ 8
Kansas City	31	44	+13
Los Angeles	35	62	+27
Minneapolis	38	96	+58
Oakland[2]	85	81	— 4
Peoria[1]	79	94	+15
Philadelphia	79	71	— 8
Sacramento	26	59	+33
San Diego	33	55	+22
San Francisco	44	50	+ 6
San Jose	42	61	+19
Washington, D.C.	49	46	— 3
Wilmington	35	58	+23

[1]Base year is 1964.
[2]Base year is 1963.

With bail amounts remaining unchanged, some increase in the ability of defendants to post bail could be expected as a result of inflation over the period from 1962 to 1971. This changes the relative value of a given bond and would make it easier to raise the necessary money. The increase might also be partly due to changes in the practices of bondsmen. The increased use of O.R. may have forced bondsmen to relax their screening of defendants in order to retain the same volume of releases. Changes in either

TABLE 6
Percentage of Felony Defendants
Released on O.R. and Bail—1971

	Percent released O.R.	Percent released Bail
Houston	2	64
Kansas City	3	34
Chicago	11	47
Denver	13	64
Boston	13	26
Minneapolis	14	73
Wilmington	14	47
Los Angeles	17	44
San Francisco	17	39
Hartford	18	45
Oakland	18	33
Peoria	19	53
San Jose	26	41
Sacramento	30	35
Philadelphia	33	46
Champaign-Urbana	37	45
Detroit	37	34
San Diego	45	30
Des Moines	47	32
Washington, D.C.	56	13

the amount of collateral required or in willingness to write bonds in higher risk cases could alter release rates even though bond amounts remain constant. Also, as will be discussed later, defendants in felony drug cases tend to post bail in a high percentage of cases, and thus the large increase in drug cases from 1962 to 1971 might be a contributing factor in the higher percentage of defendants posting bail in 1971.

Summary

The percentage of felony defendants detained in custody for the period from arrest to disposition substantially decreased in the period from 1962 to 1971. In five cities the increased use of money bonds was primarily responsible for the decrease which was observed. In seventeen of the twenty cities, however, the increased use of nonfinancial release was a major influence on the reduced custody rate. In Washington, D.C., and Des Moines, the percentage of defendants on money bail dropped sharply from 1962 to 1971 but was offset by an even more substantial increase in nonfinancial releases. In the remaining cities, the percentage of bail defendants decreased only slightly or increased, and thus the use of O.R. had a direct effect on reducing the custody percentage.

PRE-APPEARANCE DISPOSITIONS

Only those persons on whom charges were filed in court were included in this study. The detention of persons arrested on felony charges which never culminate in a felony filing are not reflected in this study. In some cities these persons represent a sizable percentage of the total felony arrests. In San Francisco in 1969, for example, it was reported that 39.6 percent of all defendants arrested on probable cause (without a warrant) for felony offenses had their charges dismissed prior to any court appearance.[4] In Los Angeles and San Diego, a similar percentage of felony cases are rejected by the District Attorney prior to the filing of a complaint. Since in most jurisdictions bail is set in felony cases only by a judge and only after a complaint has been filed, the vast majority of these defendants undoubtedly do not make bail but rather are detained until the charges are dismissed.[5] The detention of these arrestees increases the percentage of felony defendants held in custody prior to disposition in most cities.

4. The San Francisco Committee on Crime, *A Report on the Criminal Court of San Francisco; Part II, Bail and O.R. Release* (San Francisco: The San Francisco Committee on Crime, February, 1971), p. 7.
5. This was true in California at the time of the survey. Subsequently, the California legislature has mandated the creation of felony bail schedules which make it possible for bail to be set and posted prior to appearance in some felony cases.

The degree in which this unknown factor increases the custody rate varies from city to city depending upon the local practice in matters such as how closely felony cases are screened prior to court filing and how long a defendant can be held before charges must be filed.

The amount of screening by the prosecutor prior to the filing of felony criminal charges varied among the jurisdictions studied, creating a sampling problem. In cities where there was very little screening of felony arrests prior to the filing of charges, defendants would necessarily be included in the samples taken from first court appearances who would not have reached court in other cities. In thirteen of the cities studied, instances of felony cases being dismissed at first appearance were quite rare. In the remaining seven cities, however, a number of felony cases were dismissed, or "no papered," at first appearance. Inclusion of those cases dismissed at first appearance in these seven cities distorts the comparison of pretrial detention rates, since in 1971 felony bail was rarely posted prior to court and the detention rate for defendants in first appearance disposition cases was therefore high—73.4 percent.

The detention rates most seriously influenced by the first appearance terminations were in Boston and Washington, D.C. The felony detention rate in Boston was reported as virtually unchanged from 1962 to 1971—61 percent in 1962 and 62 percent in 1971. Likewise, no change was observed in the use of unsecured appearance bonds. The rate of first appearance dispositions in Boston, however, increased from 8 percent in 1962 to 35 percent in 1971. This rate is unusually high in part because the Boston Municipal Court, in addition to serving the normal function of holding probable cause hearings in felony cases, has the unusual jurisdiction to handle all felony cases that carry penalties of five years or less, plus jurisdiction over certain enumerated felony offenses such as breaking and entering during daytime and larceny from motor vehicles.[6]

6. In fiscal year 1968, 96 percent of all criminal matters in Massachusetts were finally disposed of at the lower court level. Stephen R. Bing and S. Stephen Rosenfeld, *The Quality of Justice in the Lower Criminal Courts of Metropolitan Boston* (Boston, Mass.: Lawyers Committee for Civil Rights Under Law, 1970), p. 2.

Analysis of the Boston data with these first appearance disposition cases omitted reveals that a substantial change had occurred in the detention rate in "contested" felony cases. Standing at 58 percent in 1962, the detention rate had dropped to 45 percent in 1971. Similarly, in Washington, D.C., if the 31 cases that were "no papered," or dismissed, at arraignment are eliminated from the sample, leaving only those cases in which a bail decision was actually made, the 1971 District release figures become even more impressive: 64 percent nonfinancial releases, 15 percent bail releases, and just 21 percent custody.

Two other cities in which the overall custody rate is affected by a high detention rate in cases disposed of at first appearance are San Francisco and Des Moines. In San Francisco removal of these cases decreases the custody percentage from 44 to 36 percent and increases the O.R. and bail rates to 19 and 45 percent respectively. In Des Moines the 1971 custody rate drops from 21 to 17 percent with removal of first appearance dispositions. Almost one-half—49 percent—of the defendants in cases proceeding beyond first appearance were released on own recognizance.

Virtually all of the cases in which defendants posted bonds in cases which terminated at first appearance occurred in two Illinois cities, Chicago and Peoria. These two cities accounted for 45 of the 51 cases in which this occurred. In Chicago 63 cases in our sample terminated at first appearance. Of the 63 defendants, 36 (57 percent) were in custody; 23 (37 percent) were on bail; and 4 (6 percent) were on O.R. Elimination of these cases reduces the detention rate in the Chicago sample from 42 to 38 percent and slightly increases the O.R. and bail percentages to 12 and 51 percent. Peoria was the only city in which the majority of defendants in cases not proceeding beyond first appearance were not in custody. The custody rate in these 46 cases was just 28 percent, the exact percentage of custody cases in the sample as a whole. Thus, inclusion of these cases in Peoria did not distort the overall custody rate.

The final city in which more than five cases in the 1971

felony sample terminated at first appearance was Hartford. In Hartford ten felony defendants, half of whom were in custody and half of whom had been granted O.R., had their cases disposed of at first appearance. Inclusion of these cases did not substantially affect the overall release figures in Hartford.

6

Selected Felony Offenses

PRETRIAL release rates vary considerably depending upon the alleged criminal conduct with which the defendant is charged. One concern in comparing pretrial release rates from one city to another and from one year to another is whether any changes that appear are due to changes in release practices or simply changes in other factors, such as the kind of crime or criminal involved. It is obvious, for example, that there was a tremendous increase in the number of defendants charges with drug-related offenses in the period from 1962 to 1971. Could this increase or changes in the way that alleged drug offenders were handled by the court account for the decrease in the amount of detention in 1971? To address this concern, a number of felony offenses will be analyzed separately.[1] However, it can be noted at the outset that the changes observed in the samples as a whole generally hold true for each of the offenses to be considered.

1. To facilitate the comparison of pretrial release rates among the various cities, a slight change is necessary in the manner in which the data are presented in order to take account of the cases disposed of at first appearance. In the felony samples as a whole, the small number of cases handled at first appearance affected the release and detention rates in only the few cities set forth in the preceding section. With the substantially smaller sample sizes involved in analyzing release rates for specific offenses in a single city, however, even a single case disposed of at first appearance will substantially affect the custody rate in that city. For this reason, those custody cases disposed of at first appearance are not included in the samples.

NARCOTIC AND DRUG CASES

Drug cases increased dramatically throughout the country between 1962 and 1971. This tremendous increase is reflected in this study. In 1962 just 5 percent of the felony cases involved narcotic or drug offenses. In 1971, on the other hand, these cases constituted almost one-fourth of the total. In 1962 four California cities—Los Angeles, Oakland, San Diego, and San Francisco—and Chicago had over 10 percent drug cases.[2] By comparison, in 1971 drug cases represented over 10 percent of the felony cases in all cities, with the exception of Kansas City.

In 1962 the detention rate for defendants charged with felony drug offenses was not substantially different from the overall felony custody rate. The detention rate did vary considerably from city to city, as shown in Table 7, but this is primarily owing to the limited number of drug cases in the 1962 sample. For example, the three cities in which all felony drug defendants secured pretrial release involved only three defendants in Houston, six in Philadelphia, and ten in Peoria. Likewise, Minneapolis and Washington, D.C., which our figures show had 100 percent detention rates, had only one and two defendants respectively in the samples. The small number of cases makes it impossible to attach significance to these rates.

The 1971 figures, however, reflect a high release rate for drug defendants, as shown in Table 7. In only three cities did the custody rate for drug defendants edge above 30 percent: Kansas City, 33 percent; Wilmington, 32 percent; and Boston, 31 percent. In several cities, the custody rate for felony drug defendants was particularly low: Minneapolis, 2 percent; Des Moines and Peoria, 4 percent; Washington, D.C., 5 percent; Denver, 6 percent; Sacramento, 8 percent; Philadelphia, 10 percent; Chicago and Houston, 11 percent; and Detroit, 15 percent. On the

2. In Chicago, felony narcotic, dangerous drug, and marijuana cases appear in a separate narcotics court. In selecting the case samples in Chicago, an effort was made to include cases from this court. Thus, the percentage of drug cases in the Chicago sample is not necessarily representative of the overall percentage of drug cases in that city.

TABLE 7
Percentage of Felony Drug Defendants
Detained through Disposition—1962, 1971.

	Percent detained 1962	Percent detained 1971	Change
Boston	64	31	—33
Champaign-Urbana[1]	43	19	*
Chicago	45	11	—34
Denver	40	6	—34
Des Moines	No cases	4	*
Detroit	40	15	*
Hartford	31	29	— 2
Houston	0	11	*
Kansas City	No cases	33	*
Los Angeles	50	29	—21
Minneapolis	100	2	*
Oakland[2]	31	27	— 4
Peoria[1]	0	4	+ 4
Philadelphia	0	10	*
Sacramento	64	8	—56
San Diego	71	19	—52
San Francisco	54	27	—27
San Jose	50	24	*
Washington, D.C.	100	5	*
Wilmington	No cases	32	*

[1]Base year is 1964.
[2]Base year is 1963.
*No change is indicated for those cities with fewer than 10 felony
  drug cases in the 1962 sample.

whole, the custody rate in drug cases is lower than it is in any of the other major felony offense categories.

As with all felony offenses, more releases in drug cases are attributable to the use of money bail rather than to O.R. In fact, the percentage of drug defendants securing release on bail bonds was quite high in most cities. The overall felony release rate on bonds was 44 percent, and just three cities—Minneapolis, Denver, and Houston—released over 55 percent of the felony defendants on bonds;

however, in the cases involving drug defendants, thirteen cities—Boston, Chicago, Denver, Hartford, Houston, Los Angeles, Minneapolis, Oakland, Sacramento, Wilmington, Champaign, Peoria, and Kansas City—had bail release rates of 55 percent or higher.

In nine cities, the rate of nonfinancial release in drug cases was lower than for the felony sample as a whole. In just six cities—Chicago, Des Moines, Washington, D.C., Minneapolis, San Jose, and Philadelphia—was the percentage of O.R. releases in drug cases substantially above the rate in nondrug cases. O.R. release rates in 1971 drug cases are presented in Table 8.

How, then, do the drug cases influence the overall 1971

TABLE 8

O.R. Releases in Felony Drug Cases—1971

	Number of drug cases	Number of O.R. releases	Percent released on O.R.
Boston	29	3	10.3
Champaign-Urbana	53	10	18.9
Chicago	44	13	29.5
Denver	63	3	4.8
Des Moines	28	18	64.3
Detroit	55	23	41.8
Hartford	88	6	6.8
Houston	35	0	0.0
Kansas City	9	0	0.0
Los Angeles	65	7	10.8
Minneapolis	41	14	34.1
Oakland	34	3	8.8
Peoria	24	5	20.8
Philadelphia	55	25	45.5
Sacramento	60	22	36.7
San Diego	115	53	46.1
San Francisco	62	16	25.8
San Jose	74	29	39.2
Washington, D.C.	21	17	81.0
Wilmington	70	7	10.0

release figures? Table 9 shows the 1971 release rates with all drug cases removed. The difference between this table and Table 3, which shows the overall 1971 release rates, is quite modest. With the exception of Champaign-Urbana, in which there was no change, the custody rates increased in every city with removal of the drug cases. The rate of increase, however, was largely insignificant (ranging from 2 to 8 percentage points in all cities except Sacramento), and the custody rate was still substantially below the 1962 custody rate.

TABLE 9

1971 Felony Release Rates

Exclusive of Drug Cases

	Percent released O.R.	Percent released Bail	Percent not released
Boston	13	20	66
Champaign-Urbana	44	38	18
Chicago	7	45	48
Denver	17	52	31
Des Moines	44	32	23
Detroit	35	30	35
Hartford	26	32	43
Houston	2	57	41
Kansas City	3	32	65
Los Angeles	20	37	43
Minneapolis	9	75	16
Oakland	20	27	54
Peoria	19	50	31
Philadelphia	29	47	24
Sacramento	26	25	49
San Diego	43	24	34
San Francisco	13	37	51
San Jose	19	44	36
Washington, D.C.	54	13	33
Wilmington	17	41	42

Table 10

Percentage of Felony Burglary Defendants
Detained through Disposition—1962, 1971

	Percent detained 1962	Percent detained 1971	Change
Boston	60	47	—13
Champaign-Urbana[1]	51	16	—35
Chicago	68	33	—35
Denver	48	22	—26
Des Moines	63	26	—37
Detroit	64	36	—28
Hartford	58	30	—28
Houston	60	62	+ 2
Kansas City	89	79	—10
Los Angeles	73	41	—32
Minneapolis	60	3	—57
Oakland[2]	86	66	—20
Peoria[1]	31	30	— 1
Philadelphia	44	39	— 5
Sacramento	94	46	—48
San Diego	73	32	—41
San Francisco	67	52	—15
San Jose	56	27	—29
Washington, D.C.	75	21	—54
Wilmington	61	31	—30

[1]Base year is 1964.
[2]Base year is 1963.

BURGLARY CASES

Burglary offenses constituted a sizable percentage of the felony offenses in each city. In 1962 the custody rate for burglary defendants was higher than for the felony population as a whole in most cities, ranging generally from 55 to 94 percent, as shown in Table 10.[3] By 1971 the custody

3. While in eight cities—Chicago, Denver, Minneapolis, San Diego, San Jose, Wilmington, Champaign, and Peoria—the custody rate for burglary defendants was not substantially different from the sample as a

rates in burglary cases had dropped considerably. The custody rate was below 40 percent in all but seven cities, and in most instances the rate was 33 percent or below, as shown in Table 10. The only cities in which the custody rate did not substantially decrease were Houston, Peoria, and Philadelphia.

The decrease in the detention rate for burglary defendants between 1962 and 1971 was primarily due to an increase in O.R.—from less than 3 percent to 25 percent. Burglary O.R. rates in 1971, shown in Table 11, were generally higher than for felony cases as a whole. The cities which made the greatest use of nonfinancial releases in burglary cases were those generally high in the use of O.R. over all: Washington, D.C., San Diego, Des Moines, and Champaign. Philadelphia, on the other hand, despite a high over all O.R. release rate, made little use of it in burglary cases, with an O.R. rate of just 13 percent.

That the use of bail bonds was not a major factor in the increased release rate for burglary defendants is evidenced by the fact that in nine cities the percentage of defendants released on money bail actually decreased from 1962 to 1971. In two of these cities—Houston and Peoria—the custody rate for burglary defendants was virtually unchanged, and in a third, Philadelphia, it decreased only slightly. In the remaining six cities—Des Moines, Detroit, Washington, D.C., San Diego, San Francisco, and Champaign-Urbana—the decrease in the use of bail was offset by substantial increases in the use of O.R., and thus the custody percentage did decrease substantially in each of these cities.

The decrease in the custody rate for burglary defendants was particularly dramatic in Minneapolis and Washington, D.C. In Minneapolis the decrease was the direct result of a tremendous increase in the percentage of defendants making bail—from 32 percent in 1962 to 85 percent in 1971. On the other hand, the decrease in Washington, D.C., was

---

whole, in the remaining twelve cities the burglary custody rate was from 11 to 35 percentage points higher than for the overall population.

TABLE 11
O.R. Releases in Felony Burglary Cases—1971

	Number of burglary cases	Number of O.R. releases	Percent released on O.R.
Boston	15	3	20.0
Champaign-Urbana	50	24	48.0
Chicago	39	9	23.1
Denver	27	5	18.5
Des Moines	27	13	48.1
Detroit	28	10	35.7
Hartford	40	12	30.0
Houston	21	1	4.8
Kansas City	29	0	0.0
Los Angeles	27	7	25.9
Minneapolis	34	4	11.8
Oakland	58	9	15.5
Peoria	73	15	20.5
Philadelphia	23	3	13.0
Sacramento	26	8	30.8
San Diego	31	17	54.8
San Francisco	27	7	25.9
San Jose	26	5	19.2
Washington, D.C.	28	21	75.0
Wilmington	32	7	21.9

the result of the increased use of nonfinancial releases—
from none in 1962 to 75 percent in 1971. Sacramento also
had an extremely large decrease in the custody rate for
burglary defendants from 1962 to 1971. In that city the
decrease was caused by a combination of an increase in
O.R. from 2 percent in 1962 to 31 percent in 1971, and an
increase in bail releases from 4 to 23 percent.

ROBBERY CASES

Robbery defendants had a very high rate of pretrial detention in 1962, as shown in Table 12. The rate of detention

was above 70 percent in most cities; between 60 and 70 percent in Denver, Washington, Hartford, and Minneapolis; and about 50 percent in the 1964 samples in Champaign-Urbana and Peoria.

TABLE 12
Percentage of Robbery Defendants
Detained through Disposition—1962, 1971

	Percent detained 1962	Percent detained 1971	Change
Boston	88	42	—46
Champaign-Urbana[1]	46	30	—16
Chicago	88	75	—13
Denver	64	89	+25
Des Moines	100	25	—75
Detroit	75	55	—20
Hartford	63	61	— 2
Houston	73	40	—33
Kansas City	94	79	—15
Los Angeles	91	75	—16
Minneapolis	60	39	—21
Oakland[2]	73	75	+ 2
Peoria[1]	50	37	—13
Philadelphia	90	44	—46
Sacramento	88	83	— 5
San Diego	71	63	— 8
San Francisco	72	57	—15
San Jose	78	67	—11
Washington, D.C.	65	33	—32
Wilmington	91	56	—35

[1]Base year is 1964.
[2]Base year is 1963.

By 1971 the release rate had changed somewhat in robbery cases. (See Table 12.) Although the custody rate was reduced in most cities, the magnitude of the decrease was not as great as with the burglary defendants. Since robbery cases appeared in our samples in much fewer numbers than the burglary cases, it is difficult to give much weight to the decreases shown in Table 12. This is particularly true of the cities showing the largest decrease in the custody rate. In Des Moines, for example, the tremendous decrease is based on just six cases in 1962 and eight in 1971. The Houston decrease of 33 percentage points is based on just eleven cases in 1962 and ten cases in 1971. Finally, Philadelphia's decrease is based on ten cases in 1962 and sixteen cases in 1971.

In most cities, the custody rate in robbery cases is well above the rate for the other felony offenses, excluding homicide. In 1971 the rate in most cities was well above 50

TABLE 13

O.R. Releases in Robbery Cases—1971

	Number of robbery cases	Number of O.R. releases	Percent released on O.R.
Boston	40	9	22.5
Champaign-Urbana	10	3	30.0
Chicago	48	2	4.2
Denver	19	0	0.0
Des Moines	8	3	37.5
Detroit	22	5	22.7
Hartford	31	3	9.7
Houston	10	1	10.0
Kansas City	19	0	0.0
Los Angeles	16	0	0.0
Minneapolis	28	0	0.0
Oakland	24	2	8.3
Peoria	16	3	18.8
Philadelphia	16	0	0.0
Sacramento	12	0	0.0
San Diego	8	3	37.5
San Francisco	14	0	0.0
San Jose	9	1	11.1
Washington, D.C.	45	25	55.6
Wilmington	27	2	7.4

percent. Moreover, in a number of cities—Denver, Hartford, Oakland, Sacramento, San Diego, and San Jose—the custody rate in 1971 showed either an increase or only a slight decrease from 1962.

In addition, robbery defendants were rarely released on O.R. in the cities studied, with the exception of Washington, D.C. (See Table 13.) In Washington, a robbery defendant's chances for nonfinancial release are apparently as good as those of any other felony defendant, the rate of such release being 56 percent. The only other cities

TABLE 14

Percentage of Grand Larceny Defendants
Detained through Disposition—1962, 1971

	Percent detained 1962	Percent detained 1971	Change
Boston	24	50	+26
Champaign-Urbana[1]	42	20	—22
Chicago	78	22	—56
Denver	54	15	—39
Des Moines	43	32	—11
Detroit	63	0	—63
Hartford	0	63	+63
Houston	23	28	+ 5
Kansas City	74	88	+14
Los Angeles	33	31	— 2
Minneapolis	31	0	—31
Oakland[2]	25	27	+ 2
Peoria[1]	34	6	—28
Philadelphia	50	10	—40
Sacramento	69	18	—51
San Diego	59	0	—59
San Francisco	40	17	—23
San Jose	29	10	—19
Washington, D.C.	73	33	—40
Wilmington	44	29	—15

[1]Base year is 1964.
[2]Base year is 1963.

TABLE 15
O.R. Releases in Grand Larceny Cases—1971

	Number of larceny cases	Number of O.R. releases	Percent released on O.R.
Boston	4	1	25.0
Champaign-Urbana	20	8	40.0
Chicago	40	2	5.0
Denver	27	7	25.9
Des Moines	19	7	36.8
Detroit	6	3	50.0
Hartford	8	1	12.5
Houston	18	0	0.0
Kansas City	8	0	0.0
Los Angeles	16	8	50.0
Minneapolis	17	4	23.5
Oakland	11	5	45.5
Peoria	32	7	21.9
Philadelphia	20	9	45.0
Sacramento	17	4	23.5
San Diego	6	5	83.3
San Francisco	6	0	0.0
San Jose	10	3	30.0
Washington, D.C.	12	3	25.0
Wilmington	17	7	41.2

with any appreciable number of O.R. releases in robbery cases in 1971 were Boston and Detroit.

GRAND LARCENY CASES

In most cities studied, the 1962 detention rate for grand larceny defendants was lower than for felony defendants generally.[4] (See Table 14.) Only five cities—Chicago,

4. Grand larceny is defined as theft of money or goods exceeding a certain dollar amount. Since the amount varies from one jurisdiction to another, grand larceny defendants are included in some city samples who would have been charged with petty larceny in other jurisdictions. For the purposes of this study, the charging decision made by the local jurisdiction determined whether the offense was grand or petty larceny.

Washington, D.C., Detroit, Sacramento, and Kansas City—detained more than 60 percent of these defendants. On the other hand, eight cities were detaining one-third or fewer of the grand theft defendants. The custody rate was even lower in 1971, 33 percent or below in all cities except Boston, Kansas City, and Hartford. The release and detention figures for several cities, however, are based on a very small number of grand theft defendants. The 1962 samples in Des Moines, Hartford, and Los Angeles, and the 1971 samples in Boston, Detroit, Hartford, San

TABLE 16

Percentage of Felony Assault Defendants
Detained through Disposition—1962, 1971

	Percent detained 1962	Percent detained 1971	Change
Boston	46	40	— 6
Champaign-Urbana[1]	7	13	+ 6
Chicago	50	13	—37
Denver	31	27	— 4
Des Moines	14	5	— 9
Detroit	44	50	+ 6
Hartford	28	42	+14
Houston	0	50	+50
Kansas City	36	67	+31
Los Angeles	46	56	+10
Minneapolis	53	0	—53
Oakland[2]	60	38	—22
Peoria[1]	17	19	+ 2
Philadelphia	15	15	None
Sacramento	75	57	—18
San Diego	No cases	20	NA
San Francisco	41	31	—10
San Jose	60	0	—60
Washington, D.C.	31	17	—14
Wilmington	35	60	+25

[1]Base year is 1964.
[2]Base year is 1963.

Diego, San Francisco, and Kansas City, all included fewer than ten grand theft cases.

Despite the small sample sizes, nonfinancial releases are apparently used quite frequently in grand larceny cases. In most cities the nonfinancial release rate was above 20 percent. While the cities consistently highest in the use of nonfinancial releases—Washington, D.C., and Des Moines —had relatively low O.R. rates of 25 and 37 percent in grand theft cases, several other cities had very substantial rates: San Diego, 83 percent; Los Angeles and Detroit, 50 percent; Oakland and Philadelphia, 45 percent; Wilmington, 41 percent; and Champaign-Urbana, 40 percent. (See Table 15.)

TABLE 17

O.R. Releases in Felony Assault Cases—1971

	Number of assault cases	Number of O.R. releases	Percent released on O.R.
Boston	20	4	20.0
Champaign-Urbana	30	16	53.3
Chicago	30	1	3.3
Denver	11	2	18.2
Des Moines	19	15	78.9
Detroit	16	3	18.8
Hartford	12	2	16.7
Houston	6	0	0.0
Kansas City	12	0	0.0
Los Angeles	9	0	0.0
Minneapolis	6	0	0.0
Oakland	16	3	18.8
Peoria	16	2	12.5
Philadelphia	13	3	23.1
Sacramento	14	1	7.1
San Diego	5	2	40.0
San Francisco	16	1	6.3
San Jose	8	1	12.5
Washington, D.C.	42	31	73.8
Wilmington	10	1	10.0

FELONY ASSAULT

Although felony assault is a serious crime against the person, in both 1962 and 1971 custody rates for this offense were lower than in the robbery cases. In 1962 only five cities—Chicago, Minneapolis, Oakland, Sacramento, and San Jose—detained 50 percent or more of the felony assault defendants. By 1971 a number of cities had reduced the custody percentage considerably. In nine cities, however, there was no decrease, and in six cities the detention rate was still 50 percent or greater. (See Table 16.)

Low 1971 custody rates were most often the result of a a high rate of bail bond use. In nine of the cities studied, bail bond release rates were at or above 50 percent. The use of nonfinancial releases was generally rare in felony assault cases in 1971. Houston, Los Angeles, Minneapolis, and Kansas City had none. (See Table 17.) Those cities that were exceptions were the same as in the robbery cases: Des Moines (79 percent); Washington, D.C. (74 percent); Champaign-Urbana (53 percent); and San Diego (40 percent).

7

Misdemeanor Detention Rates

In 1962 slightly more than 40 percent of the misdemeanor defendants studied did not secure pretrial release. By 1971 this detention rate had decreased to 28 percent. While this decline of nearly one-fourth in the number of misdemeanor defendants detained is smaller than the one-third drop in the felony cases, it is nonetheless a substantial decrease.[1]

1. While city-to-city comparisons of pretrial release practices in felony cases present many difficulties, for misdemeanor cases the problems are even more acute. Comparisons of release figures in misdemeanor cases must be viewed with caution, given the size of our sampling. Even in a medium-to-large city, the misdemeanor arraignment calendar will often be heard by a single judge, and when he is rotated or reassigned, the whole system may change drastically. In order to deal with this problem, samples of misdemeanor and felony defendants were selected from different months of the year. In those cities in which judges rotate to the arraignment calendar quarterly or less frequently, the 200 case samples were derived by randomly selecting fifty consecutive misdemeanor defendants from four different periods of the year. In a city such as Washington, D.C., where the judges rotate monthly, twenty consecutive misdemeanors were selected from each of ten months. Selection of twenty or fifty consecutive misdemeanor defendants represented only a single day's court calendar in several of the larger cities.

A second problem arising with the misdemeanor samples is that in several cities certain offenses tended to occur much more frequently than in other cities. So that the misdemeanor samples would not reflect only the bail practices for a single offense, in cases where a series of misdemeanor defendants were charged with the same offense only the first three defendants were included in the sample, and the coder then skipped to the first defendant charged with a different offense. Even with this precaution, however, certain offenses tended to predominate in many cities. Owing to the unavailability of court records, Oakland was not included in the misdemeanor sampling. In Philadelphia only 1971 records were available.

As contrasted with the felony cases, for which more than half the cities studied had detention rates above 50 percent in 1962, only two cities were found to be detaining well above this level in misdemeanor cases. Detention rates in the individual cities generally ranged from 35 to 50 percent as shown in Table 18. The lowest rates were: Champaign-Urbana (19 percent), Peoria (26 percent), Denver (28 percent), Houston (30 percent), and San Jose (32 percent). The highest rates were in Detroit and Sacramento—both cities with a high percentage of first appearance dispositions.

TABLE 18
Percentage of Misdemeanor Defendants
Detained through Disposition—1962, 1971

	Percent detained 1962	Percent detained 1971	Change
Boston	37	51	+14
Champaign-Urbana[1]	19	3	—16
Chicago	47	36	— 9
Denver	28	12	—16
Des Moines	43	33	—10
Detroit	90	60	—30
Hartford	36	20	—16
Houston	30	9	—21
Kansas City	42	27	—15
Los Angeles	45	46	+ 1
Minneapolis	52	29	—23
Peoria[1]	26	1	—25
Philadelphia	No sample	31	NA
Sacramento	69	37	—32
San Diego	50	25	—25
San Francisco[2]	46	42	— 4
San Jose	32	13	—19
Washington, D.C.	49	33	—16
Wilmington	37	18	—19

[1]Base year is 1964.
[2]Base year is 1963.

By 1971 custody rates had dropped substantially in most cities. With the exceptions of Boston, Detroit, Los Angeles, and San Francisco, 1971 detention rates were all below 40 percent. The two lowest rates were quite remarkable: 1 percent in Peoria and 3 percent in Champaign-Urbana. Other noticeably low custody rates included Houston (9 percent), Denver (12 percent), San Jose (13 percent), and Wilmington (18 percent).

In most cities the custody percentage dropped 15 to 25 percentage points from 1962 to 1971. In the two cities with the highest 1962 custody rates—Detroit and Sacramento—the detention percentage fell 30 points in 1971. The only city with a significant increase in the custody rate was Boston, where the number of first appearance dispositions more than doubled.

DETENTION RATES IN CASES TERMINATING AT FIRST APPEARANCE

The most serious problem in interpreting misdemeanor release rates involves the large number of cases which are handled at the defendant's first court appearance. In the felony samples, relatively few cases were disposed of at first appearance, and thus inclusion of these cases affected the overall release rates in only a few cities. The problem, however, becomes much more acute with misdemeanors. Thirty-nine percent of the 1962 and 33 percent of the 1971 cases were handled at first appearance. In both years most cases involved defendants who were incarcerated.

The percentage of misdemeanor cases not proceeding beyond a single court appearance in 1962 ranged generally from about 40 to 60 percent, as shown in Table 19. Detroit (87 percent) made far and away the greatest use of first appearance dispositions. By 1971 the rate of first appearance dispositions had dropped somewhat—generally ranging from 30 to 40 percent, as shown in Table 20. Detroit, with a rate of 67 percent, continued to make the most frequent use of first appearance dispositions.

Although most cities in 1962 offered misdemeanor defendants the opportunity to post bail shortly after their

TABLE 19

Misdemeanor Cases Terminating at First Appearance
By Defendant's Release or Detention Status—1962

	Percentage of all cases disposed of at first appearance	Percentage of defendants with first appearance dispositions		
		Released on O.R.	Released on bail	Not released
Boston	20	12	10	78
Champaign-Urbana[1]	19	0	34	66
Chicago	46	3	33	64
Denver	12	22	11	67
Des Moines	55	0	26	74
Detroit	87	0	0	100
Hartford	39	0	30	70
Houston	0	—	—	—
Kansas City	5	0	0	100
Los Angeles	39	7	15	78
Minneapolis	59	0	22	78
Peoria[1]	72	25	41	34
Sacramento	64	0	14	86
San Diego	55	0	30	70
San Francisco[2]	45	1	41	57
San Jose	27	0	29	71
Washington, D.C.	32	0	0	100
Wilmington	49	10	27	63

[1]Base year is 1964.
[2]Base year is 1963.

arrest and booking, very few defendants in cases terminating at first appearance did so. In three cities—Detroit, Washington, D.C., and Kansas City—none of the defendants in first appearance disposition cases was released prior to appearance. In all of the remaining cities, with the exception of San Francisco and Peoria, 63 percent or more of the defendants were incarcerated. The average detention rate was 74 percent.

While the detention period in these cases is generally only overnight, it can be longer, as when the defendant is arrested on a weekend. In addition, even a detention of

TABLE 20

Misdemeanor Cases Terminating at First Appearance
By Defendant's Release or Detention Status—1971

	Percentage of all cases disposed of at first appearance	Percentage of defendants with first appearance dispositions		
		Released on O.R.	Released on bail	Not released
Boston	47	0	8	92
Champaign-Urbana	0	—	—	—
Chicago	56	7	47	47
Denver	16	39	15	46
Des Moines	38	17	3	80
Detroit	67	0	22	78
Hartford	40	61	5	33
Houston	0	—	—	—
Kansas City	5	0	0	100
Los Angeles	39	0	12	88
Minneapolis	34	11	15	74
Peoria	59	17	82	1
Philadelphia	28	0	0	100
Sacramento	32	12	29	59
San Diego	32	3	30	67
San Francisco	58	33	13	54
San Jose	31	54	22	24
Washington, D.C.	21	2	2	95
Wilmington	25	46	10	44

short duration can create a serious problem for the defendant, including possible loss of job. These detentions also represent a substantial cost to the public.

The detention rate in 1971 continued to be high for cases disposed of at first appearance, declining, however, from 74 percent in 1962 to 60 percent in 1971. As compared to all but two cities in 1962, only nine cities had detention rates of 60 percent of more. However, only three cities—Peoria, San Jose, and Hartford—had rates below 44 percent. It is not known whether the release rates in cases terminating at first appearance are low because defendants who cannot afford bail opt to settle their cases

quickly rather than face the continued incarceration necessary to fight the charges, or because the defendants choose
not to pay the cost of release in cases they know will be
disposed of at first appearance.

CONTESTED MISDEMEANOR CASES

Detention in those cases which proceed beyond a single
court appearance is even more important than in first
appearance cases. Defendants in these cases may face
weeks and even months of detention if they are unable to
secure release. Considering only those misdemeanor cases
which continued beyond a single court appearance substantially reduces the percentage of incarcerated defendants. The 1962 detention rate is reduced from 40 to 21
percent, and the 1971 rate from 28 to just 12 percent. The
detention rate in contested cases in 1971 is, thus, a full 40
percent lower than the 1962 rate, a decrease similar to that
observed in the felony cases.

In 1962 most cities were detaining from 14 to 27 percent
of the misdemeanor defendants involved in cases going
beyond first appearance. (See Table 21.) Only five cities—
Kansas City, Sacramento, San Francisco, Chicago, and
Houston—had detention rates of 30 percent or more, while
three jurisdictions had rates below 10 percent: Des Moines
(5 percent), Peoria (8 percent), and Champaign-Urbana
(9 percent).

In 1971 the custody rate in contested misdemeanor cases
was lower in every city studied, as shown in Table 21.
Except for the cities with very low rates in 1962, the drop
generally was substantial. The largest decreases were in
Houston and San Diego. In ten of the nineteen cities
studied, the 1971 custody rate was below ten percent. The
rate was still over 20 percent, however, in five cities:
Sacramento (26 percent), San Francisco (25 percent),
Kansas City (23 percent), Chicago (23 percent), and
Detroit (22 percent). Given the large number of misdemeanor offenses, however, even low detention rates can
mean that a significant number of defendants are being
detained. This alone should be cause for concern when one

TABLE 21
Percentage of Misdemeanor Defendants Detained
through Disposition in Cases Proceeding
Beyond First Appearance—1962, 1971

	Percent detained 1962	Percent detained 1971	Change
Boston	26	15	—11
Champaign-Urbana[1]	9	3	— 6
Chicago	32	23	— 9
Denver	22	5	—17
Des Moines	5	4	— 1
Detroit	27	22	— 5
Hartford	14	12	— 2
Houston	30	9	—21
Kansas City	39	23	—16
Los Angeles	25	19	— 6
Minneapolis	14	6	— 8
Peoria[1]	8	1	— 7
Philadelphia	No sample	4	NA
Sacramento	38	26	—12
San Diego	27	6	—21
San Francisco[2]	37	25	—12
San Jose	17	9	— 8
Washington, D.C.	25	17	— 8
Wilmington	11	9	— 2

[1]Base year is 1964.
[2]Base year is 1963.

considers the relatively minor nature of most misdemeanor offenses.

This chapter indicates that the bail reform movement had a considerable impact on the release status of misdemeanor defendants between 1962 and 1971. The overall detention rate dropped from 40 to 28 percent. The rate for cases disposed of at first appearance decreased from 74 to 60 percent, and for "contested" cases dropped from 21 to 12 percent.

THE CAUSES OF CHANGE

Between 1962 and 1971 the O.R. rate climbed from 10 to over 30 percent for misdemeanor defendants, while money bond releases dropped from 50 to 40 percent. The decrease in detention was thus primarily due to the increased use of nonfinancial releases.

In 1962 money bail was clearly the normal method for achieving pretrial release. Compared to the 10 percent released on O.R., almost 50 percent of the 1962 misdemeanor defendants posted bonds. As in the felony cases, the cities with the lowest detention rates were those making the greatest use of money bonds. In Houston 71 percent of the defendants were released on money bail, and in Champaign-Urbana, 72 percent. In most cities the bail release rate ranged from 40 to 60 percent. Cities in which money bail was used least were those with the highest detention rate and the highest rate of first appearance terminations. Just 3 percent of the defendants in Detroit, and 29 percent of those in Sacramento, were released on money bail. The use of nonfinancial releases rivaled the use of money bail in only two cities—Boston (29 percent O.R. versus 35 percent money bail) and Peoria (27 percent O.R. versus 46 percent bail).

The sharp increase in the use of nonfinancial releases by 1971 not only reduced the percentage of defendants in custody, it also decreased the use of money bail. In 1962 bail release rates generally ranged from 40 to 60 percent. In 1971, however, only five cities had bail release rates above 40 percent. Four of these cities had lower than normal O.R. rates, and three of the five were Illinois cities with deposit bail systems. This is discussed in more detail in Chapter 16.

In eleven of the cities studied, the use of nonfinancial releases equaled or surpassed the use of money bail, and only four cities had nonfinancial release rates of less than 20 percent, as shown in Table 22. Houston, with a rate of 3 percent, was virtually unaffected by the bail reform movement. Chicago and Detroit had rates of 10 percent, and Peoria had a rate of 16 percent.

TABLE 22
Bail and O.R. Releases
in 1971 Misdemeanor Cases

	Percent released on O.R.	Percent released on bail
Boston	22	27
Champaign-Urbana	48	49
Chicago	10	53
Denver	56	32
Des Moines	41	26
Detroit	10	31
Hartford	65	15
Houston	3	88
Kansas City	20	53
Los Angeles	20	34
Minneapolis	36	35
Peoria	16	83
Philadelphia	46	23
Sacramento	26	38
San Diego	41	34
San Francisco	36	22
San Jose	56	31
Washington, D.C.	56	11
Wilmington	58	24

Not surprisingly, nonfinancial releases were used much more frequently in misdemeanor than in felony cases in 1971—33 percent as compared to 23 percent. Those cities with the highest rates of nonfinancial releases in felony cases also had high rates in misdemeanor cases: Washington, D.C., 56 percent; Des Moines, 41 percent; and San Diego, 41 percent. Several cities, however, which were not particularly high in the use of nonfinancial releases in felony cases, made very strong showings in the use of O.R. in misdemeanor cases: Hartford, 65 percent; Wilmington, 58 percent; San Jose, 56 percent; and Denver, 56 percent. Each of these cities has pretrial release mechanisms focused on the speedy release of misdemeanor defendants. The Hartford figure is particularly interesting in that the initial bail decision in that city is made by the police. It is readily apparent (and will be discussed fully in Chapter 17) that the police are quite liberal in the use of O.R. in misdemeanor cases.

Detroit's O.R. release rate—10 percent—although affected by a high rate of first appearance dispositions, was still remarkably low in view of the fact that the city's felony O.R. rate was above 30 percent. One possible reason might be the use of interim bonds in Detroit which permit prompt, inexpensive release at the jailhouse for misdemeanor defendants.[2] As this type of release requires no judge's approval, it is conceivable that many defendants seek it rather than O.R. release, which generally does require approval and a court appearance.

MISDEMEANOR BAIL AMOUNTS

With the exception of the deposit bail cities in Illinois, bail settings for misdemeanors appear to have changed no more than those for felonies. Generally, in both years bail amounts did not exceed $1,000. In 1962, 36 percent of the misdemeanor bails (excluding O.R.) were under $500. While the increased use of O.R. decreased the number of bail settings under $500, 26 percent of the 1971 bails were still in this low range. Bail amounts were often not provided in the court records, particularly when the defendant was in custody, and it is possible that there were unobserved changes.[3] There were no indications of this, however.

The major exception to the use of low bails in 1962 misdemeanor cases was Kansas City, where 74 percent of

2. In Detroit a person arrested for a misdemeanor offense may post an "interim bond" of $50 at the police station to secure his release prior to arraignment. At arraignment the magistrate will make a bail decision in each case, but apparently the interim bond is quite frequently continued as the bail in these cases.
3. The use of misdemeanor bail schedules was the reason usually given for the failure to state the bail amount in each case.

the bail amounts were in the $1,000-2,999 range. The only other cities with any substantial number of bails in this high range were Boston (28 percent), Champaign-Urbana (21 percent), and Peoria (17 percent).

By 1971 bail amounts for misdemeanor defendants had dropped considerably in Kansas City, exceeding $1,000 only 32 percent of the time. Only three other cities set misdemeanor bails in the $1,000-2,999 range in over 30 percent of the 1971 cases. All three—Chicago, Champaign-Urbana, and Peoria—were Illinois deposit bail cities. In Peoria virtually all of the final bail settings in misdemeanor cases were either O.R. (18 percent) or in the $1,000-2,999 range (64 percent). The same was true of Champaign-Urbana—48 percent O.R. and 37 percent in the $1,000-2,999 range. Although Chicago had a number of bails set at or below $250, 35 percent were set between $1,000 and $2,999.

These data confirm the suspicion of many that bail amounts have increased in Illinois since the adoption of that state's deposit bail laws. This increase, however, has not adversely affected the ability of defendants to secure pretrial release. In all three cities the percentage of defendants detained in custody was lower in 1971 than in the base year—1962 in Chicago and 1964 in Champaign-Urbana and Peoria. Peoria and Champaign-Urbana had by far the lowest 1971 custody rates of the nineteen cities studied. The percentages of defendants released on bail in each of these cities—83 percent in Peoria; 53 percent in Chicago, and 49 percent in Champaign-Urbana—were well above the national average of 40 percent. This is more fully discussed in Chapter 16.

MISDEMEANORS TERMINATING AT FIRST APPEARANCE

In most cities in 1971 defendants whose cases terminated at first appearance secured release, if at all, by posting bail. Only in Hartford, San Jose, Wilmington, Denver, and San Francisco were own recognizance or citation releases extensively used. Sixty-one percent of the Hartford defendants and 54 percent of those in San Jose went free on O.R., as compared with 5 and 22 percent on money bail. In each of these cities the police have the authority to release misdemeanants on O.R. In Hartford the police undertake this responsibility, while in San Jose the authority is delegated to the Santa Clara County Pretrial Release Program.

Two of the three remaining cities with detention rates below 50 percent in cases terminating at first appearance also had a high rate of O.R. release. Wilmington's 44 percent detention rate was achieved primarily by releasing 46 percent of the defendants on O.R., and Denver, with a detention rate of 46 percent, released 39 percent of the defendants without bond.

Quite different, but very interesting, is Peoria. Fifty-nine percent of the misdemeanor cases in Peoria in 1971 did not continue beyond a single court appearance. Less than 1 percent of the defendants involved in these cases, however, failed to secure pretrial release. Most—over 80 percent—secured release by posting a bail deposit with the court. Since this system does not require the defendant to secure the services of a bail bondsman and also returns to the defendant 90 percent of the money he posts, the defendant has a very quick and inexpensive method of securing pretrial release. The deposit bail system is obviously working quite well for misdemeanor defendants in Peoria. As will be seen later, it is also working quite efficiently in Chicago and Champaign-Urbana.

MISDEMEANORS CONTINUING BEYOND FIRST APPEARANCE

The increase in the use of O.R. is seen even more dramatically in the misdemeanor cases continuing past first appearance, going from 15 percent in 1962 to 39 percent in 1971. Along with the 10 percent increase in the release rate that this helped to generate, there was also a decline in the money bail release rate from 60 to 46 percent.

Nonfinancial releases were used surprisingly often in most cities in 1962 misdemeanor cases that proceeded

TABLE 23
Percentage of Misdemeanor Defendants Released and
Detained in Cases
Proceeding Beyond First Appearance—1962

	Percent released O.R.	Percent released Bail	Percent not released	Number of cases
Boston	33	41	26	(160)
Champaign-Urbana[1]	10	81	9	(163)
Chicago	16	52	32	(99)
Denver	12	66	22	(192)
Des Moines	33	62	5	(139)
Detroit	50	23	27	(26)
Hartford	14	72	14	(114)
Houston	0	70	30	(200)
Kansas City	10	51	39	(148)
Los Angeles	12	63	25	(128)
Minneapolis	20	66	14	(80)
Peoria[1]	32	60	8	(47)
Sacramento	7	55	38	(76)
San Diego	13	60	27	(95)
San Francisco[2]	7	57	37	(90)
San Jose	15	67	17	(144)
Washington, D.C.	2	73	25	(134)
Wilmington	22	67	11	(101)

[1]Base year is 1964.
[2]Base year is 1963.

beyond first appearance. (See Table 23.) The Vera experiment was just beginning, and the use of O.R. had not yet received the publicity it was to obtain later. With the exception of Houston, Washington, D.C., Sacramento, and San Francisco, however, all of the cities studied had O.R. rates of 10 percent or greater. The cities making the greatest use of O.R. in 1962 felony cases also made the most frequent use of nonfinancial release in misdemeanors. Although only 13 percent of the Detroit cases continued beyond first appearance, in fully half of these the defendant secured nonfinancial release. Lower but still

substantial were Boston, Des Moines, and Peoria, which
released about one-third of their misdemeanor defendants
in this way.

By 1971 the use of nonfinancial releases had greatly
increased. In ten of the nineteen cities studied, close to 50
percent or more of the defendants were freed in this way.
(See Table 24.) In three of these cities the rate exceeded
60 percent, and in Washington, D.C., it reached 70 percent.

In many cities the use of nonfinancial release far
surpassed the use of money bail. Surprisingly, while the
widespread use of O.R. had an obvious effect on detention
rates, in Washington, D.C. and Hartford—the two cities

TABLE 24

Percentage of Misdemeanor Defendants Released and
Detained in Cases
Proceeding Beyond First Appearance—1971

	Percent released O.R.	Percent released Bail	Percent not released	Number of cases
Boston	41	45	15	(103)
Champaign-Urbana	48	49	3	(196)
Chicago	14	63	23	(177)
Denver	59	36	5	(169)
Des Moines	56	40	4	(132)
Detroit	29	49	22	(65)
Hartford	67	22	12	(111)
Houston	3	88	9	(163)
Kansas City	21	56	23	(128)
Los Angeles	33	48	19	(119)
Minneapolis	49	45	6	(130)
Peoria	14	84	1	(77)
Philadelphia	64	32	4	(151)
Sacramento	33	41	26	(147)
San Diego	58	36	6	(143)
San Francisco	40	35	25	(92)
San Jose	57	34	9	(139)
Washington, D.C.	70	13	17	(159)
Wilmington	63	28	9	(147)

with the highest usage of nonfinancial releases—the detention rate was higher than in many other cities. Where nonfinancial releases have achieved such wide usage, those defendants not securing release in this manner must be considered as posing special release problems. It may be that the small profit involved in writing bonds in misdemeanor cases may not be worth the risk of bond forfeiture posed by these defendants. At least in the District of Columbia, there is some indication that bondsmen are not interested in posting low bonds in misdemeanor cases.

8

Days to Release

THERE is an obvious and important difference in being released the day of one's arrest and being held in jail for two weeks prior to release. The defendant's job, his family relationships, and often his defense hang in the balance. In the preceding chapters, defendants were considered as released if they achieved release at any point prior to final disposition of the case. In this chapter, the length of time from arrest to release will be considered.

What the data show is that those defendants who achieve pretrial release do so very quickly. Not surprisingly, releases were effectuated much faster in misdemeanor cases than in felony cases. More interestingly, release on own recognizance appears generally to be faster than release on bail. This study indicates that most nonfinancial releases are granted at the time of the defendant's first appearance in court, and often prior to court in misdemeanor cases. Since a defendant who is granted release on his own recognizance is not faced with the problems of dealing with a bail bondsman or raising money for his bail, it is easy to understand how his release is accomplished quite quickly.

It might be supposed that, with an increasing number of defendants being released, the average length of time to release would have increased during the period of the bail reform movement. Such is not the case, however. Times have actually decreased somewhat. Thus, in 1962 only 62 percent of the felony defendants who were released were freed at the time of first appearance or before. By 1971, however, this figure had risen to 70 percent. In both years about 10 percent of the released defendants were in jail over two weeks. The average times to release were 5.1 days from first appearance in 1962 and 4.5 days in 1971.

For misdemeanors the story was much the same, except that releases were much faster. Eighty-five percent of the released defendants achieved release at or before first appearance in 1962, but 92 percent in 1971. Only 1 percent of those released stayed in jail more than two weeks in both years, and over all the average time from first appearance to release was .8 days in 1962 and .7 in 1971.

It is possible, and in some cities quite common, for defendants to be released prior to any appearance in court. This is particularly true in misdemeanor cases, where the use of misdemeanor bail schedules and citation releases provide speedy release possibilities.[1] Pre-appearance release is particularly helpful for defendants on weekends and holidays, when it may otherwise be several days until they will be brought to court. It is also important to recognize that detention prior to initial appearance is serving an essentially bureaucratic purpose. A defendant who poses a substantial risk of failure to appear should be held until trial. Keeping a person in jail part of the time and then releasing him does not prevent him from skipping. If a defendant is to be given his pretrial freedom at all, the case is strong for letting him out as soon after arrest as is feasible. Thus, as discussed in Chapter 18, a few cities have established "24-hour" arraignment courts (generally operating 12 to 16 hours) or weekend and holiday courts to speed up the setting of bail. In most

---

1. Releases prior to a court appearance were quite common in misdemeanor cases in 1971 in most of the cities studied. While it was often difficult to tell from court records whether a defendant was released before or at his first appearance, it was apparent that in many cities, including Boston, Chicago, Denver, San Jose, and Peoria, a majority of all misdemeanor releases had occurred prior to any court appearance. If releases that occurred prior to first appearance were computed as negative numbers in determining the number of days from first appearance to release, the average days to release in misdemeanor cases would be even lower.

cities, however, this has not been done. In this study, days to release are counted from the date of first appearance.[2] Any pre-appearance days served would therefore increase the number of days in detention.

BAIL VS. O.R.—FELONY CASES

Releases for both bail and O.R. cases tended to be quick in 1971. Given the procedure generally required for O.R., one of the more surprising findings is that in 1971, in fifteen of the twenty cities studied, the average number of days to pretrial release was less for O.R. releases than for bail releases. (See Table 25.) With the exception of Sacramento, the five cities in which bail release was faster all had inordinately long times prior to nonfinancial release: Denver, 24.8 days; Houston, 21.3 days; Wilmington, 15.7 days; and Los Angeles, 9.7 days. In the remaining cities, the average number of days prior to release on O.R. generally ranged from a day and a half to four days. On the other hand, the average number of days to release on bail ranged from three to six days in most cities. While there was an increase in the average length of time to release on bail from 1962 to 1971, it was not great. It seems clear because of this, however, that the overall decrease in time to release is largely attributable to the increasing number of nonfinancial releases.

The short period of time prior to release for both O.R. and bail cases is the result of most defendants being released on or before the day of their first appearance in court and very few defendants being released after more than a week in custody. For example, in the 1971 felony O.R. cases, in ten cities better than 80 percent of the O.R.

2. Ideally, the time span that is most important is from the moment of arrest to the moment of release. Limits on the available data, however, forced us to compromise the ideal. If any date prior to the date of the defendant's first court appearance is recorded, it is generally the date on which the complaint was issued. While this date may, in many instances, be the same as the date of arrest, it could also be prior to or subsequent to the date of arrest. For our purposes, therefore, the date of release will have to be related to the date of the defendant's first appearance in court.

TABLE 25

Average Number of Days from First Appearance
to Release in Felony Cases—1962, 1971

	1962		1971	
	O.R.	Bail	O.R.	Bail
Boston	3.5	1.5	1.8	3.8
Champaign-Urbana[1]	20.1	5.0	3.8	5.7
Chicago	6.5	1.1	1.6	3.0
Denver	13.6	17.4	24.8	8.6
Des Moines	6.8	1.4	1.6	4.1
Detroit	0.8	1.2	1.7	4.0
Hartford	*	*	3.8	4.6
Houston	No cases	11.3	21.3	9.1
Kansas City	0.0	1.3	1.6	2.3
Los Angeles	4.3	6.2	9.7	2.8
Minneapolis	7.6	2.0	0.0	0.3
Oakland[2]	15.4	7.5	4.7	16.9
Peoria[1]	0.4	1.3	2.1	3.8
Philadelphia	No cases	*	*	*
Sacramento	1.6	2.3	3.3	2.7
San Diego	3.5	3.3	1.9	3.0
San Francisco	29.8	4.6	4.2	6.1
San Jose	9.7	9.1	4.0	6.2
Washington, D.C.	No cases	4.4	3.8	9.8
Wilmington	15.9	10.2	15.7	4.8

[1]Base year is 1964.
[2]Base year is 1963.
*Information not available.

releases occurred at or prior to first appearance: Minneapolis, 100 percent; Washington, 90 percent; Hartford, 87
percent; Peoria, 84 percent; Des Moines, 83 percent;
Chicago, 82 percent; and Kansas City, 80 percent. In
another three cities—San Francisco, San Diego, and Detroit—the percentage of O.R.'s occurring at first court
appearance was only slightly less than 80 percent. For the
remaining cities the use of O.R. at first appearance was
considerably less, and in Houston none of the defendants
was released by this stage.

Release on bail for the 1971 felony defendants also generally occurred at or prior to their first appearance in court. The rate of release at first appearance for bailed defendants was not nearly as high, however, as with the O.R. releases. The need to locate a bondsman and raise his fee was probably partly a cause of the longer delay for bail defendants. In any case, in only three cities were better than 80 percent of the bailed defendants free from custody on or before the day of their first appearance: Peoria (87 percent); Minneapolis (86 percent); and Wilmington (82 percent). In most cities the percentage of bailed defendants free by the day of first appearance ranged from 45 to 75 percent. The one notable exception was Oakland, where only 13 percent of those defendants who made bail had done so by the day of their first appearance.

The difficulty many defendants face in raising money necessary for bail also results in a sizable percentage of bail releases coming after more than a week in jail. Bail releases after one week in custody are also the result of bail being reduced in many cases.

The number of cases in which the courts were willing to reevaluate the bail originally set and to lower it at a later hearing was clearly greater in 1971 than in 1962. In the base year, only three jurisdictions—San Jose, Denver, and Champaign—lowered the initial bail amount in at least 15 percent of the felony cases.[3] In 1971, on the other hand, bail was reduced in at least 15 percent of the cases in eleven cities: Denver, Des Moines, Detroit, Hartford, Los Angeles, Sacramento, San Diego, San Jose, Wilmington, Champaign, and Peoria.

O.R. programs have played some role in this increased willingness to reconsider the original bail. In some instances, projects recommend that bail be lowered for defendants for whom they cannot recommend O.R. In other instances, judges who will not accept a project

3. The American Bar Foundation in its study of felony bail practices in 1962 found substantial variations among courts in the rate at which bail reductions occur. The median, however, was only 8 percent of the cases. Lee Silverstein, "Bail in the State Courts—A Field Study and Report," *Minnesota Law Review,* vol. 50 (1965-66), pp. 621, 633.

nonfinancial release recommendation will use the program's report in making a bail reevaluation.

BAIL VS. O.R.—MISDEMEANORS

Nonfinancial releases tend to be faster than bail in misdemeanor as well as in felony cases. The margin of difference is not great, however, and both forms of release tend to be fast. The average time to release is generally less than one day and very rarely is it over two days. (See Table 26.) The chief exception is Houston, where the average length of time prior to O.R. release is 24 days and

TABLE 26

Average Number of Days from First Appearance
to Release in Misdemeanor Cases—1962, 1971

	1962		1971	
	O.R.	Bail	O.R.	Bail
Boston	0.2	0.1	0.9	0.2
Champaign-Urbana[1]	0.5	0.1	0.9	0.9
Chicago	2.3	0.3	0.0	0.3
Denver	0.1	0.6	0.0	1.9
Des Moines	0.0	0.2	0.2	1.0
Detroit	0.0	0.0	0.3	0.0
Hartford	*	*	0.3	0.03
Houston	No cases	4.3	24.0	3.5
Kansas City	9.5	1.1	0.9	0.9
Los Angeles	0.0	0.7	1.8	1.3
Minneapolis	0.0	0.0	0.0	0.1
Peoria[1]	0.0	0.0	0.0	0.0
Philadelphia	*	*	0.4	3.5
Sacramento	0.2	0.3	1.0	0.1
San Diego	0.8	0.4	0.1	0.5
San Francisco[2]	0.4	2.0	0.04	1.4
San Jose	0.0	0.9	0.2	0.5
Washington, D.C.	3.0	0.4	0.7	0.3
Wilmington	0.0	0.8	0.2	1.8

[1]Base year is 1964.
[2]Base year is 1963.
*Information not available.

the average for bail cases is 3.5 days. Philadelphia also had an average delay of three and a half days from first appearance to release on bail.

In fifteen of the nineteen cities in the misdemeanor study, over 90 percent of the nonfinancial releases in 1971 occurred at or prior to the first court appearance. In nine cities, the same was true for bail releases. In seven other cities, first appearance bail releases exceeded 80 percent.

Virtually all pretrial releases in misdemeanor cases were secured within a week of first appearance. Thus, unlike the felony cases, misdemeanor releases after one week in jail were extremely rare. Of course, the data also show that the majority of misdemeanor defendants not securing release by their first appearance in court have their cases disposed of in some manner at that first court appearance. In misdemeanors, unlike felony cases, low initial bail amounts, the high use of O.R., and the over all ability of defendants to post the first bail set result in few adjustments being made.

9

Failure to Appear

DURING the period from 1962 to 1971, the percentages of defendants, both felony and misdemeanor, securing pretrial release substantially increased. The rate of failure to appear by defendants on pretrial release also rose during this period. In 1962 the average nonappearance rate in the cities studied was 6 percent for both felony and misdemeanor defendants.[1] By 1971 this rate had increased to 9 percent for felony defendants and 10 percent for misdemeanants.

Computing and comparing failure to appear rates, however, is a very treacherous undertaking. Other published studies have not generally taken a uniform approach to this issue. At the outset of this study, an effort was made to standardize the definition of what is a "failure to appear." Simply, failure to appear (FTA) was defined as any missed court appearance. Whenever a defendant's appearance in court was required and he was not there, this was recorded as a failure to appear.

Even with this all-encompassing definition, however, this study still ran into a serious problem in collecting standardized data. The problem stemmed from the use of court records. Since this was the only source of information available, the study could only reflect those failures

1. Nonappearance rates represent the percentage of released defendants who failed to appear at any court proceeding at which their presence was required. Such a definition does not consider either the number of court appearances involved or the number of times a single defendant failed to appear. While multiple nonappearances by a single defendant did occur, this was extremely rare. In short, each released defendant was considered as appearing if he made all scheduled court appearances, and as a failure to appear if he missed one or more appearances.

to appear which were recorded in the court minutes. While in some courts the records were quite complete, in others the minutes were very sketchy. Thus, while in some courts we could be quite confident that every time the defendant was not in court this fact would be noted, in other courts this was not the case. This difficulty is encountered not only in comparing failure to appear rates from one city to another, but also in comparing the rates in the same city from one year to another.

Part of the increase in failures to appear from 1962 to 1971 may, consequently, be the result of factors having nothing to do with the conduct of defendants that we are attempting to measure. First, court records in 1962 appear to have been less complete than 1971 records in a number of cities. Second, with fewer defendants passing through the court system, judges in 1962 may have been more lenient in declaring failures to appear, permitting defendants a second opportunity to appear before declaring a failure to appear. Third, lesser concern with the problems of court delay and nonappearance rates may have resulted in fewer failures to appear being recorded in the court minutes. For all of these reasons, it may be that in 1962 technical or inadvertent failures to appear were not being recorded in the court minutes, and thus the figures for this period reflect only true FTA's where the defendant attempted to avoid the court process. It is, however, also probably true that in 1962 there were fewer technical failures to appear owing to the faster disposition of cases, less time between appearances, and fewer court rooms. Each of these factors would lessen the confusion on the part of the defendants as to when or where they are to appear.

Whatever the shortcomings of the data, it seems clear that there has been some increase in the failure to appear rates (see Tables 27 and 28), due at least in part to the increased release rates. While there is probably some general relationship between high release rates and higher FTA rates, higher failure to appear rates do not necessarily follow a high release rate. Cities with the highest non-appearance rates in 1971 felony cases—Boston, Chicago,

TABLE 27
Percentage of Felony Defendants
Failing to Appear—1962, 1971

	1962	1971
Boston	3%	17%
Champaign-Urbana[1]	6%	5%
Chicago	*	17%
Denver	9%	15%
Des Moines	3%	3%
Detroit	11%	11%
Hartford	1%	5%
Houston	4%	4%
Kansas City	3%	8%
Los Angeles	10%	14%
Minneapolis	5%	5%
Oakland[2]	8%	6%
Peoria[1]	5%	3%
Philadelphia	4%	11%
Sacramento	2%	11%
San Diego	4%	4%
San Francisco	14%	14%
San Jose	2%	11%
Washington, D.C.	3%	9%
Wilmington	15%	11%

[1]Base year is 1964.
[2]Base year is 1963.
*Information not available.

Denver, Los Angeles, and San Francisco—were not among the cities with the highest release rates. With the exception of Denver, these cities had lower than average felony release rates. On the other hand, Minneapolis, Champaign-Urbana, and Des Moines—the cities with the highest felony release rates in 1971—had among the lowest failure to appear rates: 3 percent in Des Moines and 5 percent in Minneapolis and Champaign-Urbana. Despite an increase in the release rate, the failure to appear rate did not increase in any of these cities.

Likewise, in the misdemeanor sample, the highest failure

TABLE 28
Percentage of Misdemeanor
Defendants
Failing to Appear—1962, 1971

	1962	1971
Boston	1%	18%
Champaign-Urbana[1]	7%	9%
Chicago	7%	8%
Denver	8%	21%
Des Moines	2%	6%
Detroit	0%	9%
Hartford	2%	3%
Houston	13%	*
Kansas City	12%	7%
Los Angeles	15%	29%
Minneapolis	2%	13%
Peoria[1]	*	*
Philadelphia	*	6%
Sacramento	2%	3%
San Diego	1%	4%
San Francisco[2]	10%	17%
San Jose	4%	10%
Washington, D.C.	0%	14%
Wilmington	16%	11%

[1]Base year is 1964.
[2]Base year is 1963.
*Information not available.

to appear rates were in Los Angeles, Denver, Boston, and San Francisco. With the exception of Denver, each of these cities had release rates substantially below the national average.

FAILURES TO APPEAR ON BAIL AND O.R.

The rate at which defendants who have been released on own recognizance appear in court has been of great concern since the beginning of the bail reform movement. The success of own recognizance release projects was in a large measure contingent upon maintaining an acceptably low failure to appear rate. During the early years of the bail reform movement, O.R. projects consistently reported extremely low nonappearance rates. Generally, failure to appear rates of 5 percent or less were reported.[2] Still today most bail projects are reporting similarly low FTA rates. There have been indications, however, that in cities making extensive use of nonfinancial release, failure to appear rates have climbed to 10 percent and above.[3]

There are several explanations for the extremely low nonappearance rate for O.R. defendants during the first years of the bail reform movement. Two of the more plausible explanations are: first, that the very strict screening of defendants during the early years assured that only the very best O.R. risks were accepted for release; and second, that the limited number of releases during the early years permitted close supervision of those who were released. The close screening guarded against the possibility that someone who really intended to flee would be released, and the close supervision prevented technical failures to appear that could occur if a defendant forgot his court date or was confused as to when or where to appear. The important question is whether own recognizance release used on a large scale produces a failure to appear rate higher or lower than the traditional bail rate, or whether the type of release makes no difference.

2. Figures compiled by the United States Department of Justice and the Vera Foundation for presentation at the 1965 Institute on the Operation of Pretrial Release Projects revealed that thirty-four of the thirty-six programs reporting failure to appear information had nonappearance rates of below 5 percent. Thirteen of the projects reported no failures to appear. *Bail and Summons: 1965* (New York: U.S. Department of Justice and the Vera Foundation, Inc., 1966), p. 8.
3. In a study of pretrial release practices in 1967, the Vera Institute of Justice reported that 15.4 percent of the defendants on own recognizance in Manhattan failed to appear. S. Andrew Schaffer, "Bail and Parole Jumping in Manhattan in 1967" mimeographed (New York: Vera Institute of Justice, August, 1970), p. 4. In New Haven, Connecticut, a study of 1973 cases revealed that 34 percent of those defendants released on citations or O.R. missed a court appearance. Malcolm M. Feeley and John McNaughton, "The Pretrial Process in the Sixth Circuit: A Quantitative and Legal Analysis" mimeographed (New Haven, Conn.: Yale University, 1974), p. 30.

The extremely low failure to appear rates reported by the projects might also have been the result of how the rates were computed. Computing the nonappearance rate of defendants on pretrial release is not an easy task and it is subject to manipulation. Is any missed court date to be considered a failure to appear, or only those which cannot be explained by some good reason? If the defendant is located and returned to court promptly, was his nonappearance a failure to appear? Is the failure to appear rate computed on the number of defendants released or on the number of court appearances made?[4] Disagreement among pretrial release programs on how failure to appear rates are to be computed was reflected in the 1973 survey by the Office of Economic Opportunity, which showed that the fifty-one programs reporting FTA rates had used thirty-seven different methods of calculation.[5]

The acid test for an own recognizance release project's failure to appear rate is how the rate compares to that of surety bail. Interestingly enough, however, the failure to appear rate on surety bail is generally unavailable and thus only a matter of speculation. It is obvious that the failure to appear rate on money bail is subject to the same manipulation as is the O.R. rate. Does the failure to appear rate include all missed court dates? Only those in which a bail forfeiture is declared? Only those in which a bench warrant is issued? Or only those in which a bail forfeiture is paid? Because of the varying ways in which a failure to appear might be defined, it is dangerous to compare bail and O.R. failure to appear rates. This is particularly true when the rates have been computed by parties having an interest in the outcome.

The difficulties in comparing nonappearance rates from one year to another and from one city to another have

4. For example, if ten defendants are released and one fails to appear, this could mean that the failure to appear rate is 10 percent. If, however, these ten defendants had a total of twenty court appearances and only one appearance was missed, the failure to appear rate based on number of appearances would be 5 percent.

5. Hank Goldman, Devra Bloom, and Carolyn Worrell, *The Pretrial Release Program* (Washington, D.C.: Office of Economic Opportunity, Office of Planning, Research and Evaluation, 1973), pp. 21-22.

already been presented. Problems also arise even in comparing bail and O.R. failures to appear within a single city in a single year. In some cities, bondsmen and attorneys are able to persuade judges from declaring a failure to appear and issuing a bench warrant in cases where they feel the defendant can be promptly located. In some cities, judges will do the same for defendants released by an O.R. project. Merely counting those failures to appear noted in the court minutes will not, therefore, provide a totally accurate picture of either bail or O.R. failures to appear. It is very likely that the nonappearance rates for defendants on bail and O.R. are in many cities somewhat higher than reported in this study.

In defining a failure to appear as broadly as possible, this study should reflect the total number of cases in which the court was inconvenienced by a defendant's nonappearance. This study recognizes and will discuss, however, varying degrees of failure to appear. In addition to the overall failure to appear rates for bail and O.R. cases, three classes of FTA's will be discussed: (1) technical or inadvertent failure to appear; (2) the more serious FTA's; and (3) the fugitive. The distinction between the first two classes of failure to appear will be based solely upon the length of time the defendant remained in a failure to appear status. While recognizing that not all failures to appear which are of short duration are inadvertent or technical, most probably are. Further, such failures to appear, regardless of the reason they occurred, represent only a minor inconvenience to the court when compared to the longer more serious FTA's. The third class, fugitives, represents the most serious failing of the pretrial release system in that these defendants have never returned to the court process and thus presumably have avoided justice, at least in the case at issue.

APPEARANCE RATES

Appearance rates for defendants released on money bail in 1962 were uniformly quite high, as shown in Tables 29 and 30. Generally, these rates were at or above 95 percent in

TABLE 29
Appearance Rates for Felony Defendants
Released on Money Bail—1962, 1971

	1962	1971	Change
Boston	98	84	—14
Champaign-Urbana[1]	93	96	+ 3
Chicago	*	81	NA
Denver	92	86	— 6
Des Moines	97	96	— 1
Detroit	94	93	— 1
Hartford	99	96	— 3
Houston	96	96	0
Kansas City	97	93	— 4
Los Angeles	90	90	0
Minneapolis	98	95	— 3
Oakland[2]	92	94	+ 2
Peoria[1]	94	96	+ 2
Philadelphia	96	89	— 7
Sacramento	100	90	—10
San Diego	97	95	— 2
San Francisco	85	82	— 3
San Jose	97	94	— 3
Washington, D.C.	97	88	— 9
Wilmington	88	88	0

[1]Base year is 1964.
[2]Base year is 1963.
*Information not available.

most cities. This was true for both felony and misdemeanor defendants. In only a few cities did the appearance
rate drop below 90 percent: San Francisco had appearance
rates of 85 percent in felonies and 89 percent in misdemeanors; in Wilmington the appearance rates were 88
percent in felonies and 85 percent in misdemeanors; and in
Houston and Los Angeles the misdemeanor rate was 87
percent.

Because of the very limited use of O.R. in 1962, the
appearance rates for these defendants, shown in Tables 31

TABLE 30
Appearance Rates
for Misdemeanor Defendants
Released on Money Bail—1962, 1971

	1962	1971	Change
Boston	97	85	—12
Champaign-Urbana[1]	93	94	+ 1
Chicago	95	91	— 4
Denver	95	82	—13
Des Moines	100	96	— 4
Detroit	100	95	— 5
Hartford	98	100	+ 2
Houston	87	*	*
Kansas City	91	94	+ 3
Los Angeles	87	76	—11
Minneapolis	97	87	—10
Peoria[1]	100	*	*
Philadelphia	*	88	*
Sacramento	98	99	+ 1
San Diego	99	97	— 2
San Francisco[2]	89	79	—10
San Jose	96	91	— 5
Washington, D.C.	100	91	— 9
Wilmington	85	92	+ 7

[1]Base year is 1964.
[2]Base year is 1963.
*Information not available.

and 32, are not meaningful. That several cities had 100 percent appearance rates by defendants on O.R. is indicative, however, of how selective the use of own recognizance was.

In 1971 the appearance rates for both bailed and O.R.'d defendants were lower than the rate for bailed defendants in 1962. The decrease can be partly explained by the incomplete 1962 court records and a lesser concern with the failure to appear problem in 1962. It can also be the result of a greater percentage of defendants being released.

Although the nonappearance rates were higher for both

Table 31
Appearance Rates
for Felony Defendants Released
on O.R.—1962, 1971

	1962	1971
Boston	96	73
Champaign-Urbana[1]	100	93
Chicago	*	93
Denver	88	79
Des Moines	100	98
Detroit	76	87
Hartford	100	92
Houston	No cases	100
Kansas City	100	80
Los Angeles	86	77
Minneapolis	80	96
Oakland[2]	90	95
Peoria[1]	100	100
Philadelphia	*	89
Sacramento	94	89
San Diego	91	96
San Francisco	100	94
San Jose	100	82
Washington, D.C.	No cases	92
Wilmington	63	93

[1]Base year is 1964.
[2]Base year is 1963.
*Information not available.

bailed and O.R.'d defendants in 1971, the increased use of own recognizance may have been partly responsible for both. It is generally assumed that the increased number of defendants securing nonfinancial releases has forced commercial bondsmen to be less selective in whom they release. Own recognizance in 1971 was not limited solely to defendants who could not afford bail, but rather many defendants released without bail would have been potential clients for bondsmen had O.R. not been available. By removing some of the best pretrial release risks, own

TABLE 32
Appearance Rates
for Misdemeanor Defendants Released
on O.R.—1962, 1971

	1962	1971
Boston	98	79
Champaign-Urbana[1]	95	89
Chicago	84	100
Denver	79	77
Des Moines	94	92
Detroit	100	79
Hartford	100	97
Houston	No cases	*
Kansas City	73	89
Los Angeles	76	64
Minneapolis	100	87
Peoria[1]	100	*
Philadelphia	*	98
Sacramento	100	95
San Diego	100	96
San Francisco[2]	100	85
San Jose	96	90
Washington, D.C.	100	85
Wilmington	81	87

[1]Base year is 1964.
[2]Base year is 1963.
*Information not available.

recognizance has forced bondsmen to deal with higher risk defendants. It can be argued that one of the reasons for the increase in the nonappearance rates for bail defendants is the result of the higher risk defendants forced on bondsmen.

The failure to appear rates for defendants released on own recognizance also apparently increased by 1971. The consistently low nonappearance rates reported by O.R. programs in the early 1960s were not found in the 1971 data. This is undoubtedly in part owing to the increased use of O.R. in 1971. The increase is also, however, a result of the fact that the early figures reported by the bail projects were based solely on defendants released through their efforts. As discussed in Chapter 12, a large percentage of the nonfinancial releases in most cities in 1971 were granted by the court without the recommendation of a bail project. Studies comparing the appearance rates of defendants released on O.R. by a project with those released by the court without project involvement indicate that the latter defendants have much higher nonappearance rates. A study by S. Andrew Schaffer, of the Vera Institute of Justice, on failures to appear in Manhattan in 1967 disclosed that among those defendants released on own recognizance, defendants who had been released on the basis of a favorable O.R. recommendation by the Office of Probation had a failure to appear rate of just 9 percent. On the other hand, defendants interviewed by probation but not recommended for release, but who were nevertheless released by the court, and those defendants released by the court but not investigated by the probation department, had significantly higher rates of nonappearance—19 and 16 percent respectively.[6]

Although decreased from 1962, the appearance rates remained high in 1971. For bailed defendants, thirteen cities had appearance rates above 90 percent in felony cases. Although the cities were different, eleven cities had rates above 90 percent in misdemeanor cases as well. All bail appearance rates were above 80 percent, with the exception of misdemeanor defendants in San Francisco and Los Angeles, where the rates were 79 and 76 percent respectively.

The appearance rate for defendants on own recognizance release in 1971 varied little in most cities from the bail rate. (See Tables 33 and 34.) In felony cases, the O.R. appearance rate was higher than the bail rate as often as it was lower, but generally the variation was insignificant—5 percentage points or less. In misdemeanor cases, the O.R. appearance rate was generally lower than the bail rate, but again the variation was usually slight.

6. Schaffer, supra n. 3, p. 4.

TABLE 33
1971 Appearance Rates for Felony Defendants
Released on Bail and O.R.

	Bail cases	O.R. cases	Difference
Boston	84	73	—11
Champaign-Urbana	96	93	— 3
Chicago	81	93	+12
Denver	86	79	— 7
Des Moines	96	98	+ 2
Detroit	93	87	— 6
Hartford	96	92	— 4
Houston	96	100	+ 4
Kansas City	93	80	—13
Los Angeles	90	77	—13
Minneapolis	95	96	+ 1
Oakland	94	95	+ 1
Peoria	96	100	+ 4
Philadelphia	89	89	0
Sacramento	90	89	— 1
San Diego	95	96	+ 1
San Francisco	82	94	+12
San Jose	94	82	—12
Washington, D.C.	88	92	+ 4
Wilmington	88	93	+ 5

In a few cities, however, there is apparently a difference in the appearance rates for defendants on bail and O.R. In Chicago the appearance rate for defendants O.R.'d in felony cases was 12 percentage points above the rate for bailed defendants, and it was 9 percentage points above the bail rate in misdemeanor cases.[7] In San Francisco the O.R. appearance rate was higher than the bail rate by 12 percentage points in felony cases and 6 points in misdemeanor cases.

7. Figures compiled by the Clerk of the Circuit Court of Cook County for the year 1971, however, reveal just the opposite result: forfeiture rate of above 20 percent on "I" Bonds (O.R.), and a rate of 13 percent for deposit bonds.

TABLE 34

1971 Appearance Rates for Misdemeanor Defendants
Released on Bail and O.R.

	Bail cases	O.R. cases	Difference
Boston	85	79	− 6
Champaign-Urbana	94	89	− 5
Chicago	91	100	+ 9
Denver	82	77	− 5
Des Moines	96	92	− 4
Detroit	95	79	−16
Hartford	100	97	− 3
Houston	*	*	*
Kansas City	94	89	− 5
Los Angeles	76	64	−12
Minneapolis	87	87	0
Peoria	*	*	*
Philadelphia	88	98	+10
Sacramento	99	95	− 4
San Diego	97	96	− 1
San Francisco	79	85	+ 6
San Jose	91	90	− 1
Washington, D.C.	91	85	− 6
Wilmington	92	87	− 5

*Information not available.

On the other hand, in Los Angeles, Boston, and Detroit,
the appearance rates were substantially lower in O.R.
cases. In Los Angeles, the O.R. appearance rates were 77
percent in felonies and 64 percent in misdemeanors. These
rates are 13 and 12 percentage points below the respective
bail rates. Boston's appearance rate for O.R. defendants
was 11 percentage points below the bail rate in felonies
and 6 points below the misdemeanor rate. In Detroit the
appearance rates were very high for defendants on bail
bonds—93 percent for felonies and 95 percent for misdemeanors—but the O.R. rate was 6 percentage points lower
in felonies and 16 points lower in misdemeanors. For
felony defendants, San Jose and Kansas City had appearance rates considerably lower in O.R. than in bail cases.

The important question as to whether own recognizance release used on a large scale can maintain an appearance rate comparable to bond releases must be answered in the affirmative. Cities such as Washington, D.C., Des Moines, San Diego, Minneapolis, and Philadelphia have all expanded the use of nonfinancial releases to a sizable percentage of felony defendants and have maintained nonappearance rates of 10 percent or less. In the case of misdemeanor defendants, several cities—Des Moines, Hartford, San Diego, San Jose, and Philadelphia—had failure to appear rates of less than 10 percent, despite very high own recognizance release rates.

These figures suggest that most jurisdictions could substantially increase the number of nonfinancial releases without negatively affecting appearance rates. In the early years of the bail reform movement, O.R. programs found that they could identify and release a number of pretrial detainees and achieve a failure to appear rate lower than that attained by bondsmen. As the number of releases increased, the failure to appear rate also increased, so that in many cities it was equal to the rate achieved by bondsmen. The question remains, however, whether those defendants not eligible for O.R. and not released by bondsmen would have a failure to appear rate higher than those now being released. A severe overcrowding problem in the Santa Clara County, California, jail prompted the judges to authorize the own recognizance release program in that jurisdiction to release all misdemeanor defendants during a three-month period in 1971. The experiment did not negatively affect the failure to appear rate in Santa Clara county. This suggests that the assumption that defendants without the requisite residence, family, and employment ties to the community would fail to appear is far too broad, and that many of these cases could safely be released.

Most jurisdictions would also probably find that extending the use of nonfinancial releases to more felony defendants would not affect the nonappearance rate. The Brooklyn Pretrial Services Agency, for example, reported that the nonappearance rate did not increase during several weeks in 1974 when the rate of O.R. releases increased from an average of 42 percent to 66 percent of all defendants with nondisposed cases (cases not handled at first appearance). The more than 50 percent increase in the O.R. rate had no impact whatsoever on the rate of nonappearance. "Of all appearances of these 'expanded release' defendants, 8.7% ended in initial warrants for failure to appear, including those cases where defendants returned to court. This compares with a rate of 8.4% for aggregate failures to appear for defendants released under the prevailing ROR rate of 42%."[8] The Brooklyn report notes that the "expanded release" defendants faced more serious charges at arraignment than the "average release" defendants; 89 percent of the "expanded release" defendants were charged with felonies, compared to 66 percent of the "average release" defendants.

ELIMINATING TECHNICAL FTA'S

Since the procedures for recording failure to appear information in the court records may vary from one jurisdiction to another, the comparability of FTA rates from one jurisdiction to another might be questioned. If it can be assumed that differences in declaring a failure to appear occur primarily with those that are inadvertent or technical, eliminating all FTA's that last less than eight days would be one method for standardizing the results. Although recognizing that not all FTA's which are resolved within this period of time are in fact technical or inadvertent, this method of calculation does focus upon those failures to appear which gave the courts the most problems in terms of bringing cases to disposition. Elimination of those failures to appear which lasted eight or fewer days evens out the failure to appear rates among the cities, as Table 35 shows.

The picture that emerges is that failures to appear do not represent a major problem. The vast majority of

8. James W. Thompson, "Pretrial Services Agency Operations Report, April 1-April 28, 1974" mimeographed (Brooklyn, N.Y.: Pretrial Services Agency, May 15, 1974).

TABLE 35

Percentage of Released Defendants Failing to Appear and
Remaining in that Status for More than 8 Days—1971[1]

	Felonies		Misdemeanors	
	Percent of bail releases	Percent of O.R. releases	Percent of bail releases	Percent of O.R. releases
Champaign-Urbana	0	3	4	7
Chicago	16	3	7	0
Denver	9	21	9	14
Des Moines	4	2	4	5
Detroit	8	11	5	21
Hartford	2	8	0	3
Houston	4	0	*	*
Kansas City	6	20	3	3
Los Angeles	5	15	18	23
Minneapolis	4	4	9	9
Peoria	4	0	*	*
Philadelphia	10	9	12	1
San Diego	3	2	3	4
San Jose	3	9	8	8
Washington, D.C.	12	7	5	8

[1]Five cities are not included in this table because the court records did not
permit us to determine the date upon which a defendant who failed to
appear returned to court.
*Information not available.

defendants on pretrial release, be it O.R. or bail, appear
as scheduled, and those defendants who do miss court
appearances are very often returned to the court process
quite promptly. The percentage of defendants who fail to
appear and remain lost to the court system for over eight
days appears to be about 5 percent, and this rate is
consistent for bail and O.R. releases and felony and
misdemeanor offenses. Only Los Angeles evidenced a
failure to appear rate consistently above 10 percent. In
those cities where the rate edges above 10 percent, it is
the result not of a great number of failures to appear but
rather of limited use of the form of release being studied.

TABLE 36
Percentage of 1971 Fugitive Cases for
Defendants Released on Bail and O.R.[1]

	Felonies		Misdemeanors	
	Percent of bail releases	Percent of O.R. releases	Percent of bail releases	Percent of O.R. releases
Champaign-Urbana	0	0	1	1
Chicago	14**	0	4	0
Denver	6	4	2	10
Des Moines	1	0	2	2
Detroit	0	3	0	0
Hartford	0	0	0	1
Houston	1	0	*	*
Kansas City	2	20	0	0
Los Angeles	0	6	5	10
Minneapolis	1	0	3	7
Peoria	3	0	*	*
Philadelphia	0	0	0	0
San Diego	0	0	0	0
San Jose	0	2	2	1
Washington, D.C.	3	2	0	3

[1]Five cities are not included in this table because the court records did not permit us to determine the date upon which a defendant who failed to appear returned to court.
*Information not available.
**Not comparable.

FUGITIVES

The number of defendants who by failing to appear are lost to the court system and thereby evade justice is quite small, as shown in Table 36. Since this study was conducted in the last half of 1972 and the first half of 1973, it should be noted that the figures presented represent true fugitives in that these defendants had been missing from court for a period of at least one year. Chicago, which had the largest number of fugitives on bail release—twenty-four—is an exception, however, and is not comparable to the other cities. In Chicago, if the defendant fails to appear within thirty to thirty-five days, his file is closed as a fugitive case. In a few instances, we were able to identify the return of defendants after the bail forfeiture had been declared. In most instances, this was not the case, and thus the high fugitive rate for bail defendants in Chicago. This is discussed further in Chapter 16.

DAYS ON PRETRIAL RELEASE PRIOR TO FTA

What effect the length of time on release has on the rate of failure to appear is an important question to consider. Although the number of failures to appear in this sample is small, it is worth commenting on what our data indicate. First, the failure to appear rates in felony cases would have been significantly reduced in most cities if the cases could have been brought to disposition within sixty days after the defendant's pretrial release. (See Table 37.) Even if the cases could have been handled within ninety days of the defendant's release, the failure to appear rate would have been cut considerably. This was particularly true for those defendants released on money bail. Our data indicate that failures to appear while on O.R. generally occur sooner after release than do the bail FTA's.

In misdemeanor cases, the majority of failures to appear by both bail and O.R. defendants occurred in the first month of release. (See Table 38.) Because of the greater speed with which misdemeanor cases are processed, this is not a surprising finding. Nevertheless, a number of failures to appear did occur in misdemeanor cases after a considerable period of time on release had elapsed. It is thus evident that increased diligence in bringing misdemeanor cases to disposition will reduce the problem of failures to appear.

TABLE 37

Days on Pretrial Release Prior to Failure to Appear
Felony Cases 1971

(Percentage of FTA's occurring during each time period)

| | Bail | | | | | O.R. | | | | |
| | Days on release | | | | | Days on release | | | | |
	1–30	31–60	61–90	90+	N.	1–30	31–60	61–90	90+	N.
Boston	33	0	17	50	(6)	60	40	—	—	(5)
Champaign-Urbana	100	—	—	—	(3)	20	20	—	60	(5)
Chicago	29	42	13	17	(24)	—	50	—	50	(2)
Denver	25	25	25	25	(16)	—	—	40	60	(5)
Des Moines	33	33	—	33	(3)	100	—	—	—	(2)
Detroit	—	—	20	80	(5)	10	20	30	40	(10)
Hartford	50	—	25	25	(4)	67	—	33	—	(3)
Houston	*	*	*	*		*	*	*	*	
Kansas City	75	25	—	—	(4)	—	—	—	100	(1)
Los Angeles	63	—	12	25	(8)	75	12	—	12	(8)
Minneapolis	—	14	43	43	(7)	—	100	—	—	(1)
Oakland	33	—	33	33	(3)	50	—	50	—	(2)
Peoria	—	33	33	33	(3)	*	*	*	*	
Philadelphia	40	—	30	30	(10)	43	14	—	43	(7)
Sacramento	50	50	—	—	(6)	100	—	—	—	(6)

San Diego	100	—	—	—	(2)	50	25	25	—	(4)
San Francisco	29	21	—	50	(14)	50	50	—	—	(2)
San Jose	—	—	50	50	(4)	60	40	—	—	(10)
Washington, D.C.	25	—	—	75	(4)	46	9	18	27	(11)
Wilmington	27	9	9	55	(11)	50	—	50	—	(2)

*Information not available.

TABLE 38

Days on Pretrial Release Prior to Failure to Appear Misdemeanor Cases 1971

(Percentage of FTA's occurring during each time period)

| | Bail | | | | | O.R. | | | | |
| | Days on release | | | | | Days on release | | | | |
	1–30	31–60	61–90	90+	N.	1–30	31–60	61–90	90+	N.
Boston	100	—	—	—	(7)	50	25	—	25	(8)
Champaign-Urbana	67	17	17	—	(6)	18	18	—	64	(11)
Chicago	42	26	16	16	(19)	None	—	8	12	(25)
Denver	73	—	9	18	(11)	80	29	—	14	(7)
Des Moines	—	50	—	50	(2)	57	—	—	—	(4)
Detroit	100	—	—	—	(2)	100	—	—	—	(4)
Hartford	None					75	—	—	25	(4)
Houston	*	*	*	*		*	*	*	*	
Kansas City	50	25	25	—	(4)	33	—	—	67	(3)
Los Angeles	75	6	6	13	(16)	39	46	14	—	(13)
Minneapolis	78	11	11	—	(9)	38	50	—	12	(8)
Peoria	—	—	—	100	(1)	*	*	*	*	
Philadelphia	50	25	—	25	(4)	—	—	50	50	(2)
Sacramento	100	—	—	—	(1)	—	50	50	—	(2)
San Diego	50	—	—	50	(2)	75	—	25	—	(4)

San Francisco	89	—	—	11	(9)	92	—	—	8	(12)
San Jose	50	—	50	—	(6)	100	—	—	—	(11)
Washington, D.C.	50	—	50	—	(2)	47	41	12	—	(17)
Wilmington	67	—	33	—	(3)	85	8	8	—	(13)

*Information not available.

10

Days To Disposition

CRIMINAL cases against defendants detained in custody are brought to disposition considerably quicker than cases involving released defendants. Felony cases in which the defendant has been released generally take at least a month longer than do those cases in which the defendant has remained incarcerated. (See Table 39.) In several cities the time difference was even greater. A similar disparity in the number of days to disposition exists in misdemeanor cases, as shown in Table 40. As already noted, the majority of the misdemeanor cases involving defendants who do not secure release are handled at the defendant's first appearance in court. Misdemeanor cases in which the defendant is released take on the average one to two months to reach disposition.

1962-1971 CHANGES: FELONIES

Because of the obvious difference in the number of days to disposition for released and detained defendants, one would expect that the increased release rate from 1962 to 1971 would have substantially increased the problem of court delay in 1971. Generally, the courts did take more time in disposing of the 1971 cases, but the increase in the average number of days to disposition from 1962 to 1971 is not as great as the increased release rate would suggest.

The average number of days to disposition for felony cases did not increase substantially in many cities, and in some cities there was actually a decrease, as shown in Table 41. This is somewhat surprising in that a number of

TABLE 39

Average Number of Days from First Appearance to Disposition
By Release Status in Felony Cases—1962, 1971

	1962			1971		
	O.R.	Bail	Custody	O.R.	Bail	Custody
Boston	120	71	47	44	99	13
Champaign-Urbana[1]	221	163	53	134	127	44
Chicago	462	68	36	83	77	35
Denver	140	243	137	174	153	134
Des Moines	17	67	24	66	60	41
Detroit	82	110	83	100	123	91
Hartford	33	81	48	58	95	51
Houston	—	212	79	154	143	124
Kansas City	85	107	87	71	123	88
Los Angeles	71	113	70	103	102	70
Minneapolis	111	59	36	79	95	80
Oakland[2]	96	135	69	83	153	73
Peoria[1]	56	88	31	70	61	32
Philadelphia	*	*	*	90	82	100
Sacramento	43	46	31	55	65	44
San Diego	99	95	62	52	61	36
San Francisco	94	104	51	135	111	35
San Jose	66	93	34	69	85	46
Washington, D.C.	—	55	38	97	86	61
Wilmington	67	117	101	65	121	87

[1]Base year is 1964.
[2]Base year is 1963.
*Information not available.

factors have changed since 1962 that would make processing of felony cases more difficult. For example, in addition to the increased release rate for felony defendants, the number of felony filings obviously increased from 1962 to 1971, and this period also witnessed considerable expansion in the use of pretrial discovery, as well as other changes in criminal procedure expanding the pretrial rights of the accused.

TABLE 40

Average Number of Days from First Appearance to Disposition
By Release Status in Misdemeanor Cases—1962, 1971

| | 1962 | | | 1971 | | |
	O.R.	Bail	Custody	O.R.	Bail	Custody
Boston	80	35	11	68	19	2
Champaign-Urbana[1]	73	122	8	98	54	18
Chicago	174	55	7	44	45	20
Denver	59	77	16	142	128	6
Des Moines	17	10	.6	21	18	1.5
Detroit	10	12	.2	72	28	2
Hartford	32	18	2	23	32	9
Houston	—	107	15	61	78	44
Kansas City	80	125	25	122	42	24
Los Angeles	46	47	9	52	48	6
Minneapolis	15	17	.5	101	65	7
Peoria[1]	413	18	6	12	34	7
Philadelphia	*	*	*	67	76	6
Sacramento	9	16	.4	38	38	8
San Diego	41	32	4	50	39	3
San Francisco[2]	20	20	4	16	47	2
San Jose	18	57	5	42	42	11
Washington, D.C.	42	45	8	72	45	25
Wilmington	20	22	1	24	38	13

[1]Base year is 1964.
[2]Base year is 1963.
*Information not available.

Apparently, the courts have adapted to the increased burdens of handling felony cases by altering court procedures. In the California cities, for example, a more detailed analysis of the average number of days to disposition reflected a change in the municipal courts' role in processing felony cases. It was found that in 1971 the lower court was handling to completion considerably more felony filings by dismissals and reductions to misdemeanors than it did in 1962. Our analysis showed that this practice of handling felonies in municipal court had a

TABLE 41
Average Number of Days
from First Appearance to Disposition
in Felony Cases—1962, 1971

	1962	1971	Change (in days)
Boston	62	38	—24
Champaign-Urbana[1]	115	114	— 1
Chicago	56	59	+ 3
Denver	186	151	—35
Des Moines	49	59	+10
Detroit	92	105	+13
Hartford	66	72	+ 6
Houston	168	136	—32
Kansas City	91	99	+ 8
Los Angeles	86	88	+ 2
Minneapolis	50	91	+41
Oakland[2]	97	99	+ 2
Peoria[1]	62	54	— 8
Philadelphia	*	88	—
Sacramento	34	54	+20
San Diego	73	51	—22
San Francisco	74	75	+ 1
San Jose	58	68	+10
Washington, D.C.	44	83	+39
Wilmington	106	99	— 7

[1]Base year is 1964.
[2]Base year is 1963.
*Information not available.

significant influence on the time to disposition. It was found that while the average length of time to disposition for felony cases had not increased significantly from 1962 to 1971, this was primarily owing to the increased activity of the municipal court. In fact, for the felony cases reaching the superior court, there had been a significant increase in the days to dispostion.

The time to disposition for the 1971 felony cases is subject to two further qualifications. First, in several cities there were included in our sample a number of cases that were still active. For these cases, the days to disposition were unknown and thus not included in the tabulation of average days to disposition. If these cases had been included, the average days to dispostion would be slightly higher than the table indicates. Second, a problem developed in a few cities in that some felony cases were technically dismissed only to be refiled, either through a new complaint or by a grand jury indictment. Our sampling technique did not permit us to follow the defendant to his new case number, and thus our records will show a final disposition while in actuality the case continued against the defendant under another case number.

Generally, the average days to disposition for felonies ranged from sixty to ninety days. The only city below sixty days was Boston, where the lower court has jurisdiction to handle to disposition a number of selected felonies. This obviously affected the days to disposition in that city.

The longest periods of pretrial delay were found in Denver, 151 days; Houston, 136 days; Champaign, 114 days; Detroit, 105 days; and Oakland and Wilmington, 99 days each. Lengthy periods of pretrial delay, of course, strike hardest against those defendants unable to secure release. In most cities the period of pretrial delay for incarcerated defendants was considerably shorter than the sixty to ninety day averages for the samples as a whole. The cities with the longest periods of overall pretrial delay, however, also had considerable difficulty in bringing to disposition those cases involving custody defendants. The only exception was Champaign-Urbana, where despite an average time to disposition of 114 days, custody defendants waited only an average of forty-four days. Cities which did not bring custody cases to disposition within fifty days included: Denver—134; Houston—124; Philadelphia—100; Detroit—91; Wilmington—87; Minneapolis—80; Oakland —73; Los Angeles—70; and Washington—61.

If one of the concerns in promoting bail reform is to reduce the jail population, it must be borne in mind that the jail population is a function both of the number of defendants detained and the length of their stay in jail.

Long periods of pretrial detention can cancel out to some extent any reductions achieved by high release rates. Philadelphia, for example, though it had one of the highest felony release rates, held those defendants who were detained an average of 100 days, considerably longer than the average period for most other cities.

1962-1971 CHANGES: MISDEMEANORS

The increase in the average number of days to disposition for misdemeanor cases from 1962 to 1971 was substantial in most cities, as Table 42 shows. In eight cities the average number of days to disposition increased by twelve or more days. Two cities, Denver and Minneapolis, apparently have serious problems with increased trial delays in misdemeanor cases. The average number of days to disposition in Denver increased by sixty-two days over 1962 to a staggering 120 days average. This can be partly explained by the presence of ninety-one drunk driving cases in the Denver 1971 sample. This number of DUI cases is out of all proportion to their presence in the other city samples. Drunk driving offenses could be expected to take considerably longer than other misdemeanor crimes to handle because of the necessity for blood alcohol tests to be run and because of the serious consequences which can flow from a conviction. Thus, in drunk driving cases it will take longer for the state to prepare its case, and the defendant may well want to present a full defense to such charges. Also, Denver had a very low total custody rate of 12 percent and handled very few cases at first appearance, 16 percent in 1971.

Minneapolis's average days to disposition increased by fifty-two days. In 1962 Minneapolis had one of the lowest average days to disposition—eight days—but this increased to sixty in 1971. This was apparently owing to an increase in misdemeanor releases from 48 to 71 percent, and a drop in the number of cases handled at first appearance, from 59 to 34 percent.

Three cities reversed the general trend and significantly reduced the time to disposition in misdemeanor cases. Two

TABLE 42

Average Number of Days
from First Appearance to Disposition
in Misdemeanor Cases—1962, 1971

	1962	1971	Change (in days)
Boston	39	20	—19
Champaign-Urbana[1]	96	74	—22
Chicago	43	36	— 7
Denver	58	120	+62
Des Moines	7	14	+ 7
Detroit	1	17	+16
Hartford	14	22	+ 8
Houston	80	74	— 6
Kansas City	77	52	—25
Los Angeles	29	29	0
Minneapolis	8	60	+52
Peoria[1]	13	30	+17
Philadelphia	*	50	—
Sacramento	5	27	+25
San Diego	19	34	+15
San Francisco[2]	12	17	+ 5
San Jose	36	38	+ 2
Washington, D.C.	27	53	+26
Wilmington	13	25	+12

[1]Base year is 1964.
[2]Base year is 1963.
*Information not available.

of these cities—Champaign-Urbana and Kansas City—had extremely long delays in the base year and, though the time was reduced by 1971, the number of days to disposition still remained substantial. Boston, on the other hand, significantly reduced its average days to disposition from thirty-nine to twenty days. Boston operates with a trial de novo procedure which permits the speedy disposition of misdemeanor cases and then offers the defendant the right to a new trial in which his rights are more fully protected. Forty-seven percent of the 1971 misdemeanor cases in Boston were handled at first appearance. As a result, Boston had one of the lowest average days to disposition in the 1971 sample. What is not known, however, is the extent to which the cases are reopened under the de novo system, and the length of additional time required for these cases.[1]

In most cities the increase in the time to disposition for misdemeanor cases can be attributed to the increased release rate. As shown in Table 40, it takes considerably longer to handle cases in which the defendant has secured pretrial release. The increase in the number of defendants securing release also means that fewer cases will be handled at the first appearance in court. The rate of first appearance dispositions decreased from 39 percent in the 1962 sample to 33 percent in 1971. The increased availability of release prior to a court appearance and the increased use of nonfinancial releases, which cost the defendant nothing, enable more defendants to be released promptly and cheaply, and thus the defendants are less likely to seek an immediate disposition.

BAIL VS. O.R.

In comparing the average days to disposition for O.R. and bailed defendants, one would expect that they would be roughly the same, and in 1971 this was generally the case. (See Tables 39 and 40.) In 1962 the very small number of O.R.'s makes it difficult to attach much significance to the average days to disposition.[2] While the length of time to disposition was generally comparable for bail and O.R.

1. In fiscal year 1968 only 2 percent of all cases brought in the district courts in Massachusetts were retired under the de novo system, but of those defendants eligible to pursue their case under the de novo system, one in five did so. Stephen R. Bing and S. Stephen Rosenfeld, *The Quality of Justice in the Lower Criminal Courts of Metropolitan Boston* (Boston, Mass.: Lawyer's Committee for Civil Rights Under Law, 1970), p. 4 fn. 8.
2. It should be noted, however, that the very high average number of days to disposition in Chicago is the result of a procedure for releasing youthful defendants on what amounts to predisposition parole, after which the charges are dismissed.

cases in 1971, in some cities—Boston, Hartford, Oakland, Wilmington, and Kansas City—the days to disposition in felony cases was considerably less in O.R. than in bail cases. This gives reason to ask whether the use of O.R. in these cities is limited to defendants charged with less serious and therefore easier to dispose of offenses, or whether it is limited to defendants against whom the evidence is weak and the charges more likely to be dismissed prior to trial.

11

O.R. Projects, 1965-1970

To LOOK at the figures on nonfinancial releases in 1971, one could only conclude that the movement set in motion by Louis Schweitzer's visit to the Brooklyn jail had been a great success. Where a decade before such a thing had hardly even been heard of, by 1971 over 20 percent of the felony and over 30 percent of the misdemeanor defendants in the cities studied were being released on O.R. or some other form of nonfinancial release. And as a result, 30 to 40 percent more defendants were being released than in the early 1960s.

A look at the O.R. projects themselves would have been far less encouraging. It would have shown that many of the programs begun so boldly in the early exciting days of national conferences and Robert Kennedy had either ceased to operate or had managed to continue only on a very limited scale. O.R. projects were no longer in the forefront of legal reform, and even Vera had withdrawn from the field—turning the Manhattan Project over to the New York Probation Department.

Although a few programs such as those in Washington, D.C., and Des Moines had made substantial progress and grown into strong, effective organizations, field trips to fifteen pretrial release programs in 1970 by the Center on Administration of Criminal Justice revealed that most had made little progress and that many had encountered serious difficulties. Most projects contacted had at least one or more of the following problems:

—Serious difficulty in attracting the economic resources necessary for a strong program.

119

—A shifting in allegiance from providing a service to the defendant to that of being a service to the courts. The experimentation philosophy and the commitment to greater use of O.R. was often lost in the transition.

—Self-imposed limitations as to who would be interviewed, resulting in many criminal defendants never being considered for O.R. recommendation.

—Delays in interviewing defendants and verifying the information obtained, so that many defendants who could have been considered were never reached before the end of their case or release.

—Criteria for determining eligibility for O.R. release which were unnecessarily strict.

A mail survey in 1973 of eighty-eight pretrial release programs by the Office of Economic Opportunity indicated that, for the most part, these problems had not been solved and continued to exist.

These results were not altogether surprising; they had been foreshadowed much earlier. Even in the heady days of 1964, those most closely involved with the bail reform movement could see some serious problems ahead. It was obvious that many of the bail programs that were developing were not of the caliber of the Manhattan Bail Project. The Interim Report of the 1964 National Conference on Bail and Criminal Justice concluded:

But hundreds, perhaps thousands, of communities have not yet responded to the challenge, and of those which have, project quality varies widely. Under the heading of bail reform, some courts appear to direct r.o.r. program efforts to releasing 'substantial' or 'respected' citizens who might well afford a bail bond premium, while detaining those who are poor. Some projects are interrogating the defendant as to his involvment in the alleged crime instead of confining their questions to the nature of the defendant's roots in the community. These projects even go so far as to disqualify from consideration a defendant who refuses to discuss the circumstances of his arrest. Plainly, little ground exists for complacency; the nation-wide long-term success of pre-trial release projects is far from assured.[1]

1. *National Conference on Bail and Criminal Justice* (Washington, D.C.: U.S. Department of Justice and the Vera Foundation, Inc., April, 1975), p. XXVI.

Even more foreboding was a 1966 internal Vera Foundation memorandum. After visiting twenty O.R. programs as Field Coordinator and Consultant for Vera, Roger Baron pessimistically reported:

The five years since the Manhattan Bail Project has seen pre-trial release projects of every shape and form spring up throughout the country. Since little was known about pre-trial release projects at that time, this was envisioned as the best way to proceed. The theory was, let experimentation be the key to success. At some future point, we will sit down, analyze the strengths and weaknesses of each project, and determine what the best procedure is. Well, that time has come now and, unfortunately, this determination cannot be made with any degree of certainty.
. . . The problems posed several years ago—Who is best suited to administer pre-trial release projects? What do you do when a defendant does not meet your criteria for release on recognizance? Who do you present the information to? Do you use objective or subjective criteria?—are still unsolved today. In fact, we have not even answered the basic question, are pre-trial release projects necessary? If we were to release all defendants on their own recognizance, how many would return?[2]

THE PROBLEMS ENCOUNTERED BY O.R. PROJECTS:
1965-1970

Economics

Perhaps the most serious problem encountered by O.R. projects in the 1960s was that of economics. Although several of the early programs were funded by local government from the outset, all of the better projects, including those in New York City, Washington, D.C., Des Moines, San Francisco, and Wilmington, were financed initially by private foundations. Some projects were hardly funded at all, having been initiated by one or two individuals who, by dint of personal effort, were able to scrape together the resources necessary to get underway.

It was predictable, therefore, that at some point economics would become a major problem. For most pro-

2. Vera Foundatoin memorandum from Roger Baron to Herbert Sturz, December 14, 1966.

grams the ultimate hope necessarily had to be a takeover by local government. The Manhattan Bail Project, originally funded by Louis Schweitzer and later the Ford Foundation, was taken over by the city probation office in 1964. The projects in Washington, D.C., Des Moines, and Wilmington also had relatively smooth transitions from private to public funding.

Other programs, however, were not so fortunate. Several folded outright. In Philadelphia, an experimental three-year project was operated by the bar association with combined funds from four private foundations. The expectation was that the city would take over the project if it proved successful. According to the director of that project, Edmund E. DePaul, in 1968, at the end of the three-year period, funding for the project was written into the city's budget but was one of the first items to be scratched. In 1969 and 1970 it met the same fate. According to DePaul, Philadelphia suffered from a lack of funds the same as all large cities, and the money to finance the project was just not available. An Oakland program, funded by the Ford Foundation, also folded at the end of its experimental period.[3]

Some programs succeeded through simple perseverance and adroitness, their stories rivaling the perils of Pauline. In San Francisco, for example, the program began as a bar association project with a first year budget of under $15,000. The San Francisco Bar Association Foundation then applied for funds for the project from the Economic Opportunity Council. The EOC approved the request and funded the project for a year with a $35,000 grant. The EOC continued to fund the project for five years with similar-sized annual grants; and with the EOC money and the use of Vista volunteers, the San Francisco project developed into one of the best programs in the country. Despite the success of the project, its funding miseries began in earnest in 1970 when the EOC grants terminated. The refusal of the City and County of San Francisco to fund the program forced it to cease operating for a brief time in 1970, but

3. Pretrial release programs with substantial federal funding were reestablished and are now operating in both Philadelphia and Oakland.

the tenacity of director Ken Babb finally paid off when he obtained a $24,000 grant from a private foundation which the city agreed to match. A year later, however, with local government still unwilling to commit enough money to the program, the project was close to termination again until an impassioned plea by Babb to the California Council on Criminal Justice—the state's Safe Street Act vehicle—produced funds to carry the program for the remainder of 1971 and all of 1972. Finally, in 1973, local government picked up the project with an interim grant of $40,000 to carry the program from January to July, and in July the project was funded for $126,000 for the next fiscal year. In 1974 and 1975 the project was refunded by the local government.

Generally, two arguments have been put forward as reasons for local government to undertake the financial burden of O.R. programs. First are the merits of the program itself. Local funding should be given as a matter of fairness and justice to defendants and the community. The Evansville-Vanderburgh County Bail Bond Project in Evansville, Indiana, summarized this reasoning in a 1973 report on the project's first ten months of operation:

Beyond these financial savings, rational pre-trial release is valuable for many other less measurable reasons. A high percentage of those arrested are first offenders and most are misdemeanors. A large number will be found not guilty and many cases will be dismissed. Along with helping to alleviate the overcrowding in local jail facilities, the prevention of pretrial incarceration of non-serious offenders with hardened criminals in what many have called 'schools for crime' where inmates are subjected to loss of self-image, job, family, property bought on time, helps prevent many first offenders from becoming recidivists. As such, the project can be viewed as a crime prevention program.

By removing the punitive aspects of money bail, the project shifts emphasis from arrest to trial, thereby increasing the importance of the courts in the criminal process and upholding the fundamental concept of legality that punishment should be imposed only after guilt has been determined by the court at trial under due process. If confinement to jail is a deserved punishment (it is actually imposed in only 15% of all convictions) it should be given after guilt is properly determined and not before trial simply because of the accused's inability to afford a money bond. By returning control to the courts of one of the most important judicial decisions, that of pretrial release, the administration of justice has become more rational, efficient and fair.[4]

The second reason advanced to convince local government to undertake project funding is that of cost-savings to the jurisdiction. Conscious of the fact that their long-term existence was dependent on support from local government, experimental O.R. projects were from the beginning concerned with justifying their activities through some method of cost-benefit analysis.

The normal method for showing the cost-savings to a jurisdiction through the presence of an O.R. project involves an averaging technique. The project multiplies the number of releases it has over a certain period of time by the average number of days a defendant would have spent in jail had he not been released. This figure is the number of jail days the project has saved the city. Multiplying the jail days saved by the cost per day of housing a defendant then gives the cost-savings to the city. An example of how this works is found in the 1968 annual report of the Wilmington, Delaware, project. Figuring that the average time to disposition in Delaware is eighty-nine days in felonies and sixty-six days in misdemeanors, and the cost of keeping a defendant in jail is $6.28 per day, the project's report estimates that its 349 releases in 1968 saved the city $149,595.88 in jail costs alone.[5]

San Francisco's project, after four years of operation, estimated the amount of money it had saved the city as follows:

The impact of this program on the city has been as great or greater than the effect on the defendants released on Own Recognizance. A conservative estimate of the cost of housing a

4. Charles E. Marske, "Evansville-Vanderburgh County Bail Bond Project—The First Ten Months: Initial Results and Future Prospects," mimeographed (Evansville, Ind.: Probation Department of the Vanderburgh Circuit Court, 1973), pp. 19-20.
5. Thomas C. Maloney, "Report of the 1968 Operation of the Pre-Trial Release Program, Department of Correction, State of Delaware," mimeographed (Wilmington, Del.: Pre-Trial Release Program, 1969), p. 19.

defendant in City Prison is $5.00 per day. The average period of time that elapses before a case is adjudicated is 39 days. Therefore, each prisoner costs the city an average of $195 in detention costs before his case is completed. That means that there have been total savings to the city in custodial expenses alone of at least $1,092,975. There are additional savings to the city of incalculable amounts that would be spent for welfare payments to an incarcerated person's family. Finally, there would be a loss to the city in tax revenues from many people who would be unable to work during the period they are incarcerated. The savings to the city alone are more than ten times greater than the expenditures which have been made to finance this program.[6]

Not many cities have been fully persuaded by these statistics. In part this has been due to questions about the figures themselves. With limited budgets to begin with, O.R. projects have been unable to fund adequate research and evaluation efforts. Generally, the projects have information readily available only on the number of interviews conducted, the number of recommendations made, the number of releases granted, and the number of failures to appear by defendants they have assisted in gaining release. For the most part, they do not have data on how their activities relate to the overall system of pretrial release and detention in their jurisdiction.

The lack of more sophisticated research efforts has limited the credibility of the cost-benefit studies that have been done. Cost-savings estimates based on the assumption that all of the persons released by the project would have otherwise remained in jail, and that the average length of time to case disposition is the same for custody and released defendants, seem to exaggerate the number of detention days saved by the project. In addition, the failure to distinguish fixed from variable jail expenses in computing the detention cost-savings per inmate seems to inflate the savings.

This is not to say, however, that the jail cost-savings to be realized by a pretrial release program are insignificant, or that they do not offset the cost of operating the program.

6. San Francisco Bail Project, "The First Four Years," mimeographed (San Francisco: San Francisco Bail Project, 1969), p. 4.

While it is true that the only real savings from a single O.R. release is the price of a few meals and a little processing time, the savings from just one O.R. release a day for a year or two years are much greater. Over a period of time the marginal jail cost-savings through a pretrial release program may very likely approach the average cost of a detention. This can be seen most readily where the existence of a pretrial release program saves the jurisdiction the cost of a jail expansion—a situation not uncommon, because pretrial release programs have often been established in jurisdictions with a strong need for bail reform caused by serious overcrowding in detention institutions. In view of spiraling capital costs (and the tendency of the marginal jail costs to approach the full jail cost), the presence of O.R. programs in these jurisdictions is generally clearly justified on a cost efficiency basis. Even if no capital construction is avoided, the existence of a sizable pretrial release program active in generating significant numbers of pretrial releases over a considerable time very likely results in significant dollar savings.

In large part, therefore, the failure of the cities to be convinced by these cost-savings estimates has less to do with the accuracy of the figures than with the desperate financial situations of the cities and their hope that other sources can be found to keep the projects in operation. Even if a totally accurate cost-savings figure were to be shown, it does not necessarily follow that the jail budget would be increased by that amount if the project were discontinued. First, it is quite likely that in many jurisdictions judges, having become familiar with the use of O.R., would compensate for the loss of the program by increasing the use of nonfinancial releases on their own volition. Second, even if the jail population does increase with the discontinuance of projects, it is possible to stretch the available money further. More detainees simply mean more crowded cells, more inmates without blankets and bedding, and less food and personal necessities per inmate. Thus far, at least, there has certainly been no commitment to maintaining standard levels of care for inmates.

The economic picture for pretrial release programs has brightened considerably in the 1970s, but this has been more the result of the widespread availability of Law Enforcement Assistance Administration (LEAA) money than of increased support from local government. Safe Street funds have pumped new life into a number of older programs but have been primarily used to create new ones. The 1973 Office of Economic Opportunity study of pretrial release programs identified forty-six projects which had started since 1970 and found that over half were funded primarily by LEAA.[7] The study did report, however, that the funding of O.R. programs was about equally divided between LEAA and local government. Forty-two percent of the programs cited county or municipal government as the primary source of their funds, and 37 percent cited LEAA.[8] The report also noted, however, that a large number of programs operate on small budgets. Almost half of the programs reporting indicated that they operated on an annual budget of less than $50,000, and a quarter of the programs on less than $25,000.[9]

Clearly, the economic problems of O.R. projects have not been solved. When the period of LEAA funding runs out, projects will be forced to solicit local funds just as the 1960 projects were forced to do when the funding from private foundations terminated. Whether the second wave of projects will be any more successful than the first remains to be seen.

Bureaucratization and a Changing Role for O.R. Projects

It was obvious by 1970 that the role of O.R. programs, insofar as they were able to carve out roles for themselves, was changing from that of largely defendant-oriented experiments to that of a court staff agency. In the early years

7. Hank Goldman, Devra Bloom, and Carolyn Worrell, *The Pretrial Release Program* (Washington, D.C.: Office of Economic Opportunity, Office of Planning, Research and Evaluation, 1973), p. 10.
8. Ibid., p. 8.
9. Ibid., p. 7.

of the bail reform movement, O.R. projects were operated by a variety of organizations and individuals, such as law students, bar associations, attorneys, public defenders, district attorneys, police, Vista volunteers, and private foundations, as well as by the courts and probation offices. In 1965 approximately one-half of the programs were operated by independent agencies outside of the existing court structure.[10] With the transition to government funding, projects more and more often became part of the court staff or the probation department. In 1973 OEO reported that sixty-nine projects were run by public agencies and just nineteen by private agencies, and that 42 percent of the public programs were organizationally located in probation offices and 38 percent were under the courts.[11]

As a consequence of this shift to a court agency, a number of changes occurred in the organization and role of the projects. The concern for the defendant which sparked the early bail reform efforts was not as readily obvious in 1970. While the original Manhattan Bail Project and most of the other early programs were concerned only with identifying good risk defendants and presenting their cases to the judge, projects increasingly moved toward recommending defendants both for and against O.R. In 1965, only 38 percent (16 of 42) of the projects supplying information to the Institute on the Operation of Pretrial Release Projects were identified as recommending against O.R. release in some cases.[12] By 1973, 69 percent of the projects in the OEO survey (52 of 75) made negative as well as positive recommendations.[13] Sixty percent of the programs responding to the OEO questionnaire were also making bail as well as O.R. recommendations—generally either for bail reductions or specific bail amounts.[14] Instead of merely submitting recommendations to the court, many projects began submitting O.R. reports which included facts about

10. *Bail and Summons: 1965* (New York: U.S. Department of Justice and the Vera Foundation, Inc., August, 1966), p. 8.
11. Goldman et al., supra n. 7, p. 9.
12. *Bail and Summons: 1965*, supra n. 10, p. 8.
13. Goldman et al., supra n. 7, p. 16.
14. Ibid.

the alleged offense and and other data not relevant to the defendant's ties to the community.

By 1970 projects were also less likely to maintain contact with the defendant once he was released. Most of the early programs felt a commitment to maintain contact with the defendant to assist with any problems that might arise during his period of release. In 1973, only 61 percent of the programs required defendants to maintain contact, and only 75 percent of the projects sent letters reminding defendants of their court appearances.[15]

Institutionalized, the programs in 1970 bore little resemblance to the programs of the 1960s. In no city was the change from a private to a public organization more obviously detrimental than in New York City. In September of 1964 the Vera program was turned over to the Office of Probation and the program took on a completely different outlook.

Harry I. Subin, associate professor at the New York University School of Law and director of the school's Criminal Law Clinic, described the probation program as it operated in 1970:

Now fully bureaucratized, the bail program run by the Office of Probation bears little resemblance to the original project: it is attempting to apply release criteria useful in isolating the highly visible good risks to defendants all along the risk spectrum, and it is doing even this in a half-hearted way. The information from probation comes to the court in only about one-half of the cases, and it comes without verification, without oral advocacy, and without the promise of follow-up procedures, all of which were critical parts of the original project. The result is that the judges often do not have reports, and often do not read them when they do have them. Several judges have told me—even if they have not told their superiors—that the probation reports are useless.[16]

The change that occurred in the Manhattan program was foreseen by Roger Baron, director of the program under Vera. At the 1964 Conference on Bail and Criminal Justice, Baron was asked what changes the New York Probation

15. Ibid., p. 20.
16. Harry I. Subin, "New York's Bail Riots," *Legal Aid Review*, vol. LXVII (1970), p. 30.

Department would make in the operation of the Manhattan Bail Project. He answered:

They have started, basically, with our interview form, but they do have a different policy. As of now, the way we operate is that we only present a recommendation to the judges in cases where we are prepared to recommend that an accused be released on his own recognizance. The Probation Department, as of now, is submitting reports on every single case that they interview. In the cases that meet the standards that we have set up, they present a recommendation for release. In cases where they interview the defendant but are not able to recommend release, they present the judge with the information that they have verified without recommending anything; they simply submit the information. There is a difference in philosophy in that the Department of Probation considers itself to be an arm of the court. Its responsibility is to the judge, to present him with whatever information will be helpful to him in determining the question of bail. We feel that we should only present favorable recommendations.[17]

Generally, probation-run programs in 1970 had lower O.R. release rates than programs run by independent agencies. One hypothesis advanced to account for the lower release rates of probation programs was that probation officers, being accustomed to evaluating defendants only after conviction, did not have the proper outlook for passing on the eligibility of an arrestee for pretrial release. The assumption was that probation officers were viewing the accused as guilty and thus were not motivated to aid in his release. This was one of the conclusions expressed by Forrest Dill in his dissertation on the probation-operated project in Oakland, California.[18] According to Dill, the probation interviewers, in passing on a defendant's eligibility for O.R., considered the ultimate sentence that he was likely to receive if convicted. Dill found that whenever a defendant appeared likely to be incarcerated once convicted, he was denied O.R. by the investigator. This finding, however, is not unique to the Oakland project or to probation projects generally. The overreliance placed on the

17. National Conference, supra n. 1, p. 85.
18. Forrest Dill, "Bail and Bail Reform: A Sociological Study" (Ph.D. diss., University of California, Berkeley, 1972).

alleged offense and the defendant's prior record by most O.R. programs amounts to a presumption of guilt. In most cities in 1970 it was a rare case when a defendant on O.R. was incarcerated following a conviction.

A more likely reason for the relatively poor performance of most probation-run programs in 1970 is that they viewed themselves as performing a service to the court. As such, probation programs provided the court only that which the court desired. This meant, first, that only the very best pretrial risks were favorably recommended for O.R. release and, second, that full O.R. reports were presented to the court for all defendants. Probation-operated programs in 1970 did not generally challenge the court by presenting favorable release recommendations in tough, borderline cases. They also generally did not use an objective point scale for determining O.R. eligibility but rather relied on subjective evaluations. Exclusions based on the alleged offense or prior record were thus even more prevalent in these programs.

The institutionalization of O.R. programs also tended to induce delay. Many programs in 1970 spent considerable time verifying the information provided by the defendant and writing detailed O.R. reports, which resulted in the defendant spending additional time in jail prior to an O.R. recommendation. The problem of long delays in securing O.R. releases was not unique, however, to probation-run programs. Strict verification requirements, coupled with inadequate staffing, often caused delays of several days in verifying the information the defendant had provided. A major cause of these delays was the fact that bail programs were forced to rely on the telephone for all verifications, and it was often difficult to contact references by this means. A 1971 evaluation of the Dallas O.R. project revealed that: "On the average it took slightly more than nine days for a prisoner to be released by the Dallas Project. The traditional money bail method is faster."[19]

Today, pretrial release agencies are operating in almost

19. Robert L. Bogomolny and William Gaus, "An Evaluation of the Dallas Pretrial Release Project," *Southwestern Law Journal*, vol. 26 (1972), pp. 510, 522.

every major American city.[20] Most of these programs have
been incorporated into the existing court structure, either
as part of the probation office or as a new court agency.
Such institutionalization of bail programs represents both
success and failure for the bail reform movement. Clearly,
the courts now recognize the value of nonfinancial releases
and the need for O.R. investigations in the setting of bail.
The long-term use of O.R. appears assured. On the other
hand, the shift away from the defendant-orientation which
sparked the original bail reform movement may represent
a significant failure for the movement. Institutionalized as
long-term, ongoing agencies, the bail programs today have,
in many jurisdictions, lost the motivation or incentive to be
of maximum service to the criminal defendants. Such a
shift in philosophy may have been inevitable. The type of
dedicated, creative individual who would develop a pretrial
release program is not the type of person needed to operate
the program on a day-to-day basis. The type of organization
or foundation willing to fund a demonstration O.R. program is not willing to undertake the long-term financing of
such a program.

Several programs, however, have managed to survive
institutionalization better than most. Examples of successfully institutionalized programs would include those in
Washington, D.C., Philadelphia, and Des Moines. The
most striking similarity among these programs is their
continued use of law students and recent college graduates
in the operation of the program. Under the control of a
full-time director who maintains a good relationship with
judges, court personnel, law enforcement officials, and
local government, student staffing has two primary virtues.
First, the young people have demonstrated a commitment
to the defendant population that marked the earlier bail
reform programs, and thus the defendant orientation of the
programs has remained constant. Second, the turnover of

20. According to the OEO study, approximately 100 pretrial release
programs were operating as of March 2, 1973, and of the twenty-five
largest cities, only Boston, Cleveland, Columbus, and Milwaukee were
without programs. Goldman et al., supra n. 7, p. 7.

personnel in these programs is constant. A frequent turn-over in personnel is a virtue in that it maintains a level of enthusiasm and commitment within the staff. Once the novelty of the job wanes and the interviewing becomes too routine, there is a tendency for the interviewer to prejudge defendants and conduct superficial interviews. The injection of new blood into the programs through a regular turnover in staff can prevent this from occurring.

3. Delay in Interviewing Defendants

A number of the early projects, such as those in San Francisco, Wilmington, Des Moines, New York, and Washington, D.C., were able to interview defendants within a few hours of their arrest. These, however, were the exception. Most projects observed in 1970 were not able to interview defendants for at least a day, and many took as long as a week or more.

Poor project location and procedural requirements were two principal causes of interviewing delays. Projects in Houston and Atlanta suffered from the first problem. Although all persons arrested in these cities were taken initially to the city jails, the projects operated in the county jail. This meant that defendants were in custody at least twenty-four hours before they arrived at a facility in which they could be interviewed. In Denver the felony O.R. program in 1970 was unable to interview defendants until five or six days after their arrest because there was no place available in the jail for interviewing. In Albuquerque and in Nassau County, New York, procedural requirements were the cause of delay. In both cities, the judges required that the project not interview defendants until after arraignment.

One effect of delay in interviewing defendants was to encourage defendants who could make bail in any way whatsoever to do so. The defendants who were able to make bail were of course not those that Louis Schweitzer had first been concerned about—his concern was for those too poor to make bail at all. Very early in their development, however, the projects had sought to provide service to other defendants as well. The fact that a defendant could some-how afford to pay a bondsman was rarely considered a limiting factor, the injustice of making the defendant pay for his release being thought a sufficient justification to warrant the help of an O.R. project.

The Houston project exemplified some of the problems faced when defendants are not reached within twenty-four hours of their arrest. Thus, in 1970 both Thomas Roberson, director of the Houston Legal Foundation which sponsored the project, and Jack Cox, director of the program, felt that their biggest problem was the professional bondsman. Because defendants arrested in the city did not reach the county jail where the project was located until a day or so after their arrest, most of the "good risks" were already free on bail. From the "leftovers," the project in 1970 was able to write only about thirty bonds a month.

A 1971 evaluation of the pretrial release program in Dallas observed that: "Because the project does not see the prisoners at the first possible moment, i.e., the first moment bond can be posted, a substantial number post bond before they are interviewed by the Project."[21] The evaluators noted that in a ten-day study period slightly less than 50 percent of a potential 1,199 defendants had already posted bail prior to their names coming before the project.[22] In its 1973 survey of pretrial release programs, the Office of Economic Opportunity reported that one-third of the projects responding to its questionnaire interviewed defendants only after the initial bail determination had been made.[23]

While it seems clear that the advantages of early inter-viewing were recognized from the beginning of the bail reform movement, there were reasons why not all projects were able to achieve it. Persons concerned with starting projects were often required to make concessions to the court or to the bondsmen, agreeing that in the beginning they would interview defendants only after they had been arraigned or been held for twenty-four hours after arrest.

21. Bogomolny and Gaus, supra n. 19, p. 529.
22. Ibid.
23. Goldman et al., supra n. 7, p. 15.

In some instances, projects were even limited to interviewing only after a felony defendant had been bound over to the trial court level, which could be weeks after arrest. Projects that began operating under these concessions found themselves in the same position as Houston, that is, working with "leftovers" and not with those defendants that they were in the best position to help. Operating at this level, the projects did not have the volume of releases needed to justify their existence. Thus they were never able to expand into reaching defendants within hours of their arrest, and sometimes were eventually terminated without ever having had the opportunity to prove themselves.

An experimental O.R. program begun in Oakland, California, in 1963 was discontinued at the end of a two-year demonstration period. The final evaluation report made clear that interviewing delay was a major problem for the project.

The Oakland project operated after arraignment and primarily with misdemeanor defendants. Because of the typically low bail in misdemeanor cases, the vast majority of defendants made bail. According to the project's final report, approximately 75 percent of the defendants booked and technically eligible for O.R. continued to secure bail or enter early guilty pleas before even making application for an O.R. interview. Another 5 to 10 percent made bail or entered a plea after making O.R. application but before an investigation could be completed. "The remaining cases certainly represented a distillation of those with limited financial resources and those considered poor risks by the bail bondsmen."[24] They were clearly not the best risks for pretrial release, at least by the accepted criteria:

Most clearly, he (a male) was currently unemployed, and, when employed, worked in an unskilled occupation. He had few, if any tangible economic assets. He obviously was having difficulty raising bail and was unable to afford a private attorney. He was in his mid-twenties and a Negro. He was single (or separated or divorced), resided in Oakland, but had lived at his present address less than six months. Although he had frequent contact

24. D. L. Kuykendall and R. W. Deming, "Pretrial Release in Oakland, California," mimeographed (Oakland, Calif., March 23, 1967), p. 40.

with relatives, he had few dependents or family responsibilities. He had some history of misdemeanor convictions and had spent some post-conviction time in a correctional institution.[25]

After studying the best available research done in the pretrial release field, the National Center for State Courts concluded in 1975 that one of the few consistent findings to emerge was that a close relationship exists between the speed with which a program operates and the number of releases generated.[26] Quite consistently, the swifter a program operates in interviewing defendants and processing release recommendations, the greater the proportion of criminal defendants that will be released through the program's efforts. Conditions in American jails being what they are, it is not surprising to find that defendants tend to secure release by whatever method is fastest, rather than waiting the additional time necessary for a nonfinancial release.

Since 1970 several programs have made important gains in increasing the speed with which they operate. For example, programs in Santa Clara County, California, and Philadelphia are now functioning as a routine step in the booking process of arrestees and, thus, conduct their initial interviews within minutes of a person's arrest and booking. In addition, several pretrial release programs have been delegated the authority to release misdemeanor defendants on own recognizance without seeking prior judicial approval. Early program intervention, coupled with a grant of release authority, can drastically reduce the time from arrest to nonfinancial pretrial release. This is evidenced in the success of the Santa Clara County program in reducing the average time from arrest to nonfinancial release in misdemeanor cases from 74 hours in 1970 to 2.4 hours in 1971.[27]

25. Ibid., pp. 52-53.
26. National Center for State Courts, *An Evaluation of Policy Related Research on the Effectiveness of Pretrial Release Programs* (Denver, Colo.: National Center for State Courts, August, 1975), p. 66.
27. American Justice Institute, "Santa Clara County Pretrial Release Project Final First-Year Evaluation Report," in Ronald J. Obert, *Pretrial Release Program in an Urban Area: Final Report, Santa Clara County Pretrial Release Program* (San Jose, Calif.: Santa Clara County Pretrial Release Program, 1973), p. 53.

Early pretrial release program intervention, while clearly preferable, does, however, raise at least two significant potential problems. First, in large urban cities the number of arrests per day is often quite high, and the burden on the program to interview everyone can be prohibitive. Without adequate funding and staff, a program which attempts to handle all arrestees may find its overall effectiveness diminished. This was one of the major problems for the Manhattan project which, under the operation of the probation department in 1970, was required to interview all arrestees. If an arrestee refused the interview, as many prostitutes did, or was incoherent, as many intoxicants were, the project was still required to obtain their names and addresses. As a result, the severely overburdened operation could make only token efforts at verification, and a general program breakdown ensued.

The second and potentially more serious disadvantage of early interviewing is that a program may be able to generate an impressive number of nonfinancial releases, and therefore appear to be quite successful, but at the same time be failing those the bail reform movement was intended to benefit—those unable to post bail. The danger does exist that programs through early intervention can facilitate a substantial number of releases merely by screening off the very best pretrial release risks—ones who would be most likely to post bail if O.R. were not available—and not be successful in addressing the needs of indigents. Programs which do not intervene until after a defendant has appeared in court do have one advantage over those programs which intervene close to arrest: the former programs can be quite confident that the persons they assist in release would not have been released but for their efforts.

4. Verification Procedures

The ability of pretrial release programs to operate swiftly in securing releases was further hindered by problems in verifying the information necessary to submit O.R. recommendations. It has been an almost universal practice for projects to verify the information obtained from a defendant by phoning references he has provided. In most projects phone calls are virtually the only means by which verifications are conducted. When asked how they thought their programs could be improved, directors of several projects commented in 1970 that additional staff would permit field investigations of defendants not verifiable by phone, and would also yield more accurate information about the defendant. The exclusive use of the phone for verifications results in a number of defendants being denied a release recommendation because the information they gave was unverifiable.

A 1967 study of the D.C. Bail Agency by the U.S. Justice Department's Office of Criminal Justice addressed the Agency's verification procedures:

Having completed their interviewing, the Bail Agency staff returns to the press room of the court (a small inadequate facility) where they attempt to contact by telephone the references listed by each defendant. The calls are generally made between 8:30 and 10:00 A.M. Frequently, verification is impossible because the reference is at work, because the reference's phone number is unlisted, or because the reference had no phone. If none of a defendant's references can be reached, the information sheet for the court is typed up with the information given by the defendant. It is, however, marked 'unverified' and the defendant is not recommended for pretrial release.

We were unable to find any tabulation by the Bail Agency of the frequency with which it is unable to verify defendants because the reference lacks a phone or because the reference was not home. In the course of the verification efforts, however, 22% of the defendants in our sample proved verifiable only after a visit, and another 11% required an evening telephone call to complete verification. Thus, it appears that the Bail Agency will always have a substantial number of defendants whom it cannot verify so long as it limits its verification efforts to morning phone calls.

The researchers feel that the Bail Agency should make greater efforts to verify information given by the defendants. Evening telephone calls and visits seem the obvious answer . . .[28]

As will be discussed later, the D.C. Bail Agency has undergone a substantial revision and now has the staff to do some field verifications. However, the problem of the

28. James S. Reynolds and W. Anthony Fitch, *The Bail Reform Act and Pre-Trial Detention* (Washington, D.C.: Office of Criminal Justice, U.S. Department of Justice, September 5, 1967), pp. 23-24.

exclusive use of the phone for verification is still with most projects. In some projects, failure to contact a defendant's references within a certain period of time can keep a defendant from ever being favorably recommended because the project loses jurisdiction. In other cities, it can mean a delay in release of several days while the project continues to try to make phone contact.

Probably no project in the country suffered more from inadequate verification procedures than that in New York City. Partly as a result of trying to handle too many defendants, as discussed earlier, but more directly the result of having to comply with court procedures, the project had an enormous verification problem in 1970. The New York City arraignment court required that the O.R. investigation sheet be attached to the defendant's court records at the time he was interviewed. A police officer was at the interview waiting to take the defendant *and* his papers as soon as the verification was made. The result was that after the interview was completed, the interviewer made one phone call to the defendant's most promising reference in an effort to verify all of the necessary information. As a consequence of this token effort at verification, a vast number of the O.R. reports were going to the judges marked "Unable to Verify."

The problem of incomplete verifications still exists for most programs and is particularly acute in those programs which attempt to have their pretrial release report available for the court at the time of a defendant's initial appearance. As the bail reform movement has advanced, however, it is now questionable whether full, independent verification is necessary in every case. Many programs are now submitting pretrial release information to the court whether that information has been verified or not, and quite often defendants are granted nonfinancial releases on the basis of this unverified information. Moreover, the growing use of citation release by the police, and the granting of nonfinancial releases by judges without any program involvement whatsoever, also cast doubt on the assumption that it is always necessary to conduct independent verifications.

5. Eligibility for O.R. Release

One of the most common and most serious factors in the failure of O.R. projects to improve during the late 1960s was a set of exclusions which prevented many defendants from even being considered for nonfinancial release. Understandably, during the early period of a project's existence there is a need to gain the acceptance of judges and the public. This prompted projects to create a series of excluded offenses.[29] Defendants charged with these excluded offenses would not be eligible for O.R. consideration. As the performance of defendants on O.R. became recognized, it was hoped that the number of exclusions and qualifications could be reduced. For the most part this never occurred, and by 1970 many programs were laboring under the same set of exclusions as existed five years previously. Exclusions based on the alleged offense and sometimes the defendant's prior record severely limited the operation of many projects. This is evident from the way in which projects were generally operating in 1970.

In Houston, for example, over 50 percent of the defendants were excluded from the very beginning and were never interviewed. In Atlanta, the figure was two-thirds. Excluded were defendants accused of homicide, robbery, any violent crime, narcotics offenses, rape and other serious sex offenses, liquor control violations, and lottery violations. In addition, any defendant arrested on a peace warrant or with a bond set above $5,000 was not eligible.

In St. Louis the project was burdened with exclusions that eliminated the vast majority of defendants. Excluded were all misdemeanors, felony offenses of murder, manslaughter, robbery, arson, rape, and sale of narcotics, and cases involving serious injury to the victim. Because of these exclusions, the project director at that time called the project a "token program, in essence only for indigent first offenders."

In Nassau County, New York, the project handled no

29. The Manhattan Bail Project initially excluded a number of offenses, including narcotics charges, homicide, forcible rape, sodomy involving a minor, corrupting the morals of a child, carnal abuse, and assault on a police officer.

narcotics offenses or first or second degree felonies, except when requested to do so by a judge.

A 1971 evaluation of the Dallas Pretrial Release Project discussed this exclusion problem. It reported that during a ten-day evaluation period, a total of 1,199 prisoners were considered by the pretrial release program in the city and county jails, but only twenty-eight prisoners were released.[30] The investigators found that project exclusions were largely responsible for the low release rate:

> In its application for a grant, the Project proposed to exclude 'those prisoners charged with homicide, armed robbery, certain sex offenses, and most narcotic offenses.' During the special interview period it was found that the Project excluded not 'certain sex offenses' but all sex offenses, including indecent exposure, selling obscene material, and sometimes aggravated assault—male on female. Similarly, the Project excluded not only narcotics offenses but all drug related offenses, including driving under the influence of drugs, violation of the Dangerous Drugs Act, forging a prescription, and possession of marijuana. In addition to construing its stated exclusions broadly, the Project developed some further exclusions. . . . The project excluded all those charged with assault on police officers, armed robbery, threats, violation of peace bond, and other assaults, none of which were proposed to be excluded at the start of the Project. In addition to those prisoners who were excluded because their offense was thought too serious, prisoners were excluded if they committed a group offense, or were arrested for more than one offense, if it appeared that the prisoner had ever used an alias (other than a nickname), if the prisoner had an attorney at the time the project considered him, or if the police or some other agency requested that the prisoner not be released.[31]

In other cities more defendants were interviewed, but the same factors of offense charged and prior record often were controlling elements in the criteria used to determine whether release would be recommended or not. Thus, in Jacksonville, Florida, the project in 1970 operated with only a few excluded offenses, eliminating only those cases where no bond was set. Usually, this meant murder, rape, arson, and armed robbery. The project's 1967 report, however,

30. Bogomolny and Gaus, supra n. 19, p. 520.
31. Ibid., p. 529.

indicated that the remaining defendants who were inter-viewed but rejected for release were denied primarily because of their past record.

In Denver the felony pretrial release program in 1970 interviewed all defendants except those charged with murder. However, defendants charged with aggravated robbery, narcotics or dangerous drugs for sale, and certain sex offenses were given a minus five points on the Denver point scale—an amount sufficient to make it almost im-possible for a defendant to be qualified for O.R. One of the project investigators explained that the project was looking for "the young, 18 to 20 year old arrested for the first time; those we can verify and release back to school or a job right away."

Studies of other bail projects indicate something of the role that judges play in this emphasis on the charged offense. Andrew Schaffer, for example, in a 1969 Vera Institute of Justice study of the problem of overcrowding in the detention institutions of New York City, found:

At the present time, the nature of the offense charged (which plays no role in the ROR recommendation) and the defendant's previous criminal record (which does play such a role) *seem* to be the major countervailing influences to a favorable recommenda-tion. Of course, one cannot be sure of a judge's reasons for rejecting a recommendation for pretrial parole because they are rarely stated explicitly. Neither of the aforementioned factors, however, is demonstrably related to the question of whether the defendant will return to court for trial—the primary question in the bail setting process. Instead, they are used to make an implicit determination that the defendant is dangerous to the community and, therefore, his release is made more difficult by the imposition of money bail.[32]

In another study, Yale law student William Brockett analyzed a sample of the pretrial population in the New Haven Correctional Center. He found that, of the factors considered at the bail hearings, "the offense charged in

32. S. Andrew Schaffer, "The Problem of Overcrowding in the Deten-tion Institutions of New York City: An Analysis of Causes and Recom-mendations for Alleviation" mimeographed (New York: Vera Institute of Justice, January, 1969), p. 29.

almost all cases appears to be the main or only consideration."[33] His conclusion, based on interviews of eighty-one
accused felons, was that "nearly one-half of those held in
jail because of inability to make bond would meet the
conditions for release under the criteria of community
ties."[34]

Despite the advances which pretrial release programs
have made in educating judges in the use of community ties
as criteria in making pretrial release decisions, the alleged
offense and prior record of a defendant continue to have a
dominant role in bail hearings. According to the 1973 OEO
study, 68 percent of the pretrial release programs excluded
defendants charged with certain offenses.[35] Since a defendant's prior record and charged offense will have a
bearing on his sentence if he is convicted, they can quite
obviously be relevant in predicting the reliability of the
defendant to reappear for trial. Equally obvious, however,
in the failure to consider nonfinancial release for defendants charged with certain crimes or with serious prior
records, is concern by the court and the pretrial release
program that the defendant might commit additional
crimes while on release. Hence, in these cases the defendant's pretrial release—regardless of how extensive his ties
are to the local community—is made more difficult or
outright impossible by the imposition of a high money bail.

6. Release Criteria

One of the earliest arguments concerning the operation of
O.R. projects was whether the criteria used for recommending release should be subjective or objective; that is,
whether the judgment should be based on a clinical or
casework decision or upon a predetermined point scale.
This argument resulted in part from the experience of the
Manhattan project. In the beginning this project had no
fixed criteria, relying largely on the judgment of the
individual interviewers. Later, however, examination of the

33. William Brockett, "Pre-Trial Detention: The Most Critical Period"
(Yale University paper, 1970), p. 13.
34. Ibid., p. 15.
35. Goldman et al, supra n. 7, p. 12.

project results indicated that more uniform and faster results could be obtained through the use of a rating system in which defendants were given points for the various kinds of ties they had to the community. If they met the magic number of five, they were automatically recommended for release.[36]

This system worked well for the project and was generally accepted both by project workers and judges. As other jurisdictions began to develop new projects, some adopted the Vera point scale while others preferred a more subjective approach. The differences in approach depended in part upon who was administering the program. Probation departments in particular tended to object to the objective approach.

The criteria and point scales used by various "objective" projects are very similar, being patterned after the Vera scale. Despite this, however, some projects slip into the practice of rating defendants much harder than others. Even within a single project, it is not uncommon to find a difference in how defendants are rated based on who is doing the interviewing. For this reason, there is considerable truth in the opinion of many that all of the controversy surrounding "objective" versus "subjective" criteria is overplayed. As attorney Edmund E. DePaul, director of an early O.R. project sponsored by the Philadelphia Bar Association, explained, "The 'subjective' projects are operating with a *mental* measure or standard by which they evaluate defendants and in the supposedly 'objective' system there is considerable discretion in the granting or denying of points."

Vera's Manhattan Bail Project was operated by very talented and dedicated individuals and it was operated as an experiment, with an hypothesis that they wanted to test. Both of these factors made Vera's project as objective as any project probably could be. In regard to most projects, however, DePaul's statement is accurate. No matter how objective the standard, subjective decisions on points are always being made. For example, the defendant has been

36. The original Vera point scale is reproduced on pages 21-22.

living with his wife for fourteen months, but it is only a common law marriage and he has nothing to lose by leaving, so perhaps, it is reasoned, he should not get a point for living with his wife. "To get a point for a common law marriage I think they should have been together three years," explained one interviewer. Another defendant may have been in the area five years but with no one employer for more than a few months and living at several different residences—will he get points for residence and employment? Decisions such as these present themselves in hundreds of different ways, and it is how these decisions are made that can make a theoretically unbiased scale very biased in practice. At any rate, it seems clear that "objective" and "subjective" are not the exact opposites that they appear to be; that adding or denying a point on some objective scale is not as automatic as one would like to believe. This is why, whether a project be objective or subjective, it is critically important to have qualified individuals doing the interviewing and evaluating.

While the debate over the relative merits of the two evaluation approaches has not been resolved, the balance has shifted heavily toward the use of the subjective method. In 1973 just 11 percent of the programs employed an exclusively objective screening procedure. By contrast, 43 percent of the programs utilized a subjective screening and 46 percent employed both methods, with a subjective decision supplementing the use of a point scale in determining release eligibility.[37] With the increasing number of programs operating under the control of the courts and probation departments, such a shift is not surprising. The fact that most programs today present pretrial release recommendatoins for all defendants interviewed, and not just favorable recommendations for the most highly qualified individuals, as well as the involvement of many programs in other alternative forms of release, such as conditional and supervised own recognizance, has also prompted more programs to use the subjective, more traditional casework approach. Most programs apparently

37. Goldman et al., supra n. 7, p. 15.

believe that the objective point scale method does not permit the flexibility necessary for the more complex release decisions now being made.

In 1970, however, the subjective screening approach appeared to be clearly limiting the effectiveness of many programs. At that time, the programs that were most successful in generating nonfinancial releases—such as those in Washington, D.C., Des Moines, San Francisco, and New York—all employed the objective method. On the other hand, projects using the subjective standard, such as those in Nassau County, New York, Los Angeles, and Denver, as well as former programs in Philadelphia and Oakland, released considerably fewer defendants with no appreciable benefit in the failure to appear rate.

One possible reason for this difference in the number of releases is that, while under both standards the defendant is asked about residence, employment, family, and prior record, the objective standard forces the defendant to be judged on these criteria alone. Even allowing that there can be some leeway in how a defendant is rated on these factors, the interviewer is not free to deny the defendant his release on some other ground, such as his attitude toward the interviewer. Also, the objective standard forces the interviewer to evaluate all defendants by the same standard. In the subjective system this is not the case. As an example of this, an interviewer for the Denver project in 1970 explained that the current charge was quite important to know because it determined how hard the investigator would look at the defendant.

It must be noted, however, that the lower number of recommendations in 1970 from projects using the subjective system may not have been a result of the subjective criteria themselves, but rather of the fact that the agencies running projects using the subjective method—usually probation departments—were more conservative than the independent agencies running projects with the objective standard.

The use of a subjective standard is often justified as being more fair to the indigent defendants. Some projects felt that the Vera point scale was unduly harsh on indigents, and that if it were adjusted to fit them it would become too easy for others to qualify. Hence, many programs adopted the subjective evaluation approach. A substantial number of these programs have not forsaken the point scale entirely, however, and as a result the defendant often receives the worst features of both methods. First, he is required to meet a rigid point standard in order to be considered, and second, a release decision is made on a subjective appraisal of him. In reality, no defendant without the requisite number of points will be released, and many who have the points will be denied. Thus, the point scale only works against the defendant. In Houston the project operated in 1970 with the Vera point scale, requiring six points for release but, as the director explained, the decision to release was made subjectively. It was admitted that if the point scale had been strictly followed the number of release recommendations would probably have doubled.

The O.R. Project approach to the pretrial detention problem is subject to two further criticisms which cut much deeper—whether the present criteria are valid predictors of failures to appear, and whether the criteria are discriminatory against indigents and minorities. Over the past fifteen years pretrial release programs have demonstrated that they can identify many persons who meet the community ties criteria, and that these persons can be released prior to trial on their own recognizance while maintaining a failure to appear rate comparable to that of defendants on bail. Since own recognizance was previously a little used procedure, the result has been a considerable expansion in the use of O.R. and, in light of this result, few persons were really concerned with the validity of the assumption that these factors of employment, residence, and family ties were valid predictors of pretrial release reliability. However, as these community ties criteria are now deeply entrenched in the pretrial release decision—consideration of them is mandated by statutes and court rules in many jurisdictions—increasing concern is now surfacing regarding their validity as predictors of release reliability.

At least two things have been suggested as being wrong in the present approach. The first is that, while the Vera method has shown that persons who meet the existing criteria will return for trial if released without bail, it has not been proven that defendants who fail to meet these criteria would fail to do so. Hence, although we know that people who satisfy the Vera criteria are "good" risks, we do not know whether persons who fail to meet the criteria are in fact "bad" risks. Several recent studies which have attempted to measure the validity of the community ties criteria as predictors of pretrial release reliability have concluded that it is exceedingly difficult to find any positive correlation between the personal attributes of defendants, individually or collectively, and nonappearance.[38] What emerges is simply the fact that the vast majority of persons released prior to trial do appear as required, and research to date has been unable to isolate clearly any factor or combination of factors that either explains why failures to appear occur or identifies in advance those defendants who will not appear.

The second problem is that, even if it were possible to prove that defendants with certain characteristics are more likely to flee, not all would do so, and it is therefore unjust to detain any particular individual because it is impossible to predict which defendants will flee. In light of these problems, it can be argued that the pretrial release program approach is wrong; that a defendant should not be called upon to prove his qualifications for a nonfinancial release. The presumption should favor nonfinancial release, and the burden should be on the prosecutor to rebut this presumption with specific evidence of unreliability in individual cases.

A second, recurrent criticism of the community ties criteria has been that they are discriminatory against low-income and minority defendants. The allegation is made that the programs, in their emphasis upon employment, residence, and family stability, are middle-class oriented and that they thereby discriminate against indigents in much the same manner as the traditional bail system. Paul F. Lazarfeld, in his study of the Brooklyn Pretrial Services

38. For a discussion of these studies, see National Center for State Courts, supra n. 26, pp. 71-74.

Agency, did discover that minority defendants were under-represented in the favorably recommended population of that program: while 64 percent of the white defendants interviewed by the program qualified for a favorable release recommendation, just 49 percent of the black defendants and 45 percent of the Spanish-speaking defendants were similarly recommended.[39] Although far from conclusive, Lazarfeld's data do suggest that the ability of the programs to lessen the discriminatory nature of the traditional bail system is reduced somewhat by the release criteria presently being employed. There does appear to be an obvious correlation between indigency and factors such as employment, residence, and family stability which the programs are now using as predictors of release reliability.

It should be emphasized, however, that failure to meet the community ties criteria is not the *major* cause of pretrial detention. The alleged offense and his prior criminal record are more often the cause of a defendant's detention. In his study of the New Haven jail in 1970, William Brockett found that nearly one-half of those detained because of an inability to post bond would meet the conditions for release under the criteria of community ties.[40] New Haven had a pretrial release program in operation at that time; in a city without a program, one would expect the percentage of detained defendants who could qualify under the community ties criteria to be somewhat higher.

After observing O.R. interviews in several cities, it appears the original Vera scale that considered only whom the person was living with, how long he had been in the area, how long he had been employed, and his prior record is not seriously biased. Under this scale, the majority of defendants could achieve enough points to qualify. It is also true, however, that the manner in which the point scale has been administered in many cities has resulted in a number of defendants who should qualify for O.R. being

39. Paul F. Lazarfeld, *An Evaluation of the Pretrial Services Agency of The Vera Institute of Justice,* (Brooklyn, N.Y.: Vera Institute of Justice, 1974), p. 70.
40. Brockett, supra n. 33, p. 15.

rejected. The reason for this is that, while Vera was using its criteria of community ties to identify individuals with some measure of stability, the projects now are looking for stability in the community ties. While the longer a defendant was at one job or one residence, the more points Vera would give him, an individual could also get points by merely being employed for a certain period of time or living in the area for a certain span of time. Projects are now not so prone to give these points; a person who moves frequently, changes jobs often, or has an unstable family life will not qualify, even though he has been in the area and has been employed a considerable length of time. If the release criteria used by projects are now biased, it is because they are requiring too high a degree of stability in residence, employment, and family, a quality notably lacking in jail populations.

12

Pretrial Release Programs and Nonfinancial Releases

GIVEN the many problems faced by O.R. programs during the late 1960s, how was it possible that the use of nonfinancial releases increased so much? Were projects accomplishing more than appeared on the surface, or were there other factors at work? Some figures suggested that the projects were not as vital as had been thought. Thus, a study of pretrial release practices in New York City during the first three months of 1967 revealed that, of the 5,358 defendants granted O.R., only 28.8 percent had been interviewed by the probation department's O.R. program, and only 16.9 percent had been favorably recommended for release.[1] Even in felony cases, only 56 percent of the O.R.'d defendants had been interviewed and less than one-third recommended for O.R. Our national study of bail practices in 1971 revealed a similar pattern in most cities.

This suggests that many judges, having become familiar with O.R. through the general publicity and concern about pretrial detention, began to issue such releases without benefit of outside assistance. Not infrequently, our study showed defendants being released by the court and, in a few jurisdictions, by the police before the O.R. project could act. The court also, on occasion, released defendants who were not eligible under the project's criteria because of the offense involved or their prior record. Defendants whom the project could not recommend, either because

1. S. Andrew Schaffer, "Bail and Parole Jumping in Manhattan in 1967" mimeographed (New York: Vera Institute of Justice, Inc., August, 1970), p. 2.

they resided outside the jurisdiction or because the information they gave could not be verified, were also frequently released by the court. Finally, in some instances at least, judges granted O.R. releases despite project recommendations against release.

In Washington, D.C., and Des Moines, two cities with pretrial release programs well recognized for their excellence, nonfinancial pretrial releases were clearly not contingent upon a favorable project recommendation. In Des Moines approximately 20 percent of the felony O.R. releases in 1971 were granted without a favorable recommendation by either the O.R. Project or the Community Corrections Program of supervised release, and better than 50 percent of the misdemeanor releases were without a positive recommendation. Although the D.C. Bail Agency interviews virtually every defendant and presents a bail report at first appearance, nonfinancial pretrial releases are often granted despite the lack of a favorable agency recommendation. If the information provided by the defendant is not verified, or if the defendant is not a resident of the District, or if the present alleged offense was committed while the defendant was on pretrial release, probation, or parole, the agency will submit a report but make no recommendation. Nonetheless, many of these defendants are granted O.R. or nonfinancial conditional release. In our study of 1971 bail practices in the District, just 43 percent of the felony and 59 percent of the misdemeanor nonfinancial releases involved a favorable agency recommendation.

San Diego and Philadelphia, two other cities with high felony O.R. release rates in 1971, have pretrial release programs similar to those in Washington, D.C., and Des Moines; virtually all felony defendants are interviewed close to the time of their arrest and recommendations are presented at the defendant's first court appearance. Judges in San Diego and Philadelphia, however, were much less likely in 1971 to grant an O.R. release without a favorable project recommendation. In both cities, better than 90 percent of the 1971 felony O.R. releases had been recommended by the projects. The hesitancy of the judges in San Diego and Philadelphia to depart from the recommendations of the O.R. programs may have been due in part to the newness of the concept. Unlike Washington, D.C., and Des Moines, which have had their programs since 1964, the pretrial release programs in San Diego and Philadelphia had both just started in 1971.

In Detroit, which had the fourth highest rate of felony O.R. releases in 1971, the Recorder's Court O.R. Program was directly involved in very few of the releases. This program did not interview defendants until after their first appearance in court. As over three-fourths of the felony O.R. releases occurred at first appearance, the project was obviously not involved in the release decision. This is confirmed in figures submitted by the project to the Office of Economic Opportunity survey of pretrial release programs. The project indicated that, of 5,009 O.R. releases during an eleven-month period in 1971, 4,793 were granted by the court on its own initiative and only 216 after a recommendation by the project. The project, however, may well have had a strong indirect influence on the willingness of the court to use O.R. releases, in that it assumed the responsibility of notifying all defendants on O.R. release of their future court dates. In a quarterly report to the Law Enforcement Assistance Administration, which funded the program, Coordinator John Binford Smith noted that the use of O.R. had increased 30 percent since the program began.

Even in cities with low O.R. rates, individual judges were often responsible for most of the releases, and the projects only a few. Thus, in Chicago, which had an O.R. rate of just 10 percent in 1971, figures released by Judge Peter Bakakos, Surety Section, Circuit Court of Cook County, show that, of the 21,215 O.R. releases in 1971, just 4 percent (869) were attributable to the Circuit Court's O.R. project.

A similar pattern existed in Denver, which had a felony O.R. rate of just 13 percent in 1971. In response to the OEO questionnaire, the probation department's felony O.R. program reported that only 163 of the 1688 defendants it interviewed were favorably recommended for release. All 163 were released on O.R. by the court.

However, despite the lack of a favorable recommendation, the court released 465 additional defendants whom the project had interviewed.

The role judges have assumed in granting O.R. releases is even more obvious in cities without O.R. programs which nevertheless showed a sizable number of nonfinancial releases. Two of these cities—Sacramento and Champaign-Urbana—had felony O.R. rates considerably higher than average: 37 percent in Champaign-Urbana and 30 percent in Sacramento. Three other cities studied that did not have pretrial release projects operating in 1971—Boston, Oakland, and Peoria—had felony O.R. rates ranging from 13 to 19 percent.

The relatively minor nature of most misdemeanor offenses results in even less need for O.R. project involvement in the release decision. O.R. release rates of 65 percent in Hartford, 56 percent in Denver, 48 percent in Champaign, and 41 percent in San Diego were achieved in 1971 without the involvement of an O.R. project.

The obvious correlation which the National Bail Study shows between the development of pretrial release programs and expansion in the proportion of defendants released on own recognizance is persuasive evidence of the success the programs have enjoyed. Moreover, the data in this chapter indicate that the impact of the programs on bail practices extends far beyond those cases in which they are actively involved. In demonstrating the feasibility of own recognizance and educating judges in its use, the programs have engineered changes which run much deeper. By 1971 the use of nonfinancial releases was clearly not contingent upon the intervention of a pretrial release program. The willingness of police agencies and the courts to grant nonfinancial releases without program intervention strongly suggests that the changes which have occurred in the use of alternative forms of release will be lasting. At the same time, however, it raises questions as to the continuing need for and role of pretrial release programs.

PART III

Programs and Issues:
An Analysis of Change

13

The Call for Change

By 1971 the bail reform movement had achieved a large measure of success. The almost total reliance placed on money bail prior to the 1960s was no longer present. In misdemeanor cases, many cities were using own recognizance at least as frequently as money bail. While the impact was not as great in felony cases, many cities were nevertheless releasing at least 10 to 20 percent of these defendants without bond. As a result of the increased use of own recognizance, pretrial detention rates were substantially reduced in the period from 1962 to 1971.

Just as obvious as the success of the bail reform movement, however, was the fact that there was considerable room for continued expansion in the use of O.R. Nonfinancial release rates in most cities paled in comparison to the rates achieved in Washington, D.C., and Des Moines. In most cities, improving the operations of pretrial release programs would have been an effective way to increase the use of own recognizance. A number of problems which were limiting the effectiveness of the projects in 1970 have been previously discussed. By addressing the problems of project exclusions and qualifications, by eliminating delays in interviewing defendants and processing recommendations, and by revising the standards by which defendants were evaluated for O.R., most pretrial release programs in the early 1970s could have substantially increased the number of O.R. releases.

By 1970, however, the projects were not in a position to do this. To a very real extent, the bail reform movement had passed them by. Of the early programs, only those in

Washington, D.C., and Des Moines had significantly expanded in the period from 1965 to 1970. The remaining projects that survived from 1965, as well as those started in the interim, were limiting their services to highly qualified defendants. Many of the defendants released by these projects would likely have been released by the court anyway, either on reasonable bail or on own recognizance. By 1970 it was evident that some cities without projects had nonfinancial release rates equal to or greater than cities with projects. Furthermore, even in cities with O.R. projects, very often the courts and police released more defendants on own recognizance without project involvement than were released on a project recommendation. By 1970 courts had responded to the challenge posed by O.R. projects, and there was little discernible difference between the pretrial release philosophy of the courts and the projects.

The role of own recognizance release programs had become well defined. The projects provided a service for alleged offenders who were local residents with either no or modest prior records and who were charged with the less serious offenses. It was obvious that a number of defendants who could be released were not being aided by the programs. The following case is an example:

In New York City a nineteen-year-old man is arrested and charged with receiving stolen property, a pair of shoes having been found in his possession. The young man had recently come to New York from one of the Southern states and had been employed on Long Island for his first few weeks. He was supporting himself as a shoeshine boy when arrested. Although charged only with a misdemeanor and despite having no previous record, the young man was not released on his own recognizance. Instead, bail was set in the nominal amount of $50—sufficient, however, to result in his detention. This defendant had not been recommended for O.R. because he had no local references and had been living by himself in a hotel of transients.[1]

1. S. Andrew Schaffer, "The Problem of Overcrowding in the Detention Institutions of New York City: An Analysis of Causes and Recommendations for Alleviation" mimeographed (New York: Vera Institute of Justice, Inc., January, 1969), p. 50.

Cases such as the one above were very disturbing to those working in the bail projects. As Edmund DePaul stated in his 1967 Progress Report on the Philadelphia Project: "The screening job can be frustrating in that the screener is continually aware of the bulk of inmates who cannot be helped by the Bail Project, who must be refused even before interview, and there is the unavoidable sense of tragedy that many of these people have been refused for most of their lives."[2]

Thomas Maloney, former director of the Delaware project and later mayor of Wilmington, believed in 1970 that the only significant way to improve his program was to change the project's focus toward helping defendants who did not meet the release criteria. Maloney declared: "Right now there is nothing in the system to help people who should be O.R.'d but who do not meet our criteria. If we could get these people out and work with them on their problems, we would then be helping people who really need it."

Comments such as those by DePaul and Maloney make it evident that those involved in the operation of O.R. projects were not being fooled, as were some other people, as to just what the projects were accomplishing. That those who operated the projects were aware of their shortcomings is even more dramatically demonstrated in efforts to establish court employment and work release projects along with other forms of release in a number of cities where the projects were already operating. The young man in the New York case described earlier in this chapter was, fortunately, able to gain his pretrial freedom when Vera was able to recommend and arrange as a condition of release in lieu of bail that a poverty agency social worker keep in contact with him until his court appearance. This custodial release to a third party is one of the alternative forms of pretrial release which is being increasingly tried with considerable success.

Schaffer's report on the Problem of Overcrowding in the Detention Institutions of New York City and Brockett's

2. Philadelphia Bar Foundation Bail Project, "Progress Report, Feb. 9, 1966-Sept. 8, 1967," p. 11.

Study of Pre-Trial Detention in New Haven, Connecticut, both concluded that one way to further reduce jail populations was to make greater use of alternative forms of release. After outlining a series of changes needed to improve the operation of the O.R. agency in New York City, Schaffer's report states:

> The bail re-evaluation procedure outlined above would not end the unavailability of pretrial release without money bail for defendants who are unable to supply references, those who do not meet existing criteria for release on recognizance or those recommended for pretrial parole but denied it. To enable these defendants to obtain their freedom prior to trial, Vera would make two recommendations: first, the initiation of a program of releasing defendants in the informal custody of third parties; second, the adoption of legislation authorizing new and more complex non-financial conditions of release.[3]

The failure of O.R. projects to improve and expand in the period from 1965 to 1970, coupled with the increased willingness of judges to use own recognizance release on their own initiative, might have foreshadowed the death of these programs. The O.R. projects, however, were given new purpose and the bail reform movement new energy in the 1970s as the focus shifted from straight own recognizance to other new and more complex forms of nonfinancial release. At the forefront of the rejuvenated bail reform movement was the Washington, D.C., Bail Agency and the Federal Bail Reform Act of 1966.

3. Schaffer, supra n. 1, p. 49.

14

The Federal Bail Reform
Act of 1966

UNDOUBTEDLY the most significant legislation to date in the bail reform effort has been the Federal Bail Reform Act of 1966. The most important new departure in the Act is its basic premise—that release on personal recognizance should be the normal method of release rather than an unusual or exceptional procedure. Thus the Act states in its first section that:

Any person charged with an offense, other than an offense punishable by death, shall, at his appearance before a judicial officer, be ordered released pending trial on his personal recognizance . . . , unless the officer determines, in the exercise of his discretion, that such a release will not reasonably assure the appearance of the person as required.[1]

The adoption by the Congress of the United States of this O.R. principle as the basic premise for the entire federal court system only five years after the Vera Institute began its experiment is perhaps the high point of the entire bail reform movement.

The initial work which eventually culminated in the Federal Bail Reform Act was begun at the same time that the Manhattan Bail Project was getting underway in New York City. In 1961 the Subcommittee on Constitutional Rights of the Senate Committee on the Judiciary began its investigation of bail reform, and in November of that year the chairman of the subcommittee, Senator Sam J. Ervin, Jr., sent letters of inquiry to a number of law professors

1. Bail Reform Act of 1966, 18 U.S.C. § 3146 (a).

seeking suggestions for reform. Over the next three years, the subcommittee familiarized itself with the various studies which had been done, including that by Beeley and those of Foote, and followed with keen interest the progress of the Manhattan Bail Project.[2]

Of all the studies gathered by the subcommittee, none was more persuasive of the need for federal bail reform than the report of the Allen Committee released in February of 1963.[3] The committee reported that wide variations existed in the bail practices of the various federal courts. For example, the committee found that while the federal district court in Connecticut during the three-year period from 1958 through 1960 had released 65 percent of the defendants on own recognizance, in four other district courts there was not a single O.R. release during the same period.[4] Furthermore, the committee's study of four federal district courts revealed that the percentage of defendants unable to post bail in amounts of $500 or less ranged from 11 to 78 percent.[5] In short, the Allen Committee report confirmed that what Beeley and Foote had found in Chicago, Philadelphia, and New York was true of the federal court system as well.

The first bail reform bills were introduced in 1964 by Senator Ervin on behalf of himself and others just two weeks before the National Conference on Bail and Criminal Justice convened in Washington, D.C. At this stage the legislation consisted of three related bills. The first bill provided that no person was to be denied bail solely because of indigency and contained the presumption in favor of own recognizance release. The second bill provided for crediting days served in pretrial detention against any sentence imposed after conviction. The third bill provided for a 10 percent deposit system in the federal courts.[6]

2. Hon. Sam J. Ervin, Jr., "The Legislative Role in Bail Reform," *George Washington Law Review,* vol. 35 (1966-67), pp. 429, 430.
3. Attorney General's Committee on Poverty and the Administration of Federal Criminal Justice, *Report: Poverty and the Administration of Federal Criminal Justice* (Washington, D.C.: U.S. Government Printing Office, 1963).
4. Ervin, supra n. 2, p. 433.
5. Ibid.
6. Ibid., pp. 435-436.

Hearings on the Ervin bills were held in August of 1964; those testifying included Attorney General Robert Kennedy, Herbert Sturz, of the Vera Institute of Justice, and David McCarthy, Director of the D.C. Bail Project. According to Senator Ervin, these hearings demonstrated that isolated amendments to the existing system were not enough, and that a need existed for a comprehensive omnibus bail reform bill.[7]

The omnibus bill which followed contained all of the reforms included in the earlier bills and, in addition, provided for the use of alternative conditional releases and added appeal procedures for both the defendant and the state. Another round of committee hearings resulted in further refinement of the Act, and in September of 1965 the Federal Bail Reform Act was passed unanimously by the Senate. On June 7, 1966, the Act was passed by the House of Representatives with but fourteen dissenting votes.[8]

That the Act embodied the concepts developed by Vera in the Manhattan Bail Project is in little doubt. One of the sections added to the Act shortly before its final passage set forth those factors which the court was to consider in setting release conditions:

In determining which conditions of release will reasonably assure appearance, the judicial officer shall, on the basis of available information, take into account the nature and circumstances of the offense charged, the weight of the evidence against the accused, the accused's family ties, employment, financial resources, character and mental condition, the length of his residence in the community, his record of convictions, and his record of appearance at court proceedings or of flight to avoid prosecution or failure to appear at court proceedings.[9]

The Act, however, went well beyond what Vera had been able to accomplish in New York in a number of important respects. One of these has already been mentioned. The Vera procedure had always been a discretionary one, based on an appeal to the judge who was free to accept or reject the suggestion involved. Now the statute itself directed that personal recognizance was to be the favored resolution. In

7. Ibid., p. 437.
8. Ibid., pp. 450, 452.
9. Bail Reform Act of 1966, 18 U.S.C. § 3146 (b).

effect, the presumption was changed from no O.R. to O.R.

Secondly, the Act introduced several new concepts. By far the most important of these was the use of conditional release.[10] The idea of conditional release was developed as a means of expanding the clientele capable of receiving nonfinancial release. If there were problems which made O.R. recommendations for some defendants not feasible, these were to be cured by the imposition of special conditions. If the defendant was considered unreliable in some respect, he could be placed in the custody of "some person or organization which would agree to supervise him." If it was feared that he might leave the jurisdiction, or that association with particular persons might get him into trouble prior to the trial, restrictions could be placed "on the travel, association, or place of abode of the person during the period of release." Other conditions authorized included a 10 percent deposit bond, regular money bail, or "any other condition deemed reasonably necessary to assure appearance as required, including a condition requiring that the person return to custody after specified hours." Thus the court was authorized to impose on defendants prior to trial many of the same kinds of supervision it would be able to impose after trial—the conditions in effect including pretrial probation and, as a last resort, something akin to work release with the defendant returning to jail at night. These conditions were listed in the order given above, and the judge was instructed to "impose the first of the following conditions of release which will reasonably assure the appearance of the person for trial or, if no single condition gives that assurance, any combination . . ."[11]

The Act also provided criminal penalties for those failing to appear, and credit on any ultimate sentence for any pretrial detention served.

EFFECT IN THE DISTRICT OF COLUMBIA

The Act went into effect in September, 1966. What is known about its impact comes primarily from the District

10. Ibid., § 3146 (a).
11. Ibid.

of Columbia, where the number of cases was greatest and where earlier studies make feasible some evaluation of impact.[12]

In the District the effects were immediate. In 1965 the release rate for felony defendants was 58 percent.[13] Showing the impact of the D.C. Bail Project, one-fifth of these defendants were released on personal recognizance.[14] In 1967, the first full year of the Act's operation, the felony release rate rose to 74 percent,[15] and the proportion released on personal recognizance increased to 60 percent of those released—three times the proportion in 1965.[16]

As might be expected, this rapid expansion in the use of nonfinancial releases created some administrative confusion and, during a period of rapidly increasing crime rates, considerable concern about the effect on crime. According to one observer:

> The judges charged with the immediate and ultimate responsibility for ordering conditions of release felt constrained to release all defendants indiscriminately on personal recognizance. Little thought was given to testing the conditions enumerated in the Act and financial bond continued to be used as a means for detaining high risk accused. Some of the problems of administering the Act which had not been anticipated soon surfaced. There was no method designed to notify those released of their court dates. There was no one to supervise releasees prior to trial.

12. The effect of the Bail Reform Act in other federal courts is unclear. In 1967 it was estimated, however, that the District of Columbia accounted for 20,729 of the 51,443 bail settings in the federal courts—or 40 percent of all cases covered by the Act. Statement of Chief Judge Harold H. Greene, D.C. Court of General Sessions, *Hearings on Amendments to the Bail Reform Act of 1966* before the Subcommittee on Constitutional Rights of the Senate Committee on the Judiciary, 91st Cong., 1st Sess. (1969) (Washington, D.C.: U.S. Government Printing Office, 1969), p. 32.
13. *Report on the President's Commission on Crime in the District of Columbia* (Washington, D.C.: U.S. Government Printing Office, 1966), p. 506.
14. Ibid.
15. *Report of the Judicial Council Committee to Study the Operation of the Bail Reform Act in the District of Columbia* (Washington, D.C.: District of Columbia Circuit, May, 1968), p. 46; also printed in *Hearings on Amendments to the Bail Reform Act of 1966,* supra n. 12, p. 522.
16. Ibid.

There was no continuity of representation to insure the application of the appeal and review provisions of the statute. In short, there were very few people in the system who carefully read and tried fully to implement the Act.[17]

These concerns led to the creation of a Judicial Council Committee, chaired by Judge George Hart, to study the operation of the Bail Reform Act in the District of Columbia. In its 1968 report this committee concluded:

While fully recognizing the excellent purpose of the Bail Reform Act, your committee has found that in practice the Act has not been administered with maximum understanding and effectiveness in this jurisdiction.[18]

The majority of the committee's recommendations on improving the operation of the Act in the District centered around the D.C. Bail Agency:

An enlarged District of Columbia Bail Agency or a Pretrial Service Agency should be developed for the courts of the District of Columbia. It should have sufficient personnel and appropriations both to improve its current services and to carry out a broad new range of pretrial services.[19]

The functions the Hart Committee suggested be taken over by the D.C. Bail Agency were quite extensive. Essentially its recommendation was that the Bail Agency assume the responsibility for seeing that the bail practices mandated by the Bail Reform Act were carried out. Among other things it recommended that the Bail Agency:

—Find, coordinate and assist responsible persons and organizations, including bondsmen, who are willing to serve as third party custodians for released persons and in appropriate cases itself serve as a custodian.
—Accept responsibility from the courts for supervising the completion of release orders, instructions and warnings to releasees and acknowledgements by them prior to release; for monitoring the performance of conditions imposed on released

17. Bruce D. Beaudin, "Bail in the District—What It Was; Is; and Will Be," *American University Law Review*, vol. 20 (1970-71), pp. 432, 434-435.
18. Hart Committee Report, supra n. 15, p. 2.
19. Ibid., p. 22.

persons; for supervising the periodic check-ins of released persons; and for performing the notification of defendants and custodians as to all scheduled court appearances.

—Serve as the central check-in and information agency at the courts for all defendants released pending appearance in criminal proceedings.

—Inform the courts and prosecutors of all defaults warranting court action, and coordinate referrals to and reports from enforcement agencies engaged in the pursuit and apprehension of fugitives.

—Assist released persons in securing employment, training, medical services, counseling, residential facility, family services, and other needs prior to conviction.

—Coordinate all part-time custody programs and facilities for persons required to return to jail or reside at particular community facilities pending trial.[20]

In the absence of these kinds of services, the felony release rate declined somewhat in 1968—to around 65 percent.[21] In 1969, however, the United States Court of Appeals for the District of Columbia in the case of *United States* v. *Leathers* took a very strong stand with respect to the Act, ordering the trial judges to explore every possible avenue for release. The court stated that:

In recent months this court has experienced a dramatic increase in appeals by persons detained pending trial from the imposition of bail bonds which they are financially unable to meet. This phenomenon may or may not reflect a conscious recoil from the letter and spirit of the Bail Reform Act of 1966 on the part of those judges entrusted with its day-to-day administration. We can appreciate the disquiet a trial judge may feel on occasion in releasing a person charged with a dangerous crime because the Bail Act requires it, a feeling we have at times shared. We also understand the pressures placed on a judge who sincerely believes that pretrial release in a particular case is incompatible with the public safety, and who also knows that substantial

20. Ibid., pp. 22-23.
21. *Report of the Judicial Council Committee to Study the Operation of the Bail Reform Act in the District of Columbia* (Washington, D.C.: District of Columbia Circuit, May, 1969), printed in *Preventive Detention Hearings* before the Subcommittee on Constitutional Rights of the Senate Committee on the Judiciary, 91st Cong., 2nd Sess. (1970) (Washington, D.C.: U.S. Government Printing Office, 1970), p. 744.

modification of the Bail Act is currently under consideration by the Congress. . . .

But when the statute and its legislative history are unambiguous, as is the case with the Bail Reform Act, none of us on the bench has any serious alternative, but to put aside his personal doubts and to apply the Act as Congress has written it.[22]

After discussing the provisions of the Bail Reform Act and the facts of the two cases before the court, the opinion continued:

> In neither of the cases before us is there any indication that the District Judge gave consideration to nonfinancial conditions of release as alternatives to the imposition of a high money bond, despite the clear congressional mandate that a money bond be imposed only when no other conditions appear sufficient to guard against flight. Nonfinancial conditions, our decisions have made clear, should be used flexibly, varying with the needs of the individual defendant . . .[23]

Because the Circuit Court found that insufficient attention had been given to releases fashioned upon nonfinancial restrictions, the cases were remanded to the District Court for further consideration of nonfinancial releases.

In 1970 Congress adopted almost in total the Hart Committee recommendations and greatly expanded the role of the D.C. Bail Agency.[24] To fulfill its new role, the agency in 1970 increased its staff from thirteen to more than fifty permanent positions. On this expanded staff, thirty-five positions, according to former court coordinator Dewaine Gedney, were concerned with interviewing, investigating, and supervising defendants. This made faster and more accurate verifications possible and increased the capacity of the staff to supervise defendants after their release.

With this reorganization, a deliberate effort was made to increase the use of conditional releases as a means of increasing both the overall release rate and the rate of

22. *United States* v. *Leathers,* 412 F. 2d 169, 170 (D.C. Cir., 1969).
23. Ibid., p. 172.
24. District of Columbia Court Reform and Criminal Procedure Act of 1970, Pub. L. No. 91-358. The D.C. Bail Agency provisions are codified as D.C. Code §§ 23-1301 to 1308.

TABLE 43

Pretrial Release Rates for Felony Defendants
in the District of Columbia

	Released (percent)	Released on personal recognizance (percent of all felony defendants)	Released on personal recognizance with conditions (percent of all felony defendants)
1965	58	12	*
1967	74	44	22
1968	65	41	13
1971	79	65	50

SOURCE: The 1965 data are from the Report of the President's Commission on Crime in the District of Columbia, see note 13 supra, at 506. The 1967 data are from the first report of the Hart Committee, see note 15 supra, at 46. The 1968 data are from the second report of the Hart Committee, see note 21 supra, at 744. The 1971 data are from the National Bail Study. The 1965, 1967, and 1968 data relate to felony defendants indicted in the U.S. District Court. Between 1968 and 1971 there was a court reorganization in the District of Columbia which altered the jurisdiction of that court. The 1971 figures are consequently based on felony defendants in the Superior and Magistrate Courts whose cases were not disposed of at first appearance, rather than all indicted defendants. This figure is felt to be roughly comparable to that for indicted defendants.

*Not available but presumed to be near zero.

nonfinancial releases. Both these results seem to have occurred, as Table 43 illustrates.

From these figures it seems clear that the use of conditional releases has made it possible to increase both the overall release rate and the use of nonfinancial releases. In 1967, the first year under the Federal Bail Reform Act, the overall release rate increased to 74 percent and the use of nonfinancial releases to almost two-thirds of the total releases. By 1971 the felony release rate had increased again, to nearly 80 percent, with nonfinancial releases now accounting for over four-fifths of the total. One of the consequences, however, has been a decrease in the number of straight O.R. releases. While just one-half of the nonfinancial releases in 1967 and just one-third in 1968 included the imposition of conditions, in 1971 over 70 percent of the nonfinancial releases were with conditions.

OTHER FEDERAL JURISDICTIONS

The effect of the federal act outside the District of Columbia is much less clear. As the federal government does not have general criminal jurisdiction elsewhere, the crimes normally handled in other districts differ considerably from those handled in Washington. They also differ considerably by district.

A four-district survey in 1963 by the Attorney General's Committee on Poverty and the Administration of Federal Criminal Justice showed release rates in 1961 for four districts as follows:[25]

Sacramento	43
San Francisco	65
Illinois (Northern District)	75
Connecticut	78

No general data for the federal district courts have been developed since the adoption of the Federal Bail Reform Act. A survey by the Center on Administration of Criminal Justice of the Sacramento District, however, indicated that in 1971 the release rate there increased to over 50 percent.[26] As this district had the lowest release rate of any of those surveyed in the 1963 study, these results suggest that the Act has had some effect outside the District of Columbia as well as inside it. The districts outside of Washington have not had the staff support, however, that the D.C. courts have had through the D.C. Bail Agency, and it is likely that the effects have therefore been less.

25. Attorney General's Committee on Poverty and the Administration of Federal Criminal Justice, supra n. 3, p. 134.
26. The 1971 release rate was 52.8 percent; 44.3 percent of the defendants were given some form of nonfinancial release and 8.5 percent posted bail. At the time of the 1963 survey, the Sacramento Division was part of the Northern District of California. By the time of the 1971 study, the Sacramento court was no longer part of the Northern District but a part of the Eastern District which was created in the period between the two studies. Certain other problems, including a large number of immigration cases in the 1971 sample, raise some questions about the exactness of the comparisons.

15

Conditional Release

CONDITIONAL releases were an integral part of the Federal Bail Reform Act of 1966. The drafters of this legislation recognized that substantially decreasing the use of money bail required more than merely providing for the use of O.R. Thus, while the Act directs that a person be released on his personal recognizance or an unsecured appearance bond, except when such release will not adequately assure his appearance in court, it further provides for the nonfinancial conditional release of defendants. The Act sets forth a hierarchy of possible conditions, ranging from third party supervision to a requirement that the defendant return to custody after specified hours. Included in the list of conditions is the use of deposit and surety bail bonds, but the Act requires that the judge use the nonmonetary conditions first.[1] The clear intention of the Act was to maximize the use of nonfinancial releases and decrease reliance on the use of money bail.

The Federal Bail Reform Act has had a tremendous impact in the District of Columbia. The use of personal recognizance and conditional nonfinancial releases today far exceeds the use of money bail. Largely as a result of the District's experience, a number of pretrial release programs have begun or are considering using conditional releases as a means of increasing both the number of nonfinancial releases and the overall pretrial release rate. The experience in the District would indicate, however, that there are some drawbacks to conditional releases. Their implementation on a large scale in the District created a number of problems.

1. Bail Reform Act of 1966, 18 U.S.C. § 3146.

INITIAL PROBLEMS CREATED BY
CONDITIONAL RELEASES

The implementation on June 1, 1970, of conditional supervision by the D.C. Bail Agency had two effects on the rate of nonfinancial releases. First, it had the desired effect of increasing the rate of nonfinancial releases. In 1969, 48 percent of the defendants processed by the agency—misdemeanor and felony—were released on personal recognizance.[2] This rate of nonfinancial release increased to 57 percent in 1970,[3] 63 percent in 1971,[4] 65 percent in 1972,[5] and to 71 percent in 1973.[6] Since the Agency services nearly every criminal defendant, these rates are reflective of the overall nonfinancial release rate in the District. Furthermore, no pretrial release program in the country is involved in as many felony releases as is the D.C. Bail Agency. The use of conditions has played some role in this, although even prior to conditional release supervision, the Agency was gaining the release of many more felony defendants than most other programs.

Second, the use of conditions sharply reduced the number of straight personal recognizance releases, until it became a rare case for a defendant to receive an unconditional O.R. release. Thus, in 1971, 87 percent of the nonfinancial releases in the District included the imposition of conditions,[7] and in 1972 this figure increased to 94 percent.[8]

Hence, although conditional releases are responsive to the desire of pretrial release programs to expand the number of defendants released without bail, the implication

2. "Report of the D.C. Bail Agency for the period January 1, 1969-December 31, 1969," p. 1.
3. "Report of the D.C. Bail Agency for the period January 1, 1970-December 31, 1970," p. 3.
4. "Report of the D.C. Bail Agency for the period January 1, 1971-December 31, 1971," p. 4.
5. "Report of the D.C. Bail Agency for the period January 1, 1972-December 31, 1972," p. 2.
6. "Report on the D.C. Bail Agency for the period January 1, 1973-December 31, 1973," p. 2.
7. 1971 Bail Agency report, supra n. 4, Appendix E, p. 1.
8. 1972 Bail Agency report, supra n. 5, Appendix C, p. 2.

from the District's experience is that this is at the cost of reducing the number of straight own recognizance releases. Conditional releases offer judges a middle ground, more restrictive than straight O.R. but less restrictive than money bail, and it is probably not surprising to see that they capitalize on this middle alternative.

One of the most obvious findings from the District's experience with conditional releases is that the judges tended to overuse them. They did so in two ways: first, by imposing them on too many defendants, and second, by imposing too many conditions on a single defendant. For example, where previously over 40 percent of the defendants in the District were released on O.R. without conditions, by 1972 less than 5 percent were so released. Thus, a large segment of defendants who had established their reliability on straight O.R. release were burdened with conditions. Second, whereas the list of conditions set forth by the Bail Reform Act was designed to stimulate judges to adapt conditions to individual cases, the system clearly did not operate that way. The judges were merely checking boxes on the release order to impose conditions and quite often they overchecked. The Bail Agency reported that in 1970 the number of conditions imposed averaged 2.3 per defendant on conditional release,[9] and in 1971 averaged over three conditions per defendant.[10] Our National Bail Study showed that in 1971, 2.5 conditions were imposed on misdemeanor defendants and 3.1 on felony defendants.

The standard conditions used in the District include: (1) supervisory (third party) custody; (2) reporting weekly to the D.C. Bail Agency; (3) living at a certain address; (4) curfew requirements; (5) obtaining or maintaining a job; (6) staying away from the complaining witness; (7) staying within the D.C. area; and (8) reporting for narcotics testing.

According to Bail Agency Director Bruce Beaudin, if each of the above conditions is attached across the board in each case, the situation which results is a totally unreasonable one. Beaudin, however, sees two virtues in the condition that defendants contact the Bail Agency weekly. First,

9. 1970 Bail Agency report, supra n. 3, Appendix D, p. 2.
10. 1971 Bail Agency report, supra n. 4, p. 6.

from the standpoint of risk of flight, because of the once a week contact the defendant can be personally advised as to his future court dates. Second, it has the merit, as Beaudin sees it, of keeping the defendant in touch with a sympathetic agency within the court system which is designed and motivated to provide supportive assistance during the difficult period of pretrial release. Many bail programs, however, now use the reporting-in requirement without going to the conditional release system with all of its sanctions.

The extensive reliance on conditional releases during the period from 1970 through 1972 created additional problems in the supervision of release conditions, and in deciding how to deal with defendants who violated their release conditions.

Because of the extensive use of conditions, the job of supervising the releases was difficult even for the large D.C. Bail Agency. In 1972, at any time, there were in excess of 3,000 persons free on pretrial release.[11] According to Dewaine Gedney, the Agency's court coordinator in 1971, most conditional releases received only spot supervision. Defendants were divided into three classes: (1) Five percent of the defendants were released without any conditions at all and received only passive supervision. (2) Better than 90 percent of the defendants had one or more conditions of release. For these defendants, the Agency checked at varying intervals. The conditions were checked in whatever way this could be done most simply, and if the Agency saw something amiss the defendant was advised to comply. The Agency attempted to persuade or threaten the defendant into compliance. (3) Three to four percent of the defendants released required a casework approach. The Agency in 1971 had four persons working as a community resource section doing case work for about 100 releases.

Initially, the Bail Agency reported all condition violations. Two problems quickly developed: first, the large number of violations buried the Agency in paperwork, and second, the courts did not know what to do with the violators.

11. 1972 Bail Agency report, supra n. 5, p. 3.

Bruce Beaudin discussed this at the 1972 conference of the National Association of Pretrial Services Agencies:

We have been sending [violation] notices since 1970. The courts were generally unable to deal with them until 1971 and one of the primary reasons for beginning to look into them at that time was because of pressure from a special unit that was created in the police department. The Major Violators Unit took an interest in the fact that the Bail Agency was sending notices of violations which neither the United States Attorney nor the courts were doing anything about and the past year [1972], the courts and the United States Attorney have begun to take some limited action in a few cases.

Violation notices are brought to the court's attention on a day regularly scheduled for the defendant, his lawyer and government counsel to appear for a court proceeding. Because the courts here are reluctant to deal with a violation with only the Bail Agency and the defendant present, this procedure was deemed to be the most effective.

We also have to educate the court on what it can do short of revoking the release. We practically run the whole hearing show. The U.S. Attorney still does not know what he's really doing in a violation hearing. The defense doesn't know what to do. The defendant has never questioned the fact that there has been a violation. We haven't had one situation yet where the defendant said, 'No, they're wrong . . .' What the courts have done is place a man in the cell block for an hour to impress upon him that he has to comply with his conditions of release. They use contempt and put them in jail for 30 days. They've used the setting of money bond as punishment. They have required defendants to walk over and check in personally with the bail agency.

What emerges is the fact that conditional releases, at least as administered initially in the District, did not work particularly well and were a waste of sizable amounts of money. According to Beaudin:

The first characteristic that emerges is one that we anticipated; that over 65 percent of the people on release technically violate some condition. It seems to me ridiculous to advise a defendant that he must comply with this or that condition or face punishment and then refuse to impose sanctions for violations. On the other hand, the philosophical effect of the imposition of conditions on many defendants is certainly a good one, yet one that is difficult to measure.

Conditional releases have accomplished one thing and that is to increase the number of nonfinancial releases, but the conditions are really only an "excuse." Again, according to Beaudin:

The judges in general have accepted the fact that the law requires that defendants merely accused and presumed innocent belong on release pending trial. Using the conditions as a conscience salving escape, their thinking goes: 'I've done my job. I followed the law because I released them as the statute required me to, but I've also protected the community by setting this condition.'

Using conditional releases to expand the rate of nonfinancial release may prove to be a strategy that is successful only in the short term. While it is responsive to the desire of most O.R. programs to have defendants free of jail on nonfinancial releases, it may have serious consequences in the long run. For example, in Washington, D.C., it was obvious that conditional releases became the rule rather than the exception: most defendants who could be and previously would have been released on straight O.R. were saddled with conditional releases. Secondly, will the public accept a program of conditional release where 65 percent of the defendants violate their conditions? While many of the violations are technical and insignificant, the Bail Agency did report 2,400 substantial violations in 1972.[12] This means that one-fourth of the 9,539 defendants supervised in 1972 were reported for a condition violation.

Moreover, conditional releases were unfair to the defendant. Most defendants were released on conditions that no one really cared to enforce. While the Bail Agency reported 2,400 violations in 1972 and recommended hearings on 2,126 of these cases, hearings were actually held in only 341 cases.[13] In 1973 the Agency reported 2,608 violations, but sanctions were imposed in only 58 cases.[14] In most cases, sanctions were not imposed because they were deemed inappropriate. Since conditions are designed to assure appearance, if the defendant had not failed to

12. Ibid., p. 4.
13. Ibid., Appendix E, p. 2.
14. 1973 Bail Agency report, supra n. 6, Appendix E, p. 4.

appear, few judges chose to impose additional penalties.[15] However, once a defendant has violated one condition without being sanctioned, he is very likely to assume that he can safely violate others. This can only compound the problem of condition violations.

Sanctions for condition violations were imposed in a very discriminatory manner. Sanctions were not based on the type of condition violated or the severity of the violation, but rather on the defendant who violated. This is obvious from the fact that violation notices were largely ignored in the District until the Major Violators Unit of the Police Department became involved. This unit found that condition violations were a good justification for revoking the release of certain "target" defendants. These defendants were, according to Beaudin, the "hard criminals, the armed robbers."

While the conditional release program in the District certainly had initial flaws, there were at least two very positive effects. One which has already been mentioned is the substantial increase in the number of persons being released pending trial. A second benefit, and one which has still not been thoroughly utilized, is the ability of the courts to use information obtained during the pretrial release period as a barometer of the potential response of a defendant to court-imposed conditions after conviction. As Beaudin points out:

> It stands to reason that with the collection of accurate data, a judge at the time of sentencing should have a pretty good idea of how a defendant who has been at liberty on pretrial release conditions will react to probation. To this end the D.C. Bail Agency has been forwarding to the Director of Social Services for the Superior Court of the District of Columbia summaries of pretrial release activities. These summaries have been used by the presentence writer to fashion viable alternatives to incarceration after conviction. In more and more cases sentencing judges are giving substantial credence to these reports.

Conditional releases have an important place in the bail reform movement. Used as a supplement to own recognizance release for higher risk defendants, conditional

15. Ibid.

releases are a potentially valuable means to increase the use of nonfinancial releases, reduce pretrial detention, and protect the interests of the community. The problems which arose in the District of Columbia were the result of the overuse of conditions. As the dominant form of pretrial release, conditional releases proved unmanageable. Merely placing a number of conditions on a defendant's release accomplishes nothing, either in terms of helping the defendant or protecting the public. A conditional release program can only work if the conditions are enforced, and to be enforceable the conditions must be imposed selectively and meaningfully.

In an attempt to remedy the problem of the overuse of conditions—which occasionally included the imposition of conditions that were contradictory[16] or impossible to satisfy—the procedure for setting conditions was modified in 1974. Rather than the Bail Agency recommending conditions and the court imposing them, the Agency is now simply recommending that the defendant be released either on personal recognizance without conditions or upon conditions to be determined by the Agency. If released on conditions, the defendant is required to report to the Bail Agency, where the conditions which are to be imposed are discussed with him.

This procedure has a number of virtues. First, more time can be taken to formulate the conditions so that they will be more meaningful and realistic in the sense that the defendant will actually be able to comply with them. Second, the Bail Agency can take the time to explain adequately the conditions being imposed and impress upon the defendant the obligation he has assumed to meet these conditions. Third, since the D.C. Bail Agency is staffed with people sympathetic to the needs and concerns of the defendant, it is likely that the defendant will be motivated to cooperate with the Agency; he will thus be more likely to discuss problems that develop which would otherwise lead to the nonperformance of conditions or to a failure to

16. An example of contradictory conditions would be requiring the defendant to live at a certain address and to stay away from the complaining witness, when the witness lived at the address where the defendant was ordered to reside.

appear. Fourth, the Bail Agency, by having direct initial contact with the defendant, will be better able to supervise him while released. In the initial interview, the Agency is able to identify those defendants most likely to have difficulties while on pretrial release and structure their supervision accordingly.

As a result of this new procedure, many of the defendants are now being released on the single condition that they maintain weekly contact with the Bail Agency. This is not appreciably different from straight personal recognizance.

SELECTIVE USE OF CONDITIONAL RELEASES

Used on a limited basis, conditional release can be an effective and workable means of pretrial release. The Community Corrections Program in Des Moines, Iowa, is an example of a workable conditional release program for "high-risk" defendants. This program is successful because the number of defendants in the program remains small, allowing close supervision of each defendant by his caseworker. Because of the limited number of clients handled by the Community Corrections Program, most defendants continue to be released on straight own recognizance by the O.R. project. Consequently, although the program has successfully reduced the Polk County pretrial detention population, it has not significantly reduced the number of own recognizance releases, as occurred in the District of Columbia.

According to the third-year evaluation of the Community Corrections Program, annually in Polk County approximately 1,800 defendants are eligible for bail. Roughly 800 of these people are released on own recognizance, and another 600 post bail and are released. The remaining 400 constitute the high-risk group from which the project selects its participants.[17] In 1972 the program interviewed at least 440 defendants, and 211 were eventually released to the program.[18]

17. Peter S. Venezia, *Pretrial Release With Supportive Services For "High Risk" Defendants* (Davis, Calif.: National Council on Crime and Delinquency Research Center, May, 1973), p. 5.
18. Ibid., pp. 29-30.

The defendants in the program are often charged with very serious crimes, including drug offenses, robbery, and homicide. The results of the program over its first three years indicate that these "high-risk" defendants have a low failure to appear rate (2 percent)[19] and do not differ from defendants on money bail as to offense allegations during the release period.[20]

Defendants are recommended for participation in the Community Corrections Program on the basis of a subjective decision made by the project director, the court liaison officer, and the jail interviewer. The underlying question determining the defendant's acceptability is whether the project can be of help to the potential client. If the court accepts the project's recommendation, a bail bond form is signed by the defendant as principal and by a project staff member as surety.

A program participant receives personal, family, and group counseling and attends films and lectures on subjects such as alcoholism, drug abuse, employment, the use of legal counsel and welfare services, planned parenthood, medical insurance, vocational rehabilitation services, and remedial education. According to the project's second-year evaluation report, "The overall effort is to meet flexibly the needs of the individual defendant, upgrade him in line with his interests and potential, and encourage him to develop stable community ties."[21]

A final report is prepared on each defendant. This report will include the counselor's description of the project's experience with the defendant, as well as any positive community, family, or employment ties that have been formed or strengthened during the period of release. If the client has progressed while under the project's supervision, this is considered a good indication that further rehabilitation in the community could be continued. If this situation

19. Ibid., p. 47.
20. Ibid., p. 49.
21. Peter S. Venezia, *Pre-Trial Release To Supportive Services of "High Risk" Defendants, The Second-Year Evaluation of the Des Moines Community Corrections Project* (Davis, Calif.: National Council on Crime and Delinquency Research Center, February, 1972), p. 12.

exists, the counselor may recommend that a defendant who has been convicted receive probation with a suspended or deferred sentence.[22]

The Community Corrections program is a true conditional release program in that the defendant is still involved with making court appearances. A similar function of assisting the defendant in gaining employment and counseling is also performed in several jurisdictions by court diversion units. Such diversion programs differ from O.R. projects in that the defendant is "diverted" from the court system. While he is in a diversion program, the defendant's court case is held in abeyance and he is not required to make court appearances; if he successfully completes the program, his case may be dismissed. Because of this fact, the clientele eligible for a diversion program generally includes only minor offenders, as opposed to the more serious offenders that a conditional release program can accommodate.

CONDITIONAL RELEASE LEGISLATION

The Federal Bail Reform Act has led to the revision of a number of state statutes and court rules governing pretrial release. At least seventeen states—Alaska, Arizona, Delaware, Iowa, Kansas, Maryland, Minnesota, Missouri, Nebraska, New Mexico, North Dakota, Ohio, South Carolina, Virginia, Vermont, Wisconsin, and Wyoming—have statutes or rules setting forth conditional release options in language similar to the federal act. Only nine of these states, however—Arizona, Iowa, Maryland, Minnesota, Nebraska, New Mexico, North Dakota, Vermont, and Wyoming—adopted both the presumption in favor of personal recognizance and the requirement that the court impose the least onerous condition reasonably necessary to assure the defendant's appearance at trial.

The impact of such legislation on the use of conditional releases is difficult to measure, but it would appear that the influence of legislation alone is not great. Although data

22. Ibid., p. 13.

are not available from all of the states listed above, it is apparent that the use of conditional release varies greatly among them. Where conditional releases have gained the greatest usage, a pretrial release program is usually involved. It would appear, therefore, that the presence of a pretrial release program to present the background information on defendants by which to fashion conditional releases, and to supervise defendants to see that the conditions imposed are observed, is important to an effective system of conditional release.

The Federal Bail Reform Act succeeded in making major changes in bail practices in the District only after the D.C. Bail Agency was reorganized to provide for its administration, and only after a number of appellate court decisions made it clear that trial judges in the District were not to ignore the obvious mandate of the statute. It would thus seem that the adoption of new bail laws does not alone bring about significant changes in bail practices.

16

Deposit Bail Plans

BAIL reform efforts during the 1970s have also been marked by increasing interest in deposit bail plans. The first deposit bail system—the Illinois 10 Percent Deposit Bail Plan—was actually the first major legislative development in the field of bail reform. This system, which went into operation in Illinois on January 1, 1964, is built around shifting the fee defendants normally pay bondsmen to one that is paid to the court. In Illinois and many other states, the fee charged by bondsmen at that time was generally around 10 percent of the face amount of the bond. In return for this fee, the bondsman files a surety bond with the court. If the defendant appears at trial as promised, the surety is discharged from any further obligations. The defendant, however, is never refunded any of the fee, whether he appears for trial or not.

The combination of the success of the Vera experiment in Manhattan and a sizable bail bond scandal in Chicago (in which it was revealed that a single judge had set aside $300,000 in bond forfeitures[1]) created an opportune time for bail reform, and the drafters of a new Illinois Code of Criminal Procedure capitalized on it. They reasoned that the 10 percent fee charged by bondsmen could just as easily be paid to the court, and that if this were done, and the defendant appeared as promised, the court could return the money to the defendant. One percent of the bond amount was to be retained to cover the cost of administering the program.

1. Daniel J. Freed and Patricia M. Wald, *Bail in the United States: 1964* (Washington, D.C.: U.S. Department of Justice and the Vera Foundation, Inc., May 1964), p. 30.

The idea for this proposal came in part from Caleb Foote's study of bail in New York City, in which he reported the occasional setting of bail in alternative forms, such as $1,000 or $100 cash—meaning that the defendant could have a bondsman write a $1,000 bond for his release or he could deposit $100 in cash with an officer of the city. While this practice was not widely used in New York, investigation of its feasibility by the Illinois draftsmen, particularly Professor Charles Bowman of the University of Illinois, suggested that it could reasonably be applied across the board. Among other things, the draftsman noted that the actual amount of bond money forfeited in the Municipal Court in Chicago in 1962 was close to 1 percent of the total amount of bonds written:

We reasoned that if the State had collected as costs in the first instance 1 per cent of the amount of each bond written, it would have collected during the year $185,139.65, as compared with the actual amount collected from bail bondsmen on forfeitures of $183,938.[2]

Although the Illinois legislature was receptive to the 10 percent deposit idea, bondsmen raised considerable opposition. According to Professor Bowman:

The professional bail bondsmen and insurance company representatives were down in full force attacking the bail provisions from all angles. They accused the Joint Committee of trying to put the State into the bail bond business and of destroying private enterprise (the bail bondsmen). They predicted that jumps under the proposed 10 percent provision would be as high as 90 percent, since no defendant would bother to appear if he had no professional bondsman to fear.[3]

As a consequence of the opposition's efforts, the 10 percent plan which was implemented in 1964 was experimental. Unless renewed, it was by its own terms to expire on August 1, 1965.[4] Also, since this legislation did not prohibit surety bail, during the trial period two systems

2. Charles H. Bowman, "The Illinois Ten Per Cent Bail Deposit Provision," *University of Illinois Law Forum*, vol. 1965, pp. 35, 37.
3. Ibid., pp. 37-38.
4. Ill. Ann. Stats., ch. 38 § 110-15 (1963).

operated side by side. The fears expressed regarding deposit bail did not prove justified. During the experimental period, the 10 percent plan proved so successful—in 1964 in the Municipal Court of Chicago the forfeiture rate on deposit bonds, 8 percent, was actually lower than the surety bail rate, 11 percent[5]—that in 1965 the Illinois legislature made the 10 percent plan permanent. While during the trial period 10 percent deposit bail was not permitted on misdemeanor bonds set by the police, the law reenacted in 1965 provided that deposit bail was to be available in all instances.

Most significantly, the law adopted in 1965 totally eliminated the professional bondsman. The old bail bond laws, which permitted bondsmen who had made security deposits with the state to secure releases by simply signing their bonds, were suspended by the new law. The new law provided only two means for posting bail: 10 percent deposit or full security. Bondsmen were to have no role in the posting of 10 percent deposit bonds. First, the statute provided that only the person for whom bail had been set could execute the bond and make the deposit;[6] and second, the clerks who took the deposits were instructed to deliver the receipts to the defendants directly, and to refund the money upon completion of the case by check payable to the defendant, regardless of who furnished the money.[7]

The alternative method, posting bail with full security—either 100 percent cash deposit, a deposit of securities equal to the face value of the bond, or a pledge of real property worth twice the bond amount—was impractical for bondsmen. The result has been a complete demise of professional bail bondsmen in Illinois. Not a single commercial bail bond has been written in Cook County since September, 1965.[8]

Clearly, for those defendants who have the financial abil-

5. Bowman, supra n. 2, p. 39.
6. Ill. Ann. Stats., ch. 38 § 110-7 (1970).
7. Dallin H. Oaks and Warren Lehman, *A Criminal Justice System And The Indigent* (Chicago: University of Chicago Press, 1968), p. 102.
8. Conversation with Judge Peter Bakakos, Chief Judge of the Surety Division, Circuit Court of Cook County.

ity to post bond, deposit bail is much less expensive than surety bail. Whereas in a surety bail system the defendant receives nothing back upon completion of his case, the deposit program in the federal system returns to the defendant the full amount of his deposit; other deposit programs return to the defendant 90 percent of his deposit and thus the cost to the defendant is just 1 percent of the total bond. In the states of Michigan and Wisconsin, a defendant who is not convicted receives the full amount back, while 10 percent of the deposit is retained from defendants found guilty. The cost of release under a deposit bail system is thus less to the defendant than is surety bail. Since most criminal defendants are poor and can ill afford any expense, this is an important advantage.

The Illinois plan's retention of 1 percent of the bond amount as an administrative fee was challenged in the United States Supreme Court. The appellants did concede, however, that the plan was clearly an improvement over the old surety bail system, and recognition of this fact was explicit in the Court's decision upholding the administrative fee:

> We are compelled to note preliminarily that the attack on the Illinois bail statutes, in a very distinct sense, is paradoxical. The benefits of the new system, as compared with the old, are conceded. And the appellants recognize that under the pre-1964 system Schilb's particular bail bond would have been 10 percent of his bail, or $75; that this premium price for his pretrial freedom, once paid was irretrievable; and that if he could not have raised the $75, he would have been consigned to jail until his trial. Thus, under the old system the cost of Schilb's pretrial freedom was $75, but under the new it was only $7.50.[9]

A DEPOSIT BAIL OPTION AS OPPOSED
TO A DEPOSIT BAIL SYSTEM

The Illinois system of deposit bail allows no option with respect to surety bail. This form of pretrial release simply

9. *Schilb* v. *Kuebel,* 404 U.S. 357, 366 (1971).

no longer exists. Oregon and Kentucky are the only states that have thus far opted to pass similar legislation.[10]

A second type of deposit bail—and the one which has been most frequently implemented—is that provided in the Federal Bail Reform Act of 1966. This Act, which was the first after Illinois' to provide for deposit bail, authorizes the judge to use deposit bail as one of the conditions of pretrial release. Under the hierarchy of conditions provided in the Act, the judge, if he concludes that no combination of nonfinancial conditions will adequately assure the presence of the defendant as required, may set money bail and either permit deposit bond or require a surety bond. Unlike Illinois, where the *defendant* has the option of posting a deposit bond in every case in which bail is set, in the federal courts the option to permit a deposit bond is with the *judge*. Also, under the federal system, the amount of deposit is not a standard 10 percent of the face bond amount, but rather the amount of the deposit is set by the judge in each case. A number of jurisdictions that have adopted legislation or court rules modeled after the Federal Bail Reform Act have removed the deposit bail provision, but several states—including Alaska, Iowa, Maryland, Missouri, Nebraska, New Mexico, North Dakota, Ohio, Vermont, Wisconsin, and Wyoming—retained the Act's language, and thus, in each of these jurisdictions, the option to use deposit bail rests with the judge.

The operation of deposit bail is far different where the option rests with the judge. Among other things, the option has proved to be one that is rarely used. In the District of Columbia, where deposit bonds have been authorized since 1966, only 405 were posted in the first half of 1972, compared to more than 1,500 surety bonds.[11] In several states that have adopted the federal bail act provision, there has been virtually no use of deposit bail.

Placing the option with the judge is particularly likely to reduce the usefulness of deposit bail in jurisdictions with

10. Oregon Rev. Stats.,§§135.230-.290 (1973); Kentucky Rev. Stats., Ch. 431 (1976).
11. Bond Statistics for January through June, 1972, compiled by the Superior Court of the District of Columbia, Criminal Division.

misdemeanor or felony bail schedules. In these jurisdictions, defendants can learn immediately after booking what
the bail amount is for their offense and, if they have the
necessary funds, can secure release from the jail by posting
the scheduled amount. If these defendants must wait until
a court appearance to be able to post deposit bail, many
will undoubtedly choose to secure immediate release by
paying a bondsman's fee. Under the Illinois system, the
defendant could, of course, post a deposit bond immediately.

This second type of deposit bail is in fact so different
from the Illinois system that it is misleading to describe
both by the same name. The second type is more accurately
referred to as a deposit bail option, while the Illinois plan
can be better described as a deposit bail system.

A THIRD OPTION: THE PHILADELPHIA PLAN

A third method for implementing deposit bail is that
adopted in 1972 by court rule in Philadelphia. Under the
Philadelphia system, both surety and deposit bail are
authorized, but the option as to which will be used rests in
each case with the defendant. As might be expected, the
immediate result of placing the option with the defendant
was a preponderance of deposit bonds and almost total
elimination of surety bail. During the first six months
following introduction of deposit bail, nearly 90 percent of
the defendants released on financial bail in Philadelphia
chose deposit bail.[12] In 1974 this ratio of deposit bail to
other forms of money bonds increased to 93 percent.[13] In
the states of Michigan and Ohio, defendants in misdemeanor cases also are permitted the option of posting
deposit or surety bonds.[14]

12. Bruce Beaudin, David Lester, and J. Denis Moran, "District of
Columbia Bail Agency, Philadelphia Court of Common Pleas Pretrial
Release Program: Comparative Study," mimeographed (Philadelphia:
Court of Common Pleas Pretrial Release Program, 1973), p. 185.
13. Court of Common Pleas Pretrial Services Division, "Report for the
Period 1 January to 31 December 1974," mimeographed (1975).
14. Mich. Stats. Ann., § 28.872 (56); Ohio Rules Crim. Proc., Rule 46 (D).

ISSUES RAISED BY DEPOSIT BAIL

Critics of deposit bail, primarily bondsmen, have alleged that because the judge knows that the defendant will be released by posting just 10 percent of the bond amount, bail amounts will increase once deposit bail is adopted, and that, therefore, fewer defendants will be released. Our study of bail amounts in 1971 in Chicago, Champaign-Urbana, and Peoria does, in fact, confirm that bail amounts have increased in these deposit bail cities, particularly in misdemeanor cases. In our national survey, only four cities were found to be setting misdemeanor bails above $1,000 in a significant percentage of cases. The three Illinois cities were among these four. In Peoria virtually all of the final bail settings were either O.R. (18 percent) or in the $1,000-2,999 range (64 percent). The same was true for Champaign-Urbana: 48 percent O.R. and 37 percent in the $1,000-2,999 range. Although Chicago had a number of bails set below $250, a large number of bails (35 percent) were in amounts between $1,000-2,999. By comparison, in 1964 only 21 percent of the misdemeanor bails were above $1,000 in Champaign-Urbana, and only 18 percent were above this amount in Peoria. In Chicago, in 1962, only 15 percent of the misdemeanor bails were in amounts above $1,000.

Felony bails also noticeably increased in Champaign-Urbana and Peoria. The percentage of felony bails set in amounts of $3,000 or more increased from 24 to 41 percent in Champaign-Urbana, and from 28 to 57 percent in Peoria. In Chicago, however, felony bail amounts were slightly lower in 1971. In 1962, 63.2 percent of the settings were at or below the median of $1,000-2,999; while in 1971, 62.1 percent were at or below this same median. Felony bail settings below $5,000 increased from 68.3 percent in 1962 to 75.4 percent in 1971. This indicates that the amount of the average felony bond has stayed approximately the same or decreased slightly.

It is equally clear from this study, however, that the increase in bail amounts did not negatively affect the ability of felony defendants to post bail. In Chicago the percentage of defendants on bail increased from 26 percent in 1962 to 47 percent in 1971. In Champaign-Urbana and Peoria the rates of bail release were virtually unchanged from 1964 to 1971—around 50 percent. Coupled with a sizable increase in the use of O.R., these high rates of bail release led to a decrease in detention rather than the increase predicted by bondsmen. The custody rate for felony defendants in Chicago decreased from 60 to 30 percent in the period from 1962 to 1971.[15] Felony custody rates of 43 percent in Champaign-Urbana and 27 percent in Peoria in 1964 were reduced to 19 and 22 percent respectively in 1971.

Likewise, the increase in bail amounts did not adversely affect custody rates in misdemeanor cases. The percentage of defendants detained in misdemeanor cases proceeding beyond first appearance decreased in Chicago from 32 percent in 1962 to 23 percent in 1971; in Champaign-Urbana from 9 percent in 1964 to 3 percent in 1971; and in Peoria from 8 percent in 1964 to 1 percent in 1971. The percentages of misdemeanor defendants released on bail in these three cities in 1971 were among the highest of the cities studied: 83 percent in Peoria, 53 percent in Chicago, and 49 percent in Champaign-Urbana.

It seems obvious, therefore, that at least in Illinois, deposit bail has enhanced the ability of defendants to secure pretrial release. Since the initial cost involved in securing a bond under the 10 percent system is roughly the same as securing release through a bondsman, it could be argued that this is a surprising result. Actually it is not. There are some defendants who would be capable of

15. The decrease in the pretrial detention population in Chicago was immediate and dramatic. Dallin H. Oaks and Warren Lehman, in their book on the criminal justice system in Chicago, observed:

In recent years at least 50 per cent of the prisoners in Cook County Jail were there awaiting trial, because they were unable to make bail. It is not surprising, then, that the increased availability of bail has resulted in a dramatic decrease in the jail's population. On January 24, 1966, for example, the jail population was 1,542; exactly one year earlier the figure had been a little over 2,000. Warden Jack Johnson informed us that at least 80 per cent of this decrease was directly attributable to the new bail procedures.

Oaks and Lehman, supra n. 7, pp. 101-102.

securing release by deposit bail who could not secure release with a surety bond.

First, some defendants are capable of raising the money necessary for deposit bail but not capable of raising the same amount of money to pay a bondsman. The fact that the deposit will be largely recovered after completion of the case can influence relatives or friends of the defendant to loan the necessary money. The fact that most of the money loaned to the defendant will eventually be returned can be an important consideration to the third party asked to assist.

Second, the refundability aspect can influence some defendants in the decision whether to bail or not. As discussed in the National Bail Study, in most cities a significant percentage of misdemeanor cases are disposed of at first appearance. Defendants who intend to plead guilty at arraignment, or who recognize that the charges against them will very likely be dismissed, may not wish to pay a bondsman's fee for such a short period of pretrial release. They may, however, opt to post deposit bail.

Third, and in terms of numbers probably the largest class of defendants likely to benefit from deposit bail, are those who are capable of paying a bondsman's fees—and thus have the money necessary for a deposit bond—but are not able to satisfy other requirements, especially in regard to collateral. In a commercial bail bond system, the bondsmen are under no obligation to write bonds. Merely being able to pay a bondsman's fee does not assure a person's release. Especially difficult for many defendants are the collateral requirements set by bondsmen. In their article "An Alternative to Professional Bail Bonding: A 10% Cash Deposit for Connecticut," Paul R. Rice and Mary C. Gallagher discuss the problem of collateral requirements:

It should be obvious that one of the effects of the collateral requirement is the pretrial detention of a defendant who only has the financial resources to purchase his freedom with a premium. In our sample of 179 detainees, 33 (or 18%), specifically attributed their continued incarceration to an inability to provide collateral. Similarly, a 1957 New York City study of detainees revealed that 19% (17 out of 89 detainees interviewed) remained in jail for the same reason. Thus any alternative to collateral could be expected to result in a significant decrease in the number of accused criminals held prior to trial.[16]

It should be emphasized, however, that a deposit bail system does not throw open the jailhouse doors. Deposit bail does not affect the judge's ability to control release through his bail-setting authority. The defendant who cannot raise the bondsman's fee on a high bail will be equally unable to raise the 10 percent deposit.

Another virtue of deposit bail is that in Illinois and Philadelphia, where it has been used most extensively over the longest period of time, the system has proven that it can operate and maintain failure to appear rates as low as or lower than those achieved by surety bail. Critics of deposit bail have argued to the contrary and cited figures from Cook County to show that the failure to appear rate for deposit bail is well above the rates achieved by bondsmen in other jurisdictions. The Cook County data are, however, often misinterpreted. In Cook County a defendant who fails to appear is sent a notice advising him to appear before the court on or before a certain date, which is usually thirty to thirty-five days hence. If, for whatever reason, the defendant does not reappear within this time, the bond is forfeited. It should be understandable why Chicago would report a higher bond forfeiture rate than other jurisdictions which allow bondsmen up to 180 days to return a defendant before the bond is actually forfeited. Charles Bowman, author of the Illinois plan, stated in 1965 that: "The Joint Committee felt that if we could devise a system which would result in initial forfeitures of no more than 13 per cent and permanent nonapprehensions of no more than four or five per cent, it would not be substantially different from the actual experience in Cook County from 1959 through 1962, nor from the experience in other jurisdictions throughout the nation."[17]

Experience since the adoption of the 10 percent plan has

16. Paul R. Rice and Mary C. Gallagher, "An Alternative To Professional Bail Bonding: A 10% Cash Deposit For Connecticut," *Connecticut Law Review*, vol. 5 (1972), pp. 143, 174.
17. Bowman, supra n. 2, p. 37.

borne out the draftsman's calculations. Comprehensive bail forfeiture statistics are compiled annually by the Municipal Court of Chicago (First District of the Circuit Court of Cook County). Table 44 was compiled from these annual reports.

The table indicates that the forfeiture rate has remained fairly constant despite a large increase in the number of 10 percent bonds posted. Furthermore, the rate is not out of line with the forfeiture rate on surety bonds prior to the implementation of 10 percent. Indeed, in the one year when both surety and 10 percent bonds were being posted—1964—defendants on 10 percent bail performed better than did defendants on surety bail.

Fugitive rates are not available for Cook County, but in four downstate Illinois counties a study of 1969 cases showed the fugitive rates for felonies to be 0, 0.3, 1, and 4 percent.[18] For misdemeanors the rates were less than 2 percent for all four counties.[19] Despite dire warnings about what would happen to these rates at the time the 10 percent plan was first adopted, the rates are comparable to those available for other jurisdictions throughout the country. They indicate that rates can be kept quite low without the efforts of professional bondsmen. According to the Chief Judge of the Circuit Court of Cook County:

> The bondsmen's ominous predictions have failed to crystallize into fact. Little change, if any, can be seen between the forfeiture rate under the professional bail bond system and the forfeiture rate under the present 10 percent system. . . . The success of the 10 percent bail deposit plan is undeniable.[20]

David J. Lester, first director of the Philadelphia Court Bail Programs, reported a failure to appear rate for persons released in 1972 under the city's 10 percent plan of 7.5 percent and a fugitive rate of 2.7 percent.[21] According to the Philadelphia Court's Pretrial Services Division, the

18. Board of Student Editors, "The Administration of Illinois Bail Provisions: An Empirical Study of Four Downstate Illinois Counties," *University of Illinois Law Forum,* vol. 1972, pp. 341, 364.
19. Ibid., p. 375.
20. John S. Boyle, "Bail Under The Judicial Article," *De Paul Law Review,* vol. 17 (1967-68), pp. 267, 275.
21. Beaudin, Lester, and Moran, supra. n. 12, p. 240.

TABLE 44

Bond Forfeiture Rates in Chicago, 1962—1971

Year	Surety Bonds			Ten Percent Bonds		
	Bonds written	Forfeited	Rate	Bonds written	Forfeited	Rate
1962	51,161	5,487	10%			
1964	35,571	4,606	11%	27,956	2,154	8%
1965				46,418	4,910	10%
1966				68,355	8,106	11%
1968				81,989	8,856	10%
1969				84,202	11,402	13%
1970				90,938	12,086	13%
1971				99,112	13,172	13%

failure to appear rate on deposit bonds in 1974 was 7.4 percent.[22] The Department of Justice reported that in the first half of 1968 in the U.S. District Court for the District of Columbia, 8.1 percent of the defendants released on deposit bail had their bond revoked for failure to appear. The rate for defendants released on surety bond was 9.6 percent.[23]

Aside from claims that the failure to appear rate would skyrocket under a 10 percent system, the most constant criticism of deposit bail has been the cost involved. This question of cost was considered in Illinois, where the conclusion, in the words of the draftsman, was that "the courts handle thousands of bonds each year for professional bondsmen and defendants, and get nothing as costs. The administrative burden of handling the bonds is not substantially different under either system."[24] Observation of court practices and discussion with court officials in Chicago, Champaign-Urbana, and Peoria confirm that there is no appreciable difference in the cost of the two systems.

Another consideration sometimes raised is that of revenue from bond forfeitures. It should be observed that the purpose of the system is to produce appearance at trial rather than revenue, and that this factor should not properly be a consideration at all. The record shows, however, that in 1962 total collections for bond forfeitures in the Municipal Court of Chicago amounted to $183,938.[25] In 1966, after the adoption of the 10 percent plan, $339,881 was collected from the 1 percent retained under the plan, and an additional $312,130 from 10 percent deposits on forfeited bonds.[26] These revenues are, of course, additional to whatever savings there are from reduced jail detention

22. Court of Common Pleas Pretrial Services Division, "Report for the Period 1 January to 31 December 1974," mimeographed (1975).

23. *Hearings on Amendments to the Bail Reform Act of 1966* before the Subcommittee on Constitutional Rights of the Senate Committee on the Judiciary, 91st Cong., 1st Sess. (1969) (Washington, D.C.: U.S. Government Printing Office, 1969), pp. 694, 697.

24. Bowman, supra n. 2, p. 37.

25. Boyle, supra n. 20, p. 274.

26. Ibid.

costs, and indicate clearly that costs pose no problem toward adoption of the 10 percent plan.

Lester's data on the first seven months of the Philadelphia deposit program led him to conclude:

> The 10 percent Cash Bail Program has earned substantial revenue for the City of Philadelphia. It is anticipated that the City of Philadelphia will earn approximately $500,000 per year through the 10 percent Cash Bail Program. If effective judgement enforcement can be implemented, it is probable that the figure will exceed $1,000,000.[27]

DEPOSIT BAIL AND OWN RECOGNIZANCE

Another possible criticism of deposit bail is its potential impact on the use of nonfinancial releases. Deposit bail provides a mechanism for retaining the use of money bail but at a significantly reduced ultimate cost to the defendant. As such, it can be viewed as a middle alternative between nonfinancial release and surety bail, raising the possibility that, as with conditional releases, deposit bail might reduce the use of own recognizance. In a deposit bail system in which the option for its use rests with the judge, it would seem quite possible that judges would continue to use surety bonds as they have in the past, and set deposit bails in many cases in which the defendant could be safely released on own recognizance.

It was obvious in observing felony arraignments in Chicago in 1973 that deposit bail was considered preferable to own recognizance. If a defendant appeared to be a poor pretrial release risk, the judge, with little or no inquiry into the defendant's financial status, set a high bond amount. If the defendant appeared to be a good risk, the judge asked the defendant if he could post $100 as security. If the answer was no, he then reduced the amount until the defendant indicated that the amount of deposit was within his means. Only if the defendant indicated that the $25 minimum deposit was beyond his capabilities would the judge consider a nonfinancial release.

27. Beaudin, Lester, and Moran, supra n. 12, p. 109.

The result of such a practice is a low percentage of nonfinancial releases. Our study of 1971 bail practices in Chicago disclosed just a 10 percent O.R. rate in both felony and misdemeanor cases. In 1972 only 19.2 percent of all bonds *posted* in Chicago were O.R. bonds, and in 1973 the figure was 22.7 percent.[28] Since such calculations do not include defendants detained for failure to post bail, the overall percentage of criminal defendants granted nonfinancial release is even lower.

While the possibility exists that deposit bail might reduce the use of nonfinancial releases, such a result is by no means automatic. Indeed, our National Bail Study showed that those jurisdictions making the greatest use of nonfinancial releases in 1971 felony cases were Washington, D.C., and Des Moines. In both jurisdictions, deposit bail is available but rarely used, as judges rely primarily upon own recognizance and nonfinancial conditional releases. This result is very likely due to two factors: (1) statutory requirements that the judges use nonfinancial releases except when such release will not adequately assure the defendant's appearance; and (2) effective pretrial release programs which facilitate the court's use of nonfinancial releases.

Moreover, the fact that deposit bail might reduce the number of O.R. releases is not necessarily a bad feature of deposit bail—even from a perspective advocating the widest possible use of pretrial release. The more basic questions would seem to be: (1) Does the use of deposit bail in conjunction with nonfinancial release options decrease the overall release rate from that which would be obtained in a system of O.R. without deposit bail? (2) Is the combined system a less satisfactory method of making decisions with respect to pretrial release?

As to the first question, there are no conclusive data one way or the other. However, since not all defendants will be

28. Deborah A. Sperlak, "Bail: A Legal Analysis of the Bond-Setting Behavior of Holiday Court Judges in Chicago," *Chicago-Kent Law Review*, vol. 51 (1974-75), pp. 757, 763 fn. 45. (Figures were provided by Judge Peter Bakakos, Chief Judge of the Surety Division, Circuit Court of Cook County.)

found qualified for nonfinancial release and since, as a matter of constitutional law, bail must be set in all but capital cases and a few other instances, it seems likely that some form of financial bail must be maintained, and that the combined system probably increases the rate of pretrial release. Whatever the answer to this question, the Illinois experience would suggest that the difference is not great.

The answer to the second question concerning decision making seems similarly in doubt. Either system can be used skillfully and precisely by judges and others to achieve the results they desire. Either can be abused. Both, however, seem to have clearcut advantages over surety bail in that they give more control over the release decision to the judge and less to the bondsman.

In a system of deposit bail, the judge knows the exact amount of money that a defendant must raise to secure release and, by asking appropriate questions at arraignment, can determine very accurately whether the defendant can, in fact, afford to buy his release. In a surety bail system, this is not always the case. The judge's role is limited to the setting of a bond amount, and the ultimate fact of release is often left to negotiations between the defendant and a bondsman. Judge J. Skelly Wright accurately described the problem:

Certainly the professional bondsman system as used in this District is odious at best. The effect of such a system is that the professional bondsmen hold the keys to the jail in their pockets. They determine for whom they will act as surety—who in their judgment is a good risk. The bad risks, in the bondsmen's judgment, *and the ones who are unable to pay the bondsmen's fees,* [italics in original] remain in jail. The court and the commissioner are relegated to the relatively unimportant chore of fixing the amount of bail.[29]

Once the defendant has posted the bond amount, whether there is any difference between release on deposit bail or own recognizance is also not clear. Obviously, there is some difference in terms of cost to the defendant in those

29. *Pannell* v. *United States,* 320 F. 2d 698, 699 (D.C. Cir., 1963) (concurring opinion of J. Skelly Wright).

jurisdictions which retain 1 percent of the bond amount as an administrative fee. In terms of ensuring appearance in court, however, it is not clear whether one method is superior to the other. It can be argued that there is an advantage to the deposit bail system because the defendant does have a true financial incentive to appear. Whether this makes any significant difference has not been tested, however, and the question remains unanswered.

CONCLUSION

The 10 percent deposit bail system is one which has worked well in Illinois and is being adopted in one form or another in an increasing number of jurisdictions. The American Bar Association's Standards for Criminal Justice and the National Advisory Commission on Criminal Justice Standards and Goals favor adoption of such a procedure. Ten percent deposit bail is thus an important facet of bail reform. It must be recognized, however, that deposit bail is a system of money bail and, as such, has the same capacity as surety bail to discriminate on the basis of wealth. Although it is a less onerous form of money bail for those defendants who must rely on financial bail to secure release, it is not a solution to the pretrial detention problems of indigents.

17

The Police Role

EACH day thousands of persons are swept into American jails charged with relatively minor criminal offenses. Detention of these persons is usually unwarranted and, in most cases, unwanted. Little controversy is stirred by their release. Despite the fact that many are ultimately released prior to trial, all suffer some period of detention, and the majority are out the cost of a bail bond.

For the most part, these arrestees are jailed not because someone has decided that there is a need for their incarceration, but because the traditional method of beginning criminal cases is by arrest, the taking of the person into physical custody. To be sure, courts have long had the authority to issue summonses directing the defendant to come to court, rather than ordering the physical arrest of the person.[1] This process is rarely used, however, and requires the action of the court. Most criminal cases are begun by the police without court involvement.

Since the criminal justice process normally begins with an arrest, the police are often in the best position to provide for the speedy release of criminal defendants. Historically, however, pretrial release has not been viewed as a police function. Yet, there is one notable precedent for involving the police in the release decision. Sixty years ago, before

1. A summons is a written order issued by a court which commands a person to appear before a court at a stated time and place. See, e.g., Fed. R. Crim. P. 4(b) (2). This procedure is to be distinguished from the police practice of citing arrestees and releasing them on written promises to appear. In some jurisdictions, this is also referred to as a summons, but it is more frequently called a citation.

the traffic infraction became a common occurrence, police made physical arrests of all traffic violators.[2] Once the automobile became the dominant form of transportation, it was no longer feasible to rely on traditional arrest practices for handling traffic violation cases, and the practice of citing and releasing traffic offenders was developed. It is difficult now to perceive how the system could operate otherwise.

The virtues of this type of police release procedure were also applied, at an early date, to the violation of regulatory statutes. Arthur Beeley, for example, noted such procedure in Chicago in 1927, lamenting, however, the infrequency with which it was used.[3] Often the practice was somewhat informal and without specific statutory authority.[4]

Despite the obvious success of the police citation procedure in securing the appearance of millions of traffic violators in every state in the Union, there was very little movement to extend these procedures to more ordinary criminal cases or to rethink the necessity for physical arrest. A few writers, such as Beeley and the draftsmen of the Uniform Arrest Act in 1939, did make suggestions along these lines, but for the most part they were ignored.[5] Only three states—New Hampshire and Rhode Island in 1941 and Delaware in 1951—adopted police summons provisions modeled on the Uniform Arrest Act.[6] By 1960 only one additional state—California—had adopted a police citation release statute.[7] Even with the passage of these statutes, however, release of criminal defendants by the police was a procedure which existed largely on paper but not in practice.

2. Floyd Feeney, "Citation in Lieu of Arrest: The New California Law," *Vanderbilt Law Review,* vol. 25 (1972), p. 367.
3. Arthur L. Beeley, *The Bail System in Chicago* (Chicago: University of Chicago Press, 1927; reprinted 1966), pp. 13-23.
4. See, e.g., *Mormon* v. *Baran,* 35 N.Y.S. 2d 906 (Sup. Ct., 1942).
5. See Beeley, supra n. 3, p. 154; Sam B. Warner, "The Uniform Arrest Act," *Virginia Law Review,* vol. 28 (1942), pp. 315, 346.
6. Del. Code Ann., tit. 11, §1907 (1974); N.H. Rev. Stats. Ann., §549.14 (1974); R.I. Gen. Laws Ann., §§12-7-11 and 12-7-12 (1969).
7. Act of July 8, 1957, ch. 2147 §6 (1957) Cal. Stats. 3808 (repealed 1969).

The major breakthrough in this area, as in bail, came in New York, where the Vera Institute of Justice and the New York City Police Department combined to launch the Manhattan Summons Project in the spring of 1964.[8] This project sought to apply the techniques of the already successful Manhattan Bail Project to misdemeanor defendants at the police precinct level. Law students were located in a few stationhouses in Manhattan and instructed to apply the by now familiar Vera point scale. If a defendant received the necessary five points, the desk sergeant was asked to release him on his promise to appear.

Within six months the project had demonstrated that defendants released in this way would appear in court over 90 percent of the time, and that the police could save considerable amounts of time and money. The law students were soon replaced by line police officers and the project expanded—in 1966 to all of Manhattan and in 1967 to the whole city.[9] By 1969 the New York City police were releasing over 20,000 persons a year in this manner.[10]

Meanwhile, in California a number of smaller departments had begun to experiment with citation release procedures. By the mid-1960s citations were being frequently used in Contra Costa County, and were attracting attention elsewhere in the state.[11] In 1969 the California statute was amended to require police to evaluate all misdemeanor arrestees for citation release.[12]

This new law, plus problems of overcrowding in local jails, has led to a considerable expansion in the use of citations in California. A 1971 survey by the Center on Administration of Criminal Justice indicated that nearly all of the fifty largest police departments were making some

8. See Criminal Justice Coordinating Council of New York City and Vera Institute of Justice, *The Manhattan Summons Project* (1969).
9. Ibid., p. 4.
10. Vera Institute of Justice, "Manhattan Summons Project—Activity Report for the Second Year of City-Wide Operation—July 1, 1968 through June 30, 1969" (August 25, 1969).
11. See Feeney, supra n. 2.
12. Cal. Pen. Code §853.6 (1970).

use of the citation procedure, and that many were using it extensively.[13] Rates of citation usage in eight large California departments varied from 1 percent to nearly 50 percent of all misdemeanor defendants.[14] Since 1971 the use of citations has continued to increase.

Usage of citations has also increased nationally. The number of states with authorizing statutes has increased dramatically from the five which had such statutes in 1965,[15] and the number of citations appears to have increased proportionally. While fully accurate figures are not available, the number of citations nationally may have been as high as 400,000 in 1974.[16] Usage in the most frequently committed misdemeanor offenses appears to have doubled between 1969 and 1974.[17]

13. Robert Bachman, "Misdemeanor Citation Release: A Study After Two Years of Trial in California" (unpublished paper, Center on Administration of Criminal Justice, University of California, Davis, 1971).
14. Ibid.
15. Wayne LaFave listed five citation statutes as in effect in 1965. These included those listed in notes 6 and 7 supra, plus an Illinois statute adopted in 1963. Ill. Rev. Stats., ch. 38 §107-12 (1970). Wayne R. LaFave, *Arrest: The Decision to Take a Suspect into Custody* (Little, Brown and Company, 1965), p. 204 fn. 133.

Since 1965 a number of states have adopted citation statutes. Included among these states are Arizona (Ariz. Rev. Stats. §13-1422 (1969)); Connecticut (Conn. Gen. Stats., §54-63c (1967)); Minnesota (Minn. R. of Cr. P., Rule 6.01 (1975)); Montana (Mont. Rev. Code, §95-614 (1967)); New York (N.Y. Crim. P. Law, §§ 140.20, 150.10-150.70 (1971)); Ohio (Ohio R. Cr. P., Rule 4(F) (1973)). Oregon (Oregon Rev. Stats. §133.110 (1969)); Vermont (Vt. R. Cr. P., Rule 3(c) (1973)); as well as the District of Columbia (D.C. Code, §23-610 (1967)).
16. In 1969 the Uniform Crime Reports published by the FBI began to carry some data on the use of summonses and citations as opposed to arrests. These data do not cover the entire country, to some extent cover different jurisdictions each year, and do not distinguish between the use of court-issued summonses and police-issued citations. It does seem likely, however, that a high proportion of the totals given for thefts and for some misdemeanors are police citations. Projections based on the 1974 Uniform Crime Report, pp. 175 and 179, would indicate over 400,000 citations.
17. Compare 1969 Uniform Crime Report, p. 103, with 1974 Uniform Crime Report, p. 179.

FIELD VS. STATIONHOUSE RELEASE

Citation release procedures may be broadly categorized as providing for the release of persons in the field by the arresting officer or at the police stationhouse following booking. Most statutes authorize either procedure.

Many police departments have developed guidelines to assist officers in the use of citations. In Oakland, California, for example, officers are instructed to issue field citations to adults arrested for a misdemeanor offense, unless one of the following circumstances exists:

1. The suspect requires medical care or is unable to care for his own safety.
2. There is a reasonable likelihood that the misconduct would resume, or that persons or property would be endangered.
3. The suspect cannot or will not offer satisfactory evidence of his identity.
4. The prosecution of the offense for which the suspect was arrested or of another offense would be jeopardized.
5. A reasonable likelihood exists that the arrested person will fail to appear in court as promised (a warrant check is mandatory).
6. The misdemeanant demands to be taken before a magistrate or refuses to sign the citation.[18]

Even under these guidelines, it is sometimes necessary to remove the defendant from the scene of the arrest. Cases where the person cannot satisfactorily identify himself to the arresting officer, and cases of assault or disturbing the peace where it is necessary to remove one or both combatants to prevent the criminal conduct from reoccuring, would be examples of this. Typically, however, the factors which require removal from the scene do not prevent release from the jail. Thus, in Oakland the departmental guidelines require issuance of a jail citation for adult misdemeanants who have promised to appear, except where the circumstances indicate either a reasonable likelihood that the suspect will fail to appear in court as promised or that the suspect, if released, will commit an offense causing or threating injury to persons or property.[19]

18. Feeney, supra n. 2, p. 385.
19. Ibid., p. 386.

Oakland's use of citation release has been extensive. In the program's first fifteen months, 4,374 of the 7,993 eligible misdemeanor arrestees (54.7 percent) were issued citations.[20] The majority of the citations were issued by the arresting officer in the field.[21]

The experience with field citations in California and elsewhere indicates that, for many defendants, even temporary detention is unnecessary. The relatively minor nature of most misdemeanor offenses and the "on-view" requirement for a misdemeanor arrest obviate any need for further investigation. If an identification problem exists, the arrestee can be required to produce suitable identification, and a warrant check can be run to determine whether there are any outstanding warrants or detainers. Finally, if police policy is to require that all arrestees be booked, the arrestee can be required to report to the jail for booking prior to appearing in court. The use of a field citation can save a defendant several hours or even days of detention. At the same time, the procedure will save considerable police time and money spent in transporting, booking, and jailing defendants for whom there is no custodial need.

Although field citations have the obvious advantages of eliminating custody entirely and reducing police time and expense in transporting and booking defendants, stationhouse citation procedures may generate more releases. Field citations necessarily involve more police officers than stationhouse release and, as with any new program, there is likely to exist some hesitancy and confusion on the part of some officers involved. In addition, many defendants who could not be released on the street may qualify for a jail citation. The first year experience with citations in New Haven, Connecticut, for example, was that 10.8 percent of all misdemeanants, excluding intoxication defendants, were released on field citations, but 33.3 percent were granted stationhouse release. Mark Burger, Legal Advisor to the New Haven Department of Police Service, concluded

20. Jeffrey M. Allen, "Pretrial Release Under California Penal Code Section 853.6: An Examination of Citation Release," *California Law Review,* vol. 60 (1972), p. 1339, 1359.
21. Ibid.

that, "A police citation procedure operating without the needed support of a stationhouse release program will provide some suspects with extremely speedy release from custody; but it will also result in a much higher overall detention rate."[22]

Citation releases are currently used for a wide variety of misdemeanor offenses. Perhaps their most frequent use is in shoplifting and other petty theft cases and for minor assaults. Other offenses in which citations are frequently used include drunk driving, disturbing the peace, and malicious mischief. The rate of citation usage for each of these offenses varies widely, however. In 1971, for example, the Los Angeles Sheriff's Department was using citations extensively—in over two-thirds of the cases—for drunk driving arrestees. Other major California police agencies were not using this procedure at all in this type of case.[23]

WIDER POLICE INVOLVEMENT

In a few states, the police have been brought more fully into the pretrial release area. The most extensive police powers exist in Connecticut. Here the police have the authority to grant O.R. release in felony as well as misdemeanor cases, and are, in addition, empowered to set bail amounts in those cases in which they do not grant a nonfinancial release.[24]

The Connecticut procedure generally is for the police to advise the defendant upon his arrest of his right to be interviewed for pretrial release and, unless the defendant waives or refuses, to conduct a prompt interview. Unless they conclude that custody is necessary to assure appearance in court, the police then release the defendant on a promise to appear, or set a bail amount.

Experience under this statute indicates that this type of police authority does promote early release. Studies of pretrial release practices in New Haven and Hartford reveal

22. Mark Burger, "Police Field Citations in New Haven," *Wisconsin Law Review*, vol. 1972, pp. 382, 396.
23. See nn. 13 and 16 supra.
24. Conn. Gen. Stats., §54-63c (a) (1975 supp.).

that the police are, in fact, capable and willing to release defendants prior to court. Analyzing all criminal cases filed in the Circuit Court for New Haven during a three-month period in 1973, Malcolm Feeley and John McNaughton of Yale University found that 86 percent of the defendants had been released prior to trial.[25] Remarkably, only 6 percent of the defendants were detained longer than twenty-four hours. Seventeen percent were released almost immediately on citations, and another 44 percent within three hours.[26] Over 70 percent of those freed within three hours were released on citations or promises to appear.[27] While it was not possible to identify from the records the specific cases released by the police, it was clear that the majority of the releases were attributable to the police, rather than to later action.

Most of the cases in the New Haven study were misdemeanor or minor felony arrests. The more extensive data on felony cases in Hartford contained in the National Bail Study indicate that, while the felony release rate is not as high as that in misdemeanor cases, it is nevertheless substantial. In 1971, 25 percent of the felony defendants in Hartford were released by the police prior to court. Forty percent of these persons were released on promises to appear, and the remainder on bond.

The National Bail Study also shows that the rate of misdemeanor releases by the Hartford police is similar to that in New Haven. Although the Hartford police only rarely used citations, 63 percent of the misdemeanor defendants were released prior to court, 57 percent on promises to appear. Over 90 percent of all misdemeanor nonfinancial releases in Hartford were issued prior to a court appearance.

The experience in Hartford and New Haven would suggest that many of the releases now generated by pretrial release programs could, in fact, be handled by the police.

25. Malcolm M. Feeley and John McNaughton, "The Pretrial Process in the Sixth Circuit: A Quantitative and Legal Analysis," mimeographed (New Haven, Conn.: Yale University, 1974), p. 14.
26. Ibid., pp. 19-20.
27. Ibid., p. 22.

The delays inherent in a project's process of interviewing, collecting information, verifying, and presenting a release recommendation could be eliminated if the police assumed the task of making the release decision. The police know the circumstances of the alleged offense and the arrest, have ready access to at least the person's local arrest record, and should know whether the person is a local resident. If the police can assume the responsibility of releasing on O.R. the most qualified defendants, the project's time can be more properly focused on preparing information for the tougher release decisions.

Two functions performed by O.R. programs are lacking when the police make the decision to release on O.R., but neither may be necessary, and if they are, both could be easily accommodated. The first is the problem of verification. In most instances where the defendant is charged with a minor offense and carries sufficient identification papers on his person, further verification should be unnecessary. Indeed, the growing use of police citations strongly suggests that full, independent verification of the information given by a defendant is often unnecessary. If the police were, however, skeptical of the information given by a defendant, they could request a verification by the O.R. program. This procedure has been used successfully in the District of Columbia.

Second, the follow-up procedures to remind defendants of their court dates could not be expected to be performed by the police. This procedure could easily be assumed, however, by the bail project, which would be notified of all police releases.

FELONY CITATION AUTHORITY

While citations have gained wide national usage in misdemeanor cases, they have been used only infrequently in felony arrest situations. Although two early citation statutes in Illinois and Montana did not distinguish between felony and misdemeanor defendants in providing that notices to appear may be issued whenever a peace officer is author-

ized to arrest a person without a warrant,[28] most statutes
have been limited to misdemeanor arrestees. Two more
recent statutes adopted in Vermont and Minnesota have,
however, made citation releases mandatory in many misdemeanor arrest situations and discretionary in felonies.[29]

While misdemeanor arrests often occur in situations not
requiring any detention of the accused, the more serious
felony offenses are generally thought to require that the
defendant be taken into at least some period of custody.
The greater seriousness of the alleged offense often gen-
erates a more thorough investigation and interrogation.
While recognizing that citation releases are not as likely to
be used by the police in felony as in misdemeanor cases, it
would nevertheless seem that there are some felonies for
which such authority would be appropriate. There are
many felonies which are not dangerous crimes, a large
number of offenses that may be either a felony or a
misdemeanor, and a large number of felony arrests that are
eventually reduced to misdemeanors. If the police can be
trusted with the authority to make felony arrests in the
first instance, there would seem to be no reason why they
could not be trusted with discretionary release authority as
well.

CONCLUSION

Perhaps the best summary of the need and potential for
police involvement in the pretrial release process was that
given by Professor Wayne LaFave at the 1965 Institute on
the Operation of Pretrial Release Projects:

I don't think it is realistic to expect that after the fact judicial
review of need for custody can ever be brought into play soon
enough to eliminate all unnecessary pretrial detention.

Although we may hope to improve somewhat on the prevailing
practice of bringing the arrested person into court only on the
morning of the first business day following the arrest, it seems to
me that we still are going to have to rely on police release.

28. See n. 15 supra.
29. See n. 15 supra.

It is unlikely there will ever be sufficient judicial manpower such that it would be possible to have an immediate judicial pretrial release decision. We must, then, turn to the police. They operate around the clock and they are close to the situation with which we are concerned.[30]

Considerations such as these led the American Bar Association's Minimum Standards for Criminal Justice Project to conclude that "every law-enforcement agency" should issue "citations in lieu of arrest or continued custody to the maximum extent consistent with the effective enforcement of the law," and that for offenses for which total imprisonment does not exceed six months, issuance of citations should be required except where the accused fails to identify himself, refuses to sign the citation, has no ties to the jurisdiction, has previously failed to appear, or where an arrest is necessary to prevent imminent bodily harm to the accused or another person.[31]

30. *Bail and Summons: 1965* (New York: U.S. Department of Justice and the Vera Foundation, Inc., August, 1966), p. 129.
31. American Bar Association Project on Minimum Standards for Criminal Justice, *Standards Relating to Pretrial Release* (New York: Institute of Judicial Administration, 1968), pp. 31, 33.

18

Reaching the Defendant Quickly: Bail Schedules, Bail Commissioners, and Night Courts

UNDER traditional practice, the setting of bail is a judicial act, accomplished when the arrested person first appears in court. In some jurisdictions, this occurs almost immediately upon arrest, and in others at a somewhat later time. As a practical matter, however, a person arrested late in the day or at night is often forced to wait in custody at least until the following morning, or if he is arrested on a weekend until Monday morning.

Attorneys and bondsmen are able to produce some relief from this situation by contacting a judge at home and having him set bail out of court. This is obviously a cumbersome and expensive procedure, however, and relatively few defendants benefit from it. Much more important are the police release procedures discussed in the last chapter and fast-acting pretrial release programs. These are also not always available, however.

BAIL SCHEDULES

Another method for dealing with the situation is that of a pre-set schedule of bail amounts. In California such a system was first developed for misdemeanor defendants in 1945.[1] Under this system, the court sets the bail required for each offense, these amounts are posted in the jail, and the jailor is authorized to release defendants upon the

1. Cal. Pen. Code §1269b (1970).

posting of the required amount of bond without any contact ever having been made with the court. Under this system, many defendants in states like California secure release prior to appearance in court.

This use of a bail schedule *prior* to court appearance must be distinguished sharply from the use of a bail schedule after the defendant is already in court and before the judge. As long as the defendant has not yet appeared, the schedule helps by making it possible to know immediately what bail is required and to secure release if he can afford the cost. Once the defendant appears in court, there is much less justification for determining the bail amount solely by the offense charged. The defendant is present, and the court can make an individual determination. Hence, the in-court application of pre-set schedules has been criticized as highly inconsistent with the best judicial practice.

While the use of pre-set bail schedules prior to court appearance in misdemeanor cases presents relatively few operational problems, and has worked fairly well in jurisdictions such as California which use them, the situation is much more complicated with felonies. These are more serious crimes and require greater attention. It is not surprising, therefore, that the development of pre-set schedules for felony offenses has been much slower. In California felony bail schedules were adopted in 1973.[2] Under the California law, the judges of each county are required to establish a schedule of bail amounts for felony offenses but, unlike the misdemeanor schedule, the police are given the authority to refuse to apply the schedule for any defendant for whom they think it is inappropriate. While the bail amounts established in most California counties have tended to be high, the system seems to have had a major impact in the state, and many defendants have been released under the schedules.

Although the use of misdemeanor bail schedules predates the bail reform movement, the increasing concern with the problems of bail has led to other alternatives to

2. Cal. Pen. Code §§1269b, 1269c (1975 supp.).

decrease the time from arrest to bail determination. While a bail schedule provides a prompt method of release, many defendants cannot afford the cost involved. In addition, many defendants who do secure release through a bail schedule suffer unnecessary financial hardship because they could, and should, have been released on own recognizance. Implementation of police citation releases, discussed in the last chapter, is one solution to the problem. Other remedies have included night courts and bail commissioners to set bail during noncourt hours.

NIGHT COURTS

One obvious method for reducing the delay between arrest and a judicial bail decision is simply to increase the length of court hours. Night courts, such as the one operating in New York City, can provide prompt bail decisions for persons arrested during the early evening and nighttime hours. In New York City the procedure in night court is the same as in day court, with the defendant being arraigned and a bail determination being made.

Chicago, on the other hand, established a night court in 1973 that operates from 8:00 P.M. to 3:00 A.M. for the sole purpose of setting bail. According to General Order 73-1 of the Circuit Court of Cook County, Illinois, First Municipal District, whenever any person is arrested for a misde- meanor offense which is punishable by fine only, and he is unable to post bail as set by a schedule, he must be released upon a notice to appear. Other misdemeanor defendants unable to post the schedule bail amount, and felony defendants arrested during evening hours, are to be pre- sented without undue delay before a judge regularly assigned to the Bond Court. Unlike defendants in New York, however, he does not actually appear in court. The defen- dant is presented in court through the use of a picture telephone from the police district station. The only defen- dants not to be presented in Bond Court are those arrested on warrants and any persons held for their own "safekeep- ing." The latter qualification, however, appears applicable to felony defendants only.

A major drawback in the creation of night courts to

shorten the delay from arrest to bail determination is the cost involved. The cost of employing judges and other court personnel for a night court is substantial. While the number of arrests in large cities such as New York and Chicago can justify such expenditure, most cities would find night courts impractical. On the other hand, the higher incidences of crime on Fridays and Saturdays make the establishment of weekend bail-setting courts practical in most major cities, and several jurisdictions now provide for court hours at least on Saturday mornings. While night courts can save defendants several hours of unnecessary detention, Saturday courts can save days of detention. Without weekend courts, persons arrested on Friday evenings must wait at least until Monday morning for a judicial bail determination. Aside from benefiting the arrestee, weekend courts also aid the court by reducing the normal congestion that occurs on the Monday bail calendar.

BAIL COMMISSIONERS

Another alternative to provide for bail settings during noncourt hours is the use of bail commissioners. These are nonjudicial officers empowered to set bail amounts. Their chief benefit is that they may be less expensive to employ and more readily available than judges during noncourt hours. In the last decade, at least three quite different commissioner systems have been tried.

The Massachusetts System. The least satisfactory of these commissioner systems has been that used in Massachusetts. Massachusetts law permits a variety of persons aside from judges to set bail out of court.[3] Such persons include clerks and assistant clerks of the Superior and District Courts, Masters in Chancery, Justices of the Peace, and bail commissioners. The state, however, does not pay these persons to set bail, but rather their fee is paid by the prisoner who requests a bail setting. A "Person Authorized to Take Bail," other than a judge, may charge $5 for

3. Mass. Gen. Laws, ch. 276 §57 (1972).

setting bail on each misdemeanor offense, and between midnight and 6:00 A.M. he may charge $10 for setting bail on the first misdemeanor offense and $5 on each one thereafter.[4] While the statute does not mention the fee to be charged for setting bail in felony cases, 1972 court rules provided that in the absence of statutory regulations of bail fees on felonies, the fees shall be the same as those for misdemeanors.[5] Thus, under the commissioner system in Massachusetts, the defendant must pay a fee to have bail set prior to a court appearance. Even if he is released on own recognizance, he must pay this fee.

According to a 1973 report to the Chief Justice of the Superior Court and the Chief Justice of the District Courts of Massachusetts, the lack of effective control over bondsmen and "Persons Authorized to Take Bail" created major problems:

> The greatest problem with 'Persons Authorized to Take Bail,' . . . is one that everybody seems to know but nobody wants to talk about and that is collusion between professional bondsmen or surety agents and 'Persons Authorized to Take Bail.' It has been admitted to members of the Bail Committee that certain surety agents have 'favorites' among Bail Commissioners or other 'Persons Authorized to Take Bail.' It has been told to us by one Suffolk County Bail Commissioner that the only way to stay in business is to become 'favorite' of a particular surety agent![6]

Rather than the desired procedure of a commissioner setting bail and the defendant then calling a bondsman, in Suffolk County, at least, it was found that the "Persons Authorized to Take Bail" were actually following the surety agents or bondsmen from jail to jail. The bondsmen were the first to see who was incarcerated and who had enough money or adequate credit to be released on bail:

> What often occurs . . . is that the bondsman or surety agent decides what amount of bail will be set, according to the defen-

4. Mass. Gen. Laws, ch. 262 §24 (1972).
5. Dermot Meagher, *The Final Report of the Percentage Deposit Bail Project to the Chief Justice of the Superior Court and the Chief Justice of the District Courts* (1973), p. 8 fn. 5.
6. Ibid., p. 10.

dant's ability to pay, calls his 'favorite' 'Person Authorized to Take Bail' and dictates this decision to that 'favorite' 'Person Authorized to Take Bail.' The 'Person Authorized to Take Bail' is given his fee by the bondsman or surety agent who may have already collected it from the defendant or given the defendant credit. It has been told to us that certain bondsmen give more than the fee not only to the 'Person Authorized to Take Bail' but also to whoever called them.[7]

Collusion between bail commissioners and bondsmen is obviously not conducive to the liberal use of nonfinancial releases. When bondsmen have a dominating influence on out-of-court bail settings, one would expect money bail to be set in a high proportion of cases. Furthermore, since the bonding fee increases in proportion to the amount of the bond, the obvious tendency would be for bondsmen to set bails as high as the defendant could be expected to bear. Such a practice is contrary to Massachusetts law, which creates a presumption in favor of personal recognizance.[8] While there is an automatic review of all bail settings by commissioners within forty-eight hours of the initial determination, such review is of no benefit to the defendant who has already signed a contract with a bondsman and paid his fee. Releasing such a defendant on personal recognizance in court will not alter the fact that he has already paid a bond fee.

In order to improve the commissioner system, Massachusetts in 1972 began to exert a greater control over bondsmen, surety agents, and "Persons Authorized to Take Bail." As late as 1974, however, the commissioner system was still being severely criticized. A weekly Boston newspaper reported:

The system's abuse begins with the amount of bail set by the commissioner who is under great temptation to act in collusion with the bail bondsman. Faced with a defendant who has the means to buy his release, a commissioner is often unlikely to follow the Bail Reform Law's instructions on personal recognizance—especially if he can split the profit with a bondsman. If

7. Ibid., p. 11.
8. Mass. Gen. Laws, ch. 276 §58 (1972).

the commissioner sets a $10,000 bail, he can split $1,000 for a short night's work.

As this is written, the three-judge Superior Court panel is in the midst of an investigation into possible collusion . . .[9]

The Connecticut System. The present Connecticut commissioner system is a limited one. The initial release decision is made by the police, and a commissioner becomes involved only if the police decide that custody is necessary and the defendant is unable to post the bail they have set. If these conditions exist, the police must notify a commissioner immediately, and the commissioner must conduct his own investigation and make an independent decision. Unless he finds custody to be necessary to assure appearance in court, the commissioner must release the person on his own promise to appear, on an unsecured appearance bond, or upon a bond with sureties.[10]

As originally conceived, and as it operated from October, 1968, through June, 1969, the Connecticut Bail Commission exercised much wider powers, including the authority to make all initial bail decisions. During this period, the Commission operated much like a statewide O.R. project, but with the important additional authority to make releases rather than simply recommendations. Although no formal point system was used, the release standards of the Commission were patterned heavily after those developed by the Manhattan Bail Project.[11] By statute the Commission was instructed to favor the use of nonfinancial releases over surety bonds, and a commissioner imposing a money bond was required to state his reasons for doing so.[12]

While the bail decision of a commissioner could be reviewed by the court, the defendant was in the meantime free from custody on the decision made by the commissioner. The only qualification placed on the commissioner's release authority was that if a serious dispute arose, the

9. *The Boston Phoenix,* May 7, 1974, p. 14.
10. Conn. Gen. Stats., §54-63c (1975 supp.).
11. Thomas O'Rourke and Robert F. Carter, "The Connecticut Bail Commission," *Yale Law Journal,* vol. 79 (1969-70), pp. 513, 517.
12. Ibid.

police could request the prosecuting attorney to delay the release until the next regular court session.[13]

The effect of the Bail Commission, in the words of Chief Commissioner Thomas O'Rourke, was "immediate and dramatic."[14] After two months of operation, 60 percent of all bailable defendants statewide were released on either written promises to appear or nonsurety bonds, and this rate of nonsurety release remained constant for the duration of the Commission's unrestricted operation.[15]

According to O'Rourke, the primary motivation for curtailing the Commission was one of economy.[16] In order to perform the large task it was delegated, the Bail Commission required a sizable staff. The Commission employed a bail commissioner in each of the eighteen circuits in the state, and every circuit had at least two or more assistant commissioners. The total staff of commissioners numbered 61.[17] The estimated total budget for the first year of operation, including three months of reduced activity, was $400,000.[18]

The Wilmington, Delaware, System. A much more economical commissioner system is that operated in Wilmington, Delaware. As commissioners are employed only in the evenings and on weekends when judges are unavailable, fewer bail commissioners are necessary. In addition, the Wilmington system uses commissioners in conjunction with an O.R. project, thus reducing the number of commissioners necessary since the project and not the commissioner serves the fact-finding, investigative function. The commissioner's principal role in Wilmington is to pass on the recommendations made by the O.R. project. If the project does not favorably recommend a defendant for nonfinancial release, the commissioner will generally set money bail based on a schedule of recommended bail

13. According to Chief Bail Commissioner Thomas O'Rourke, this procedure to challenge a commissioner's bail decision occurred only once. Ibid., p. 516 fn. 17.
14. Ibid., p. 517.   15. Ibid., pp. 517-518.   16. Ibid., p. 523.
17. Ibid., p. 517.   18. Ibid., p. 524 fn. 43.

amounts prepared by the court. Since only a single commissioner and one O.R. investigator are on duty during the
evenings, the two work closely together in making bail
decisions, and the O.R. report is given considerable weight.
However, if there is any doubt as to the propriety of an O.R.
release, or if the police register objections, the commissioner generally opts to impose money bail and allow the
court to reevaluate nonfinancial release at the following
morning court session.

CONCLUSION

The American criminal justice system normally begins with
the physical arrest of the accused. Whether or not there
exists any real need for immediate or continued custody,
the criminally accused is detained until he satisfies the
conditions imposed for his release. The reforms discussed in
this chapter are designed to reach defendants quickly for
the purpose of setting the conditions of pretrial release.

The case for doing so is quite strong. Detaining a
defendant for several hours or days prior to a court
appearance serves an essentially bureaucratic purpose. If a
defendant will be released anyway, the period of detention
from arrest to initial court appearance is not going to
prevent his flight to avoid prosecution. On the other hand,
even short periods of detention following arrest can be very
damaging to the person because of its effect on his job and
family situation. If a defendant is to be released at all, there
are compelling reasons for doing so as quickly as possible.

The major virtue of using pre-set bail schedules prior to
court is that they operate automatically and provide an
immediate method of release for defendants who can afford
the cost. Their obvious shortcoming is reliance on money as
the sole criterion for release. Many arrestees will be unable
to post the bail amount, and many who do so will suffer
unnecessary financial hardship because they should have
been released on own recognizance.

The use of bail commissioners can resolve this problem by
providing an individualized bail decision. The principal

virtue in the use of commissioners is in providing quick nonfinancial releases prior to court for defendants who represent the best pretrial release risks. A liberal use of field and stationhouse citation releases by the police can accomplish the same thing, however, and using police is less expensive than the employment of bail commissioners.

If the majority of misdemeanor defendants and some felony defendants are released either on citations by the police or on bail as set by a bail schedule, the involvement of bail commissioners can be limited to those defendants with serious bail problems. By conducting a pretrial release evaluation himself or in conjunction with a pretrial release program investigator, the commissioner may find other defendants qualified for immediate release. Even in those cases which require a judicial bail decision, however, the commissioner's investigation will serve a valuable purpose in providing the judge with background information for the court bail setting.

19

Pretrial Services Agencies and Diversion Programs

THE development of the various methods of pretrial release discussed in the preceding chapters has made the pretrial release and detention issue much more complex. No longer are bail decisions made exclusively by judges in court; no longer is the bail decision based solely on the offense charged or the prosecutor's recommendation; no longer is money bail the only method of release. Because of the greater complexity, pretrial release programs have assumed a much larger role in several jurisdictions, evolving into comprehensive pretrial services agencies charged with monitoring the entire system of release.

This change from O.R. project to pretrial services agency began in Washington, D.C., with the D.C. Bail Agency. Recognizing that the Bail Reform Act of 1966 had "not been administered with maximum understanding and effectiveness" in the District, the Hart Committee recommended in 1968 that the D.C. Bail Agency be expanded and assume a much greater responsibility in seeing that the bail practices mandated by the Act were carried out.[1] The Hart Committee recommendations were accepted by Congress, and in June of 1970 the D.C. Bail Agency assumed its larger role.

In addition to interviewing all persons arrested in the District, verifying the information obtained, and presenting written reports and pretrial release recommendations to the

1. *Report of the Judicial Council Committee to Study the Operation of the Bail Reform Act in the District of Columbia* (Washington, D.C.: District of Columbia Circuit, May, 1968), pp. 2, 22.

court, the Agency also supervises all persons released on personal recognizance, conditional release, and cash and deposit bonds. The determination of what conditions to impose, and the supervision of defendants to see that the conditions imposed are met, constitute an important area of the program's expanded activity. In addition, the Agency is charged with verifying information prior to issuance of police citations, when requested to do so by the police, and reviewing its initial recommendation when defendants appeal from the original release conditions imposed. Its role as an overall system monitor is seen in its further duties: to coordinate the activities of other organizations and agencies which serve as third party custodians for defendants; to inform the court and U.S. Attorney of any failure by a defendant to comply with his pretrial release conditions; to notify the court of the arrest of any person released under its supervision; and to prepare in cooperation with the U.S. Marshal and the U.S. Attorney biweekly pretrial detention reports listing each defendant and witness who has been held in custody pending indictment, arraignment, or trial for a period in excess of ten days, and stating the reason for the detention. Finally, the D.C. Bail Agency prepares an annual report in which it details the pretrial release and detention practices in the District.[2]

Similar comprehensive pretrial services agencies have also been implemented in Minneapolis, Brooklyn, and Philadelphia. The Pretrial Court Services Division in Philadelphia is unique in several respects. First, it gives much greater attention to bail reevaluation procedures. In Philadelphia each defendant is interviewed immediately following booking, and a point scale is employed to identify those qualifying for own recognizance. While a pretrial release report is submitted for each defendant at initial appearance, it is generally only those defendants who qualify on points that receive a favorable nonfinancial release recommendation from the program. However, those defendants who are not released on O.R., and who cannot post the initial bail set, are reevaluated by the program and,

2. See D.C. Code §§ 23-1301—23-1307 for regulations governing the D.C. Bail Agency.

in appropriate cases, a motion is made by the Court Representatives Unit that the court reconsider the bail decision. The program's second evaluation is subjective and, while some defendants are then recommended for O.R., more often the recommendations are for supervised release to a community agency, conditional release, or a reduction of the bond amount.

Second, the Philadelphia program is unique in that it operates in a jurisdiction which relies heavily on deposit bonds and with very little use of surety bail. As a result, the program is directly involved in the release and supervision of defendants on money bail as well as own recognizance. The program has, thus, divided its staff between the two areas of responsibility, one section handling the non-financial releases and the second in charge of the deposit bail program.

The third distinguishing characteristic of the Philadelphia program, and one which has been controversial, is its Apprehension Unit. Once a defendant has failed to appear, most pretrial release programs will attempt to locate him by telephone and advise him of the need to report to the program and the court immediately. If the defendant cannot be located, the programs will generally contact the references he provided during the initial interview to see if they can assist in locating the defendant. In a majority of the cases this procedure proves sufficient, but if it is not, the programs turn the case over to law enforcement agencies.

Philadelphia's Apprehension Unit is considerably different. Authorized to make arrests and licensed to carry guns, this unit goes into the community to locate defendants who have failed to appear. Director Dewaine Gedney considers this unit an important asset to the program. He sees the unit as part of the program's obligation to ensure that persons it has assisted in release do return for trial. Since the use of deposit bail has drastically reduced the involvement of bondsmen, the apprehension unit is performing the recapture function which is often felt to be the most significant feature of surety bail. Gedney feels the unit has worked well and notes that, because the pretrial release program is recognized as an important defendant service agency, the program has broad community support and is, therefore, able to locate fugitives more easily than the police, and is able to return some defendants peacefully who would resist police arrest. While the apprehension unit is armed, Gedney says that, as yet, guns have never been used in the apprehension of a fugitive.

Other pretrial release program directors are not so convinced that an apprehension unit is a necessary or desirable component of the programs. They shudder to think what might happen were a shooting to occur in the program's apprehension of a fugitive. More than this, however, they question whether apprehension of fugitives is not a police function and better left to them, and whether apprehension units will not decrease the program's overall effectiveness. Emphasizing that their ability to obtain quick and accurate information about a defendant is contingent upon the defendant's desire to cooperate and the community's response to verification efforts, many program directors feel that apprehension units will convert the program to another prosecutorial agency in the eyes of the community and reduce their effectiveness in processing release recommendations.

PRETRIAL DIVERSION PROGRAMS

During the past ten years, advances in the bail reform area have been paralleled by the rise in innovative correctional strategies known as pretrial diversion or intervention programs. Since the success of pretrial release programs was surely a consideration in the creation of diversion programs, and to the extent that pretrial release and diversion programs interact in the local jurisdiction, it is important to recognize this development.

Pretrial diversion programs operate on the general assumption that, in many cases, the needs of the defendant and society can be met without invoking the full judicial process. Thus, if a defendant meets the guidelines for participation in a diversion program, and the prosecutor and/or court approve, he is offered the opportunity, usually at arraignment, to participate. If he agrees to the program, his criminal case is continued for from three to six months. During this period, the defendant receives employment and family counseling and job placement and educational services. If he successfully completes the program, a recommendation will be submitted to the court that his criminal case be dismissed. If the defendant fails to meet his program obligations, he is returned to court and the prosecution resumes.

The first formalized diversion program was started in Flint, Michigan, in 1965, but the movement began in earnest in 1968 when the U.S. Department of Labor became involved. The Department of Labor initially funded two pilot programs: Project Crossroads in the District of Columbia, and the Manhattan Court Employment Project in New York City. In 1971 the Department of Labor funded additional programs in Atlanta, Baltimore, Boston, Cleveland, Minneapolis, San Antonio, and the San Francisco Bay area in California. By 1974 it was estimated that at least twenty-five urban areas had active diversion programs and were providing services to more than 10,000 persons annually.[3]

Since most of the communities in which diversion programs operate also have a pretrial release program, the two programs interact frequently. The most common interaction is referral of defendants by the pretrial release program to the diversion program. When this occurs, the diversion program will generally conduct its own interview and make an independent decision as to whether the defendant meets the requirements for program participation. Since the information needs of the pretrial release program and the diversion program are basically the same, in some jurisdictions the information for both is gathered in a single interview. In a few jurisdictions, the pretrial services agency, in fact, administers both the pretrial release and diversion program.

3. National Pretrial Intervention Service Center, *Legal Issues and Characteristics of Pretrial Intervention Programs* (Washington, D.C.: American Bar Association Commission on Correctional Facilities and Services, April, 1974, monograph), p. ii.

This issue of whether pretrial release and diversion should be operated by two separate agencies or within the same agency is one that has surfaced at several meetings of the National Association of Pretrial Services Agencies, whose membership is comprised of representatives of both programs. While recognizing that, to the extent their information needs overlap, there is considerable virtue in combining efforts, there has been a general consensus that the release and diversion issues must be kept separate and apart, and that the two programs should not be combined under one agency.

From the standpoint of the defendant, it is important that the pretrial release and detention issue be resolved first. While diversion has obvious advantages to the defendant in the services provided and the avoidance of a conviction if the program is successfully completed, there are also disadvantages. The defendant must waive his right to a speedy trial; in addition, some programs require guilty pleas, and some have even required restitution to the victim. Furthermore, the defendant is always subject to being returned to the court process if he fails to satisfy the program's requirements. In balancing these considerations, the custody issue can be critical to the defendant. If he is on pretrial release, he may opt to stay in the court process; if he is detained, he might choose diversion. Since diversion programs are generally directed toward young offenders charged with minor criminal offenses and without serious prior records, most will undoubtedly qualify for own recognizance. In fairness to the defendant, this decision should be made prior to his decision on diversion program participation.

20

Crime on Bail:
The Preventive Detention Issue

FROM the beginning, one of the most serious impediments to bail reform has been the fear that a greater number of pretrial releases would mean a greater amount of crime, particularly serious crime. It was the existence of such fears that led the Vera Foundation to concentrate, in the early days of the Manhattan Bail Project, on defendants whom almost no one saw as dangerous, and to exclude from the project defendants charged with crimes such as homicide, robbery, rape, and sales of narcotics. Eventually, however, it became apparent that, even in these categories, many defendants were being detained more because of their inability to pay a bondsman than because someone had determined that they were too dangerous to be loose. As a consequence, a number of bail reform projects came to include serious felony defendants within their scope.

Given the rising crime rate of the 1960s and the growing national concern about crime, it was probably inevitable that the pretrial release of defendants charged with serious crime would become controversial. And given the fact that the most dramatic impact of the Federal Bail Reform Act, with its liberal pretrial release philosophy, was in the District of Columbia—a city in which crime was a particularly hot issue—it was probably also predictable that the controversy would arise in its sharpest form there.

Even prior to passage of the Federal Bail Reform Act, there had been some discussion about danger to the public and the possible need to include language in the Act that would allow this factor to be taken into account in the setting of bail.[1] As passed, however, the Act omitted such a provision and allowed consideration only as to whether the conditions of release would reasonably assure the appearance of the defendant.[2]

Almost immediately, the commission of crime by persons on pretrial release became a major issue. The Report of the President's Commission on Crime in the District of Columbia defined the problem late in 1966:

> As the bail system was reformed to permit the pretrial release of more defendants, only limited consideration was given to the protection of the public from crimes which may be committed by persons released prior to trial. In the course of its efforts to improve the system of pretrial release, Congress specifically postponed consideration of issues relating to crimes committed by persons released pending trial. The seriousness of the problem, however, is amply documented by newspaper reports of the more sensational instances in which persons released on bail allegedly committed additional crimes. In one 6-week period in early 1966, three separate homicides and a related suicide in the District were attributed to persons released on personal recognizance or on money bond.[3]

The majority of the Commission recommended that "legislation be adopted to authorize the pretrial detention of those defendants who present a truly high risk to the safety of the community."[4] A minority, however, vigorously dissented.[5]

The debate was picked up the following year by a committee of the District of Columbia Judicial Council, chaired by Judge George L. Hart, Jr., which was charged with studying the operation of the Bail Reform Act in the District of Columbia and evaluating the problem of crime committed by defendants on bail. The experiences of the Hart Committee typify the deep split in opinion on the

1. *Report of the President's Commission on Crime in the District of Columbia* (Washington, D.C.: U.S. Government Printing Office, 1966), p. 513.
2. Bail Reform Act of 1966, 18 U.S.C. § 3146.
3. *Report of the President's Commission,* supra n. 1, p. 513.
4. Ibid., p. 529.
5. Ibid., p. 930.

issue of preventive detention. In May, 1968, the committee reported that it was unable to make a recommendation on preventive detention and requested an additional year to study the issue. A year later, in May, 1969, a deeply divided committee produced two reports. The six-member majority recommended that a preventive detention statute be adopted: "A proper balance between the rights and interests of the individual and those of society requires such a statute."[6] The five-member minority was strongly opposed: "We believe that a preventive detention measure should not be enacted at this time. The right to pretrial release should not be the sacrificial lamb of an inadequate system of justice."[7]

Before the Hart Committee made its second report, however, President Nixon had taken much more direct action, proposing on January 31, 1969, that the Federal Bail Reform Act be amended to permit the "temporary pretrial detention" of criminal defendants whose "pretrial release presents a clear danger to the community."[8]

While the bill containing the specifics of this proposal was not sent to Congress by the Department of Justice until July,[9] Senator Ervin did not wait that long. At the time of the Nixon address, he had already responded with a series of hearings in January and February before his Subcommittee on Constitutional Rights. Later, in May and June of 1970, the subcommittee held additional hearings specifically on preventive detention. The reports on these hearings, particularly the 1970 hearings, represent the most complete

6. *Report of the Judicial Council Committee to Study the Operation of the Bail Reform Act in the District of Columbia* (Washington, D.C.: Judicial Council of the District of Columbia Circuit, May, 1969); printed in *Hearings on Preventive Detention* before the Subcommittee on Constitutional Rights of the Senate Committee on the Judiciary, 91st Cong., 2nd Sess. (1970) (Washington, D.C.: U.S. Government Printing Office, 1970), p. 736. (Hereinafter cited as 1970 Preventive Detention Hearings.)

7. Ibid., p. 738.

8. 27 *Cong. Q. Weekly* 238, Feb. 7, 1969.

9. The bill was introduced as S.2600, 91st Cong., 1st Sess., by Senators Hruska, Dirksen, and Thurmond. See also John N. Mitchell, "Bail Reform and the Constitutionality of Pretrial Detention," *Virginia Law Review*, vol. 55 (1969), p. 1223.

compilation to date of materials dealing with the preventive detention issue.[10] The subcommittee did not report favorably on the preventive detention proposals. Subcommittee Chairman Ervin stated his position quite explicitly at the start of the 1970 hearings:

Manifestly, these proposals would authorize the imprisonment and punishment of persons for crimes which they have not yet committed and may never commit. Preventive detention is not only repugnant to our traditions, but it will handicap an accused and his lawyer in preparing his case for trial. It will result in the incarceration of many innocent persons.

If America is to remain a free society, it will have to take certain risks. One is the risk that a person admitted to bail may flee before trial. Another is the risk that a person admitted to bail may commit crime while free on bail.

In my judgment, it is better for our country to take these risks and remain a free society than it is for it to adopt a tyrannical practice of imprisoning men for crimes which they have not committed and may never commit merely because some court may peer into the future and surmise that they may commit crimes if allowed freedom prior to trial and conviction.[11]

This was not the end of the matter, however. Recognizing the hostility of Senator Ervin and apparently fearful of the subcommittee's ability to block legislation applicable to the whole federal system, the Department of Justice had persuaded the House District of Columbia Committee to include similar preventive detention legislation in the D.C. Crime Act of 1970.[12] While testimony on the merits and

10. *Hearings on Amendments to the Bail Reform Act of 1966* before the Subcommittee on Constitutional Rights of the Senate Committee on the Judiciary, 91st Cong., 1st Sess. (1969); *Hearings on Preventive Detention* before the Subcommittee on Constitutional Rights of the Senate Committee on the Judiciary, 91st Cong., 2nd Sess. (1970) (Washington, D.C.: U.S. Government Printing Office, 1970).

11. 1970 Preventive Detention Hearings, supra n. 6, p. 3.

12. House District Committee Chairman McMillan introduced the preventive detention provisions on October 14, 1969 (H.R. 14334). These were later incorporated into the D.C. Crime Bill, H.R. 16196. See H.R. Rep. No. 91-907, 91st Cong., 2nd Sess., p. 5. This bill was passed by the House in March, 1970. Apparently, part of the House Committee report dealing with preventive detention was inadvertently omitted in the printing and later printed in the Congressional Record (daily ed., March 19, 1970, pp. 2078-80).

constitutionality of this legislation was negligible, and Senator Ervin fumed about the evasion of his subcommittee, the Senate as well as the House agreed in July to a conference report on the D.C. bill containing the preventive detention provisions.[13] The Act went into effect on February 1, 1971.[14]

As adopted, the statute authorizes the pretrial detention for sixty days without bond of defendants charged with a "crime of violence" (including murder, rape, robbery, burglary, arson, and serious assaults) or a "dangerous crime" (including robbery, burglary, rape, arson, and sale of narcotics), if a hearing determines that there is a substantial probability that the person committed the offense charged and that no condition or combination of conditions of release will assure the safety of the community. To be held without bond, defendants charged with a "crime of violence" must also have been convicted of another crime of violence within the previous ten years, be on pretrial release, probation, or parole for another crime of violence when arrested, or be an addict. Persons so detained are entitled to have their cases expedited for trial and to be given a pretrial release if their trial is not in progress by the end of sixty days.[15]

The early experience with preventive detention in the District of Columbia is discussed in a monograph written jointly by the Georgetown Institute of Criminal Law and Procedure and the Vera Institute of Justice. This study's major finding was the "virtual non-use" of preventive detention:

13. The Senate bill on D.C. Court Reorganization had not contained the preventive detention provisions. In the conference, however, the Senate conferees acceded to the House bill with minor modifications. See H.R. Rep. No. 91-1303, 91st Cong., 2nd Sess., pp. 239-40. For a discussion of the history of the bill, see Paul D. Borman, "The Selling of Preventive Detention 1970," *Northwestern Law Review*, vol. 65 (1970-71), p. 879. See, also, Carl S. Rauh and Earl J. Silbert, "Criminal Law and Procedure: D.C. Court Reform and Criminal Procedure Act of 1970," *American University Law Review*, vol. 20 (1970-71), pp. 252, 287-302.

14. District of Columbia Court Reform and Criminal Procedure Act of 1970, Pub. L. No. 91-358, 84 Stat. 473. The pretrial release and detention provisions are codified as D.C. Code §§ 23-1321 to 1332.

15. D.C. Code §§ 23-1321 through 23-1332.

The chief finding of the first ten months of observation has been the virtual non-use of the preventive detention law. The law was invoked with respect to only 20 of a total of more than 6,000 felony defendants who entered the D.C. Criminal Justice system during the period. Of the 20, nine were subjected to preventive detention hearings, and eight of the nine were ordered preventively detained. Two others were held in preventive detention at judicial initiative, without a detention hearing. Of the ten preventive detention orders, five were reversed on review or reconsideration, and one was dismissed when the grand jury refused to return an indictment on the underlying charges.[16]

Furthermore, the study revealed that during the last seven months of the ten-month study period, only five preventive detention motions were made, and two of these five motions were only 'stop-gap' measures to detain the defendants for a day or two while the government secured revocation of bond pending sentencing.[17]

The most obvious question raised by the District's experience with preventive detention has to be why it was not used more. The authors cite several causes. A letter from U.S. Attorney Harold H. Titus, Jr., appended to the report, explains that a major reason why the prosecutor's office had not presented more preventive detention motions was the questionable constitutionality of the statute. According to Titus, the prosecutor's office was forced to be very selective in using the section because each case in which it was used might turn out to be the test case upon which the constitutionality issue would be decided.[18]

A second explanation for the infrequent use of preventive detention, according to Titus, was a May, 1971, decision by the District of Columbia Court of Appeals requiring exhaustion of the five-day hold provision of Section 23-1322(e) before a preventive detention motion could be made. Section 23-1322(e) of the D.C. Code provides that persons charged with *any* offense may be ordered held up to five days "if it appears that such person is presently on proba-

16. Nan C. Bases and William F. McDonald, *Preventive Detention in the District of Columbia: The First Ten Months* (Washington, D.C.: Georgetown Institute of Criminal Law and Procedure and the Vera Institute of Justice, March, 1972), p. 69.

17. Ibid., p. 70.

18. Ibid., p. 89.

tion, parole, or mandatory release pending completion of sentence for any offense under State or Federal Law and that such person may flee or pose a danger to any other person or the community if released." In his letter, Titus states that about 250 five-day hold motions were made in 1971. "Included in these 250 cases," according to Titus, "were undoubtedly a number in which, but for the ruling by the District of Columbia Court of Appeals, we would have requested pretrial detention."[19]

A third reason for the non-use of preventive detention, according to the study, is that it was often unnecessary. The time-consuming and case-divulging preventive detention hearing can be avoided if the defendant is simply detained by the imposition of high money bail requirements. If the courts are willing to continue to impose substantial money bail requirements, there is no need to resort to the preventive detention statute. In a random sampling of 200 felony defendants from the period of February 1 through May 31, 1971, the authors identified sixty-seven defendants eligible for preventive detention. The government, however, moved for preventive detention against only 1.4 percent of these potentially eligible defendants.[20] The study showed, however, that despite the non-use of preventive detention, "about one-third of the [preventive detention] eligible defendants are continuously detained throughout the pretrial period in excess of 60 days almost exclusively because of an inability to post the required bond."[21] Of the thirty-five defendants for whom money bail was set, only six obtained pretrial release.[22]

What conclusion is to be drawn from preventive detention in the District? The final paragraph of the study seems particularly appropriate:

Perhaps the most prophetic were those who felt that the statute would simply create a time-consuming additional layer in the pretrial process without giving a prosecutor a result not otherwise achievable in most cases under the bail system. For the time being, lawmakers who have been advised to consider preventive detention legislation have little reason to hurry.[23]

19. Ibid., p. 90. 20. Ibid., p. 61. 21. Ibid., p. 68.
22. Ibid., p. 63. 23. Ibid., p. 73.

ISSUES RAISED BY PREVENTIVE DETENTION

While the failure to make extensive use of preventive detention legislation has quieted to some extent the debate about crime committed by defendants on pretrial release, the issues that surfaced continue to be important. The most critical are: (1) How serious is the problem—how much crime is committed by defendants on pretrial release? (2) Is it possible to identify in advance those defendants who are dangerous and likely to commit crimes? (3) Is some form of preventive detention constitutionally permissible? (4) Are there methods other than preventive detention which might be used to minimize the problem of crime on bail?

1. How much crime is committed by
defendants on pretrial release?

The most extensive data in this area come from the District of Columbia. The first systematic study undertaken was that of the President's Commission on Crime in the District of Columbia. Examining a group of 2,776 felony defendants who were released on either bail or O.R. during 1963, 1964, and the first nine months of 1965, the Commission found that 7.5 percent had been rearrested while on release and held for grand jury action on new felony charges.[24] The rearrest rate was found to be highest among those released on surety bail (7.7 percent) and lowest for those released on O.R. (4.7 percent).[25]

Later studies based on 1967 and 1968 felony cases reported by the Hart Committee found generally similar rates of rearrests for defendants on pretrial release.[26] Other studies examining specific types of defendants and using different measures of criminal involvement found a much higher percentage of defendants to be involved in pretrial criminal acts. Thus, a Metropolitan Police Department study limited to indicted armed robbery defendants in 1967-1968 found that about 30 percent had been reindicted

24. *Report of the President's Commission on Crime in the District of Columbia,* supra n. 1, p. 514.
25. Ibid., p. 515.
26. Hart Committee Report printed in 1970 Preventive Detention Hearings, supra n. 6, p. 723.

while on release,[27] and a 1968 U.S. Attorney's Office study of over 500 indicted robbery defendants reported a 70 percent rearrest rate while on release.[28]

These seemingly contradictory findings generated a considerable debate about the validity of the specific studies, about whether the proper measurement of reinvolvement was arrests or indictments or convictions, and about the significance of the findings. This argument was intensified with the release in April, 1970, of a new and more extensive study by the National Bureau of Standards.[29]

Deputy Attorney General Richard Kleindienst, testifying before the Ervin subcommittee, described the findings:

This study was made to analyze what could be learned from criminal justice records about the rearrests of a small sample of defendants given pretrial release. . . .

The study focused on 426 defendants who were released before trial during 4 weeks in the first half of 1968. The report revealed that 17 per cent of 147 felony defendants were rearrested during pretrial release. . . . Altogether, 11 percent of the 426 defendants, including those charged with misdemeanors, were rearrested for new offenses.[30]

Kleindienst lost no time in claiming that the Bureau of Standards study supported the administration's position:

If nothing else, the NBS report confirms our contention that a substantial amount of crime is being committed by persons released on bail; correspondingly, it undermines the frequent assertion that 'offenses committed by persons released on bail are approximately 6 per cent of the total crime figure.'[31]

Kleindienst also suggested that since many crimes go unreported, and the clearance rate for crimes that are reported is not 100 percent, the number of crimes represented by the rearrest figures might be three or four times greater than the figures themselves.

27. Ibid., p. 726.
28. Ibid., p. 724.
29. National Bureau of Standards, *Compilation and Use of Criminal Court Data in Relation to Pre-Trial Release of Defendants: Pilot Study* (Washington, D.C.: U.S. Government Printing Office, August, 1970).
30. 1970 Preventive Detention Hearings, supra n. 6, p. 74.
31. Ibid.

Senator Ervin, as might be expected, took a sharply contrasting view. Noting that the study showed that only 5 percent of those defendants eligible for preventive detention under the administration's bill were rearrested for dangerous or violent crimes during the period of their release, he asserted:

One of the primary assumptions which is disproved by the study is that the rate of pretrial dangerous and violent crime is very high and thus justifies preventive detention. I think it will be useful to view that assumption in light of the low rearrest rate shown in the study.[32]

Although the results of these different studies are somewhat confusing, the picture they present is more consistent than the arguments have sometimes indicated. If the count is made on the basis of a relatively loose measure, such as rearrests, and is made with respect to the most serious defendants, as for example those who have been indicted, the rate of recidivism tends to be very high. If, on the other hand, the count is made on the basis of a stringent measure, such as convictions or reindictments, and covers a wider group of defendants, such as all felony arrestees, the rate of recidivism tends to be much lower. Thus, the rate of *rearrest* of *indicted* robbery defendants in the U.S. Attorney's office study was over 60 percent,[33] while the rate of *reindictment* of *all felony defendants* in the D.C. Crime Commission study and the two studies reported by the Hart Committee was 7 to 10 percent,[34] and the more accurate data presented by the Bureau of Standards even lower.[35]

What then is the accurate amount of crime on bail? Is there a single figure that gives an appropriate picture? Unfortunately, there is not; the question of the appropriate figure depends primarily upon the purpose for which the question is asked. If the concern is about assaultive crime, then the question is how many assaultive crimes are

32. Ibid., p. 12.
33. See n. 28 supra.
34. See nn. 24 and 26 supra.
35. National Bureau of Standards, supra n. 29, p. 134. This study shows a 7 percent felony rearrest rate for defendants released in felony cases, and presumably the reindictment rate is lower.

committed by defendants on pretrial release—not how many felonies are committed or how many crimes are committed. If the concern is how much assaultive crime is attributable to persons who are already in contact with the criminal justice system, then the base must be broad—total arrestees or total felony defendants. If the concern is whether it is possible to identify a small group of defendants who are committing a large percentage of the crime, as in the preventive detention debate, then the base must be much narrower—defendants charged with particularly heinous crimes, having reached a certain stage in the criminal justice process or some other limitation.

The question of how much crime is committed by persons on bail thus depends largely on what kind of crime one is talking about. For the District of Columbia, during the period of the preventive detention controversy, the concern was clearly about violent crime. Extrapolating from the available data about robbery—one of the crimes on which there was particular focus—it would be possible to conclude that:

—The arrest rate of indicted robbery defendants on a second robbery charge while on release may be relatively high, perhaps as much as 30 percent.[36]

—The arrest rate of felony defendants, as a group, on robbery charges while on release is much lower, about 2 percent.[37]

36. The D.C. Police study, printed in 1969 Hearings on Amendments to the Bail Reform Act of 1966 (supra n. 10, p. 670), showed a 34.6 reindictment rate on felony charges for indicted robbery defendants. The forty-five persons who were reindicted had allegedly committed a total of seventy-six crimes, and fifty of these subsequent crimes were robberies or assaults with intent to rob. If these charges bear the same proportion to the number of defendants reindicted for robbery charges as the total charges bear to the total number of reindicted defendants, the number of defendants reindicted on robbery charges would be thirty, or about 23 percent. As this figure is based on reindictments, it is increased to reflect rearrests. While the methodological criticisms of the police study during the 1969 Ervin hearings (p. 676) have some validity, the study results seem generally in line with other studies available. The lower number of robbery rearrests in the Bureau of Standards study can be attributed to the fact that it is based on defendants charged rather than defendants indicted.

37. National Bureau of Standards, supra n. 29, Table 13, p. 135.

—The arrest rate of all criminal defendants, as a group, on robbery charges while on release is even lower still, around 1 percent.[38]

—If all criminal defendants were detained throughout the pretrial period, the total number of robberies prevented would be relatively small, about 5 percent of the total.[39]

The data also suggest that shortening or lengthening the amount of time between release and disposition strongly affects the amount of crime committed on pretrial release. If the time is shortened, crime decreases; if lengthened, it increases. The average number of crimes committed by felony defendants during the Bureau of Standards study was one crime for every 1,000 days of release.[40] The average number of felony crimes by felony defendants was .5 per 1,000 days on release.[41]

2. Is it possible to identify in advance those defendants who are likely to commit crimes?

This was one of the major issues raised by the opponents to the Nixon bill, the argument being that even if crime on bail was a problem—which they did not concede—it was one about which very little could be done, since neither judges nor anyone else was very good at predicting in advance which of the many defendants would commit crimes.

The problem of making sure that one detains all defendants who will commit crimes is obviously solved if one is prepared to detain all defendants. Unless all defendants will commit crimes while on release, however, this method detains many persons who will not commit crimes. The problem essentially is that of separating the two groups with accuracy.

38. Ibid.

39. According to the Bureau of Standards study, there were six subsequent arrests for robbery defendants released during the four-week study period. (National Bureau of Standards, supra n. 29, p. 135.) If this figure is multiplied by 13, it suggests a total of seventy-eight such arrests for the year. In 1968 there were 1,519 arrests for robbery by the D.C. Police Department. (Metropolitan Police, Annual Report-1968, p. 48.) Seventy-eight is 5.1 percent of 1,519.

40. National Bureau of Standards, supra n. 29, Table 14, p. 160.

41. Ibid., Tables 13 and 14.

One of the purposes of the National Bureau of Standards study was to test how the administration's bill might work in practice—to test the predictive powers of the categories chosen. Focusing on those defendants who could be preventively detained under the bill, but who had been given pretrial release under the existing system, the study found that 17 to 25 percent had been subsequently rearrested.[42] Only 5 percent, however, had been rearrested for dangerous or violent crimes.[43] A later study by the Harvard Civil Rights-Civil Liberties Law Review of persons on pretrial release in Boston in 1968 essentially confirmed the 5 percent figure of the Bureau of Standards study.[44] This figure, argued the bill's opponents, meant that, in order to prevent one violent or dangerous crime, the bill categories required the detention of nineteen defendants who were not dangerous or violent.

Proponents countered that the legislation did not mandate the detention of defendants eligible for preventive detention, but merely allowed judges this option in individual cases. The question thus becomes, in part, whether judges can successfully identify in advance those defendants who will commit additional crimes. Judge Charles Halleck of the D.C. Court of General Sessions told the Ervin subcommittee in 1969 that they could: "I am convinced that in many cases, indeed with a high degree of predictability, we can select those persons who are likely to commit offenses."[45]

When put to an actual test, however, these predictive powers seemed much less impressive. The D.C. Bail Agency had earlier completed a comparison of over 200 cases handled by Judge Halleck with a similar number handled by Judge Alexander of the same court. While Judge Alexander had set bails allowing pretrial release in 80 percent of the cases, only 49 percent of the defendants

42. Ibid., p. 2.
43. Ibid.
44. "Preventive Detention: An Empirical Analysis," *Harvard Civil Rights-Civil Liberties Law Review*, vol. 6 (1971), p. 291.
45. 1969 Hearings on Amendments to the Bail Reform Act of 1966, supra n. 10, p. 124.

handled by Judge Halleck had secured release. The rearrest rates for defendants handled by the two judges were, however, almost identical: 9 percent for Judge Alexander and 8 percent for Judge Halleck.[46] In effect, Judge Halleck had detained 30 percent more defendants for no appreciable benefit in crime reduction.

Left open is the question of whether further research might develop criteria which have a better predictive capability. The National Bureau of Standards study explored a number of possible approaches. While none proved particularly successful, the Bureau was optimistic about what might be done. It concluded that, "developing an accurate predictive instrument requires acquiring a sufficient data base and also more adequate testing of the predictability of criminal behavior from specified factors."[47] Other observers, noting the general lack of success in parole and probation prediction efforts, where much more extensive work has been carried out, have been much less hopeful.[48]

3. Is preventive detention constitutional?

Even sharper than the debate about the wisdom of preventive detention as a policy matter has been the controversy concerning the constitutionality of any legislation authorizing the detention without bail of persons charged with criminal offenses but not yet convicted. Most legal scholars who have addressed this issue have concluded that this kind of legislation is not constitutional. The Nixon administration and some other scholars have argued to the contrary.

The starting point for both sides is the Eighth Amendment. It says simply: "Excessive bail shall not be required . . ." Hidden within these cryptic words are at least three different questions: (1) Must bail be allowed in every case, or is it simply not to be excessive when it is made available? (2) Even if not available in certain historically distinct categories such as capital cases, is bail required in all other

46. 1970 Preventive Detention Hearings, supra n. 6, p. 149.
47. National Bureau of Standards, supra n. 29, p. 41.
48. See, for example, the testimony of Professor Hans Zeisel of the University of Chicago. 1970 Preventive Detention Hearings, supra n. 6, p. 149.

cases? (3) How is excessiveness to be determined? Does this mean excessive as compared to other crimes and defendants of the same type, or does it mean excessive as to the amount that this particular defendant can pay?

The case for constitutionality of preventive detention was put most strongly by Nixon's Attorney General John Mitchell in a Virginia Law Review article:

> To resolve the ambiguity of the abbreviated language of the eighth amendment, it is necessary to examine the historical context in which it was adopted in 1791 on the assumption that those concerned with drafting and ratifying the amendment generally intended to conform the law to contemporary practices. The only Supreme Court opinion which discusses the history of the eighth amendment and its application to the right to bail clearly adopts the interpretation which permits denial of bail prior to trial in some situations. . . .
>
> The prevalent practice when the amendment was proposed by the First Congress . . . and ratified by the states in 1791 was denial of bail in death penalty cases. . . .
>
> This pervasive practice of denial of bail in capital cases when the eighth amendment was ratified in 1791 is particularly significant because at that time the great majority of criminal offenses involving a threat of serious physical injury or death to the victim were punishable by death under state laws. . . .
>
> The considerations which led to the gradual repeal of the death penalty . . . are largely irrelevant to the question whether a defendant should be detained pending trial. . . . As a class, persons held to answer for such dangerous offenses as robbery, rape or burglary if released pending trial pose as great a danger to the community today as they did in 1791. Accordingly, since the eighth amendment when adopted clearly permitted pretrial detention for capital crimes because of danger to the community, it should not today prohibit pretrial detention for such dangerous crimes merely because they are no longer capital . . .[49]

Scholars taking the opposite view were quick to rebut.

---

49. John N. Mitchell, supra n. 9, pp. 1224-1230. Other writers supporting the constitutionality of preventive detention include: Frederick D. Hess "Pretrial Detention and the 1970 District of Columbia Crime Act— The Next Step in Bail Reform," *Brooklyn Law Review*, vol. 37 (1971), p. 277; Janet R. Altman and Richard Cunningham, "Preventive Detention," *George Washington Law Review*, vol. 36 (1967), p. 178.

Professor Laurence Tribe challenged what he took to be the Mitchell thesis as to the purpose of the Eighth Amendment:

The most comprehensive compilation of the statutory and case law on the English bail system in the late eighteenth century nowhere suggests that fear of danger to the community before trial motivated the distinctions between bailable and nonbailable offenses. On the contrary, the underlying assumption seems to have been that certain classes of offenders, particularly those whose lives were at stake, ought to be detained simply to assure their presence at trial.[50]

Contributing significantly to the general uncertainty as to the meaning of the Eighth Amendment is the absence of any definitive ruling by the Supreme Court. Neither of the two principal cases on bail are determinative. Those supporting the constitutionality of preventive detention tend to rely, as did Attorney General Mitchell, on *Carlson* v. *Landon*. This was a 1952 case in which four alien Communists were accused of Smith Act violations and arrested for deportation. The aliens claimed that the government was not entitled to deport them and that they were entitled to bail pending a hearing. As it had in other cases, the Court held that the deportation proceedings were not criminal and that the aliens could be deported. On the bail issue, the Court said it could find no cases indicating "that the Constitution requires . . . the same reasonable bail for alien Communists under deportation charges as it accords citizens charged with bailable criminal offenses." The Court then went on to say:

The bail clause was lifted with slight changes from the English Bill of Rights Act. In England that clause has never been thought to accord a right to bail in all cases, but merely to provide that bail shall not be excessive in those cases where it is proper to grant bail. When this clause was carried over into our Bill of Rights, nothing was said that indicated any different concept. The Eighth Amendment has not prevented Congress from defining the classes of cases in which bail shall be allowed in this country. Thus in criminal cases bail is not compulsory where the

50. Laurence H. Tribe, "An Ounce of Detention: Preventive Justice in the World of John Mitchell," *Virginia Law Review,* vol. 56 (1970), pp. 371, 400-401.

punishment may be death. Indeed, the very language of the Amendment fails to say all arrests must be bailable.[51]

Earlier in the same term of court, however, the Supreme Court had decided *Stack* v. *Boyle*. In this case, bail had been set at $50,000 each for twelve defendants awaiting trial on Smith Act conspiracy charges. The defendants sought to have the bail amount lowered. The Court agreed that the bail had not been set properly:

From the passage of the Judiciary Act of 1789 . . . to the present Federal Rules of Criminal Procedure . . . federal law has unequivocally provided that a person arrested for a non-capital offense *shall* [italics in original] be admitted to bail. This traditional right to freedom before conviction permits the unhampered preparation of a defense, and serves to prevent the infliction of punishment prior to conviction. . . . Unless this right to bail before trial is preserved, the presumption of innocence, secured only after centuries of struggle, would lose its meaning.

The right to release before trial is conditioned upon the accused's giving adequate assurance that he will stand trial and submit to sentence if found guilty. . . . Like the ancient practice of securing the oaths of responsible persons to stand as sureties for the accused, the modern practice of requiring a bail bond or the deposit of money subject to forfeiture serves as an additional assurance of the presence of an accused. Bail set at a figure higher than an amount reasonably calculated to fulfill this purpose is 'excessive' under the Eighth Amendment.[52]

It is the emphasis in this case, and in the history of the Eighth Amendment, that the purpose of bail is to ensure the presence of the defendant at trial that has led the majority of scholars to conclude that a preventive detention statute going beyond capital cases would be unconstitutional.[53]

While the matter is certainly not free from doubt, the fear that the District of Columbia preventive detention statute might be unconstitutional has been one of the contributing

51. *Carlson* v. *Landon,* 342 U.S. 524, 545-546 (1952).
52. *Stack* v. *Boyle,* 342 U.S. 1, 4-5 (1951).
53. See, e.g., Tribe, supra n. 50. See also Caleb Foote, "The Coming Constitutional Crisis in Bail," *University of Pennsylvania Law Review,* vol. 113 (1965), pp. 1164-1188.

factors to its infrequent use.[54] A decision on the statute was avoided when a civil class action suit seeking a declaratory judgment as to the statute's constitutionality was dismissed on jurisdictional grounds in 1972 by the U.S. District Court for the District of Columbia.[55] A more recent decision by the highest local court in the District also avoided ruling on the constitutional question.[56]

4. Are there other methods for dealing with crime on bail?

Even the most rigid opponents of preventive detention do not deny that there is some amount of crime being committed by persons on pretrial release, and some attention has been devoted to developing alternative solutions to the problem. Perhaps the most constructive approach concerns the possibility of speeding up the trial process and thereby reducing the amount of time that defendants spend on pretrial release. This idea played an important role in the adoption by Congress of the Speedy Trial Act of 1975. This Act, applicable to all federal courts, provides that after 1979 all felony cases must be brought to indictment within thirty days and to trial within sixty days.[57] Somewhat longer limits are allowed in the interim period.

While it is clear that this measure is not a complete answer to the problem, and little is known of any effects to date on pretrial crime, the principle upon which it is based seems sound. The National Bureau of Standards study shows clearly that the amount of crime while on release is directly related to the amount of time the defendant is free

54. See n. 18 supra.
55. Bases and McDonald, supra n. 16, p. 5 fn. 10.
56. *Blunt* v. *United States,* 322 A. 2d 579 (D.C., 1974). This decision upheld the validity of D.C. Code § 23-1322 (a) (3) permitting the pretrial detention of a defendant who threatens a prospective witness. Such authority was held to be within the inherent power of the court to protect a witness and safeguard the integrity of its own process.
57. Speedy Trial Act of 1975, 18 U.S.C. § 3161-3174 (Supp. IV 1975). The House report makes clear that one of the central purposes of the Act is to reduce crime. See H.R. Rep. No. 93-1508, 93rd Cong., 2nd Sess. (1974).

in the community. The longer the time on release, the greater the amount of crime.[58] Shortening that period would consequently seem to mean lessening the amount of crime committed.

Another approach is to provide more intensive supervision to persons on pretrial release, and to offer family and drug abuse counseling, as well as job placement services, to address personal difficulties that might have led to the initial criminal involvement. Hence, the increasing use of conditional and supervised pretrial release for "high risk" defendants in a number of jurisdictions. A study of the Des Moines Community Corrections Program reported that, over a three-year period, the "high risk" defendants released to that program did not differ from other released defendants in terms of offense allegations during the pretrial period.[59] The impact of conditional releases on reducing pretrial crime, however, is unknown. We do not know, for example, whether the number of rearrests for participants in the Des Moines program would have been any different without the intensive supervision which was given.

SUB ROSA PREVENTIVE DETENTION

While the concept of preventive detention has not fared too well in the clear, sparkling air of a highly publicized national debate, it continues to thrive in the less visible atmosphere of the jails and courtrooms of the country. Here the fear of further crime is often an important consideration in the amount of bail that is set.

Pretrial release programs have had some impact in this area, but not a great deal. Generally, the development of ground rules for the programs themselves has brought a greater explicitness as to which types of defendants in what kinds of cases can be safely released, and the programs have given greater visibility to the release decision itself. Usually,

58. See n. 40 supra.
59. Peter S. Venezia, *Pretrial Release With Supportive Services for "High Risk" Defendants* (Davis, Calif.: National Council on Crime and Delinquency Research Center, May, 1973), pp. 48-49.

however, the programs have felt themselves in no position to make substantial challenges to pretrial detention practices in the most serious cases.

The ambiguity of attitudes about the proper role of pretrial release programs in this area is illustrated by the responses to a 1974 National Center for State Courts survey of pretrial release program directors, police chiefs, sheriffs, district attorneys, public defenders, judges, and county officials. This questionnaire survey, which called upon the respondents to evaluate the relative importance of several possible end goals for pretrial release programs, disclosed a remarkable consensus that the programs should give high priority to four goals—making sure that released defendants return for trial, lessening the inequality in the treatment of rich and poor by the criminal justice system, obtaining speedy release for defendants who are eligible for release, and producing cost savings to the public. By contrast, the survey showed considerable disagreement among the respondents on the importance of three other possible goals which implicitly raised the issue of what role, if any, pretrial release programs should have in protecting the public safety—maximizing the number of persons at liberty between arrest and disposition, helping to ensure that persons who might be dangerous to the community are not released, and minimizing the potential danger to the community from persons released prior to trial by maintaining supervision in appropriate cases. While some respondents felt that these goals should be of prime importance, others felt that they should not be a concern of the programs at all.[60]

Regardless of whether the risk of future crime *should* be a permissible consideration in the bail decision, there is little question but that it *is* treated as important by judges. The pretrial release of criminal defendants is hindered, and often totally frustrated, by the imposition of high money bail. *Sub rosa* preventive detention practices are a formidable barrier to significant expansion of nonfinancial releases.

60. National Center for State Courts, *An Evaluation of Policy Related Research On The Effectiveness of Pretrial Release Programs* (Denver, Colo.: National Center for State Courts, August, 1975), p. 59.

SHOULD THE SYSTEM BE MORE EXPLICIT?

The present situation gives something to almost everybody. Liberals retain the belief that preventive detention is illegal, and risk of flight is the only permissible consideration in the setting of bail. Conservatives obtain a considerable amount of actual preventive detention. Detained defendants are clear losers but lack the muscle to change matters through the political process.

Indeed, without some clear ruling from the Supreme Court as to whether danger to the public may be considered in setting the bail amount or in denying bail altogether, it is unlikely that anyone will be able to change the situation very much. There is even some question, given the problems associated with review of bail decisions, whether a clearcut ruling by the Supreme Court would result in much change. The experience in the District of Columbia with the Federal Bail Reform Act suggests that a clearcut ruling, enforced by a vigorous appellate bench, would make a difference. The issue is not free from doubt, however. A 1973 ruling by the California Supreme Court that the state constitution prohibited consideration of the public safety in the setting of bail does not appear to have resulted in any substantial increase in the number of pretrial releases.[61]

Leaving aside the constitutional problems involved, this general situation raises the policy question of whether defendants, as well as the public, might not be better off with a system which allowed preventive detention of dangerous defendants, but which released all others without money bail. The principle virtue of such a system would be to make any decisions about dangerousness explicit. While adoption of such a system would not solve the prediction problems already discussed, it would bring these into the

61. The California Supreme Court in the case of *In re Underwood*, 9 C. 3d 345 (1973), stated that:

> The purpose of bail is to assure the defendant's attendance in court when his presence is required, whether before or after conviction. . . . Bail is not a means for punishing the defendant . . . nor for protecting the public safety. Such objectives are provided for otherwise.

Avoiding the Eighth Amendment issue, the court concluded: "The Constitution of California prohibits the denial of bail solely because of petitioner's dangerous propensities."

open where dangerousness might be the subject of an evidentiary hearing. If such a system were thought to be weighted against defendants, it could be coupled with a presumption in favor of release which the state would have to overcome before pretrial detention could be approved.

It would seem considerably fairer to detain a defendant without bail after a full hearing on the issue of dangerousness than to detain him on a judicial hunch of dangerousness through the deceitful practice of setting bail beyond his financial capabilities. Such a system would also remove the obvious discrimination on the basis of wealth inherent in the use of money bail.

On the other hand, it is not difficult to imagine how a system such as that described could be abused. The experience in some European countries, and in the juvenile courts of this country, which have systems not too far different from that described, shows that it is very easy for the fine language of the statute to be ignored and the requisite finding of dangerousness to be made routinely in a majority of cases.

As a practical matter, given the uncertainties involved, it is not very likely that this kind of system will be considered very seriously. The question nonetheless remains: Would a more explicit system be better for all concerned?

21

Bail Reform: Present and Future

THE bail reform movement began in 1961 in New York City with the creation of the Manhattan Bail Project. The project was developed and funded initially by chemical industrialist Louis Schweitzer after he had seen the realities of the American system of bail during a visit to the Brooklyn House of Detention. Schweitzer was struck with the realization that bail, a mechanism to provide for the release of defendants prior to trial, was in fact doing just the opposite—causing the detention of vast numbers of indigent persons who could and should have been released but were not because bail, even in modest amounts, was beyond their capabilities.

The situation Schweitzer discovered was certainly not unique to the Brooklyn House of Detention. A quarter of a century earlier, Arthur Beeley, in his landmark study of bail practices in the Chicago criminal courts, described a similar situation. In the mid-1950s Professor Caleb Foote directed studies of bail practices in Philadelphia and New York City which disclosed a number of the abuses and problems in the American system of money bail. In a sense, these studies, which documented the unfairness and irrationality of the money bail system, were the foundation for the bail reform movement.

The rapid proliferation of own recognizance release projects modeled after the Manhattan Bail Project is indicative of the fact that dissatisfaction with the American system of bail was indeed widespread. This, plus the fact that own recognizance was such an easy, workable solution to the most obvious inequities of money bail, gave the bail reform movement considerable early success. By 1965 over fifty O.R. programs were operating in jurisdictions across the United States, and in 1964 and 1965 national conferences were held on the problem of bail and criminal justice and on the implementation of O.R. programs.

After the 1965 conference, national interest in O.R. projects waned considerably. In the period from 1965 to 1970, many of the programs ceased to operate, and most of those that remained made little progress. While the O.R. projects were struggling, however, important bail reform legislation and further innovation by the Vera Foundation in New York City kept the movement alive and laid the groundwork for a resurgence in the 1970s.

In 1964 Senator Sam Ervin introduced a series of bills to reform bail practices in the federal courts which eventually culminated in the Bail Reform Act of 1966. Most important of the many changes brought about by the Federal Bail Reform Act was the presumption it created in favor of the use of personal recognizance release. A second important change was the development of a series of nonfinancial conditions which could be imposed in lieu of surety bail.

As a result of the Federal Bail Reform Act, and the activities of the District of Columbia Bail Agency in administering it, the release rate in the District surpasses that being achieved in other jurisdictions, particularly for felony defendants. Moreover, in the District close to two-thirds of all criminal defendants are released on nonfinancial conditions, and less than 20 percent on money bail.

The second important legislative development of the 1960s was passage in Illinois of a 10 percent deposit bail provision. Influenced by the success of the Manhattan Bail Project, and prodded by a considerable bail bond scandal in Chicago, drafters of a new Illinois Code of Criminal Procedure sought to eliminate the professional bondsman by providing that the 10 percent bonding fee which defendants normally paid a commercial bondsman would instead be paid to the court. While the fee paid to a bondsman was nonrefundable, the court, under the new law, would return to the defendant 90 percent of his deposit upon completion of the case.

The 10 percent deposit system has worked well in Illinois, and has now been adopted, either by statute or court rule, in a number of other jurisdictions. Oregon, Kentucky, and Philadelphia have followed Illinois' lead and give the deposit bail option to every defendant. Other jurisdictions have simply added deposit bail as an option for the judge to use in appropriate cases. Experience indicates, however, that judges tend to use this option only infrequently.

While the desire to eliminate, or at least drastically reduce, the role of commercial bondsmen is one motivation for deposit bail, its principal justification is the same as that for conditional releases—a realization that straight own recognizance is available to only a select class of criminal defendants. Deposit bail is seen as a less onerous form of money bail for those defendants forced to rely upon money bond to secure release. Clearly, for those defendants with the financial ability to post bail, deposit bonds are much less expensive than surety bonds.

A third innovation of the 1960s that has become increasingly important in the 1970s is police citation release. In 1964 the Vera Foundation assisted the New York City Police Department in implementing stationhouse citation releases in selected precincts in Manhattan. This was later extended to all of Manhattan, and eventually to the city as a whole. During this same period, a number of police agencies in California were experimenting with the use of citations both at the jail and in the field. Since then, citation releases for misdemeanor defendants have grown in usage and become commonplace in many jurisdictions across the country.

Citation releases are important in that they offer the speediest release possibility. Thus far, however, the use of citations has been generally limited to misdemeanor defendants. A major issue for the future is whether such releases can be extended to felony defendants as well.

NATIONAL BAIL STUDY

Clearly, the bail reform movement has accomplished much. Perhaps its major success has simply been the education and enlightenment of judges as to the importance of the bail decision, the need to consider individual factors in the setting of bail, and the consequences of pretrial detention. The obvious correlation which the National Bail Study showed between the development of pretrial release programs and the substantial increase both in the overall percentage of defendants released and the proportion released on own recognizance and other forms of nonfinancial release clearly bespeaks the success these programs have collectively enjoyed in reforming American bail practices.

In felony cases, the proportion of defendants released prior to trial increased by nearly a third—from less than 50 percent in 1962 to over 65 percent in 1971. This change was almost entirely due to an increase in the use of nonfinancial releases. Release on money bail had remained about the same, 44 percent of all defendants. Release on O.R. and other forms of nonfinancial release increased from 5 to 23 percent.

Similar change also took place with respect to misdemeanor defendants. The overall release rate increased from 60 percent in 1962 to over 70 percent in 1971. For misdemeanor cases continuing beyond first appearance, the release rate increased from 79 to 88 percent. Again, nonfinancial releases accounted for most of the change, increasing from 10 to 30 percent of all defendants. Moreover, in misdemeanor cases, the use of nonfinancial releases had replaced money bail as the predominant form of pretrial release in several cities. By 1971 the use of nonfinancial releases was equal to or exceeded the number of bail releases in eleven of the nineteen cities studied. Considering only those misdemeanor cases which advanced beyond a single court appearance, the study showed that in ten cities close to 50 percent or more of the defendants were released without money bonds.

By 1971 it was evident that the use of nonfinancial releases was not contingent upon the intervention of a pretrial release program. In cities with pretrial release programs, the programs were actively involved in only a fraction of the total number of nonfinancial releases. Moreover, cities without pretrial release programs often had nonfinancial release rates comparable to and sometimes greater than cities in which programs were operating.

The long-term use of nonfinancial releases appears assured. Indeed, since 1971 all evidence points to the fact that the use of nonfinancial releases has continued to expand. Two areas where growth is most evident are in the use of police citation releases and conditional own recognizance releases.

The National Bail Study showed that, not only were more defendants being released in 1971, but they were also securing releases more quickly than in 1962. It was found that nonfinancial release is generally faster than bail release and that, as a result of the considerable increase in nonfinancial releases, the average time from first appearance to pretrial release was reduced from 1962 to 1971.

The effect of the increase in the proportion of defendants on pretrial release on the problems of failure to appear and pretrial delay is not totally clear. There was an increase in the rate of nonappearance from 6 percent in 1962 to about 10 percent in 1971, and there probably exists some general relationship between the higher release rate and the increase in the percentage of defendants failing to appear. However, it was also observed that cities with the highest rates of pretrial release and the highest rates of nonfinancial release did not have the highest nonappearance rates. As to the relative effectiveness of bail and O.R. in terms of ensuring appearance in court, there is no conclusive evidence as to whether one method is more effective than the other. The nonappearance rates for defendants on these two forms of release did not vary significantly in most of the cities studied.

Not surprisingly, the National Bail Study showed an obvious relationship between a defendant's release or detention status and the time it takes to bring cases to dispostion. In both felony and misdemeanor cases, it took the courts considerably longer to dispose of cases in which the defendant had secured release. Consequently, one would expect that the increased release rate from 1962 to 1971 would have resulted in longer periods of pretrial delay in 1971. While this was found to be the case, the increased delay in felony cases was not as great as the expanded release rate would suggest. Apparently, many courts have adapted to the increased problems of handling felony cases by altering court procedures. With misdemeanor cases, the problem of increased delay from first appearance to disposition was more serious. It was found that fewer cases were disposed at first appearance—39 percent in 1962 but 33 percent in 1971—and that continuing cases took longer. The increased availability of release prior to court and the increased use of nonfinancial releases, which cost the defendant nothing, apparently resulted in fewer defendants choosing to settle their cases quickly.

THE FUTURE OF BAIL REFORM

In assessing the past and looking to the future of bail reform, three questions seem pertinent: (1) What is the future of surety bail? (2) How should the various pretrial release options which now exist be integrated into a cohesive scheme of pretrial release? (3) What should the role of a pretrial release program be in this system?

1. The Future of Surety Bail

The future of surety bail can be summarized simply: It has no future. It does not now perform any important system function and will not long remain a part of the criminal justice system.

Commercial bail will not, of course, go out without a fight, and its political power should not be underestimated. In the end, however, its demise seems sure because its principal claims have been stripped away. Two major states—Illinois and Oregon—and the nation's fourth largest city—Philadelphia—have already demonstrated conclusively that the deposit system of bail works, and that the bondsman is unnecessary.

The obvious advantage to the defendant of a system in which his security is returned if he appears for trial, rather than being absorbed by the fee of a bondsman, makes it certain that, in the absence of any real benefit to the state from the commercial surety arrangement, in time deposit bail will totally replace commercial surety bail.

Two principal arguments have thus far been advanced by the bondsmen to justify their continued existence: (1) Without their services, the failure to appear rate of defendants would skyrocket; and (2) They are necessary to apprehend defendants who skip out on their bail and flee prosecution. Both claims are quite clearly false.

All the evidence is that the failure to appear rate in Illinois, which has the longest experience with deposit bail, is not noticeably different from that in other jurisdictions, or from what it was in Illinois during the time the state allowed surety bail. Whatever changes there have been seem more a function of increasing release rates, rather than of the change in the method of release. The experience in Philadelphia and Oregon is much less, but to the extent that there is evidence available it is much the same: no adverse effect.

Less information is available concerning the apprehension of persons who fail to appear, but what there is strongly suggests that the role of a bondsman is more of a clerk than a policeman. A high percentage of those who fail to appear return to court voluntarily or in response to a phone call. The police apprehend the majority of the remainder. For the most part, the bondsman simply makes sure that the court is aware that a previously bailed defendant has now been apprehended by the police or otherwise returned to the court process.

These facts are illustrated by a 1972 study of over 1,000 bailed defendants who had failed to appear in Los Angeles County. Conducted by the Office of the County Counsel in Los Angeles, the study was designed to determine the extent of positive actions on the part of bondsmen to return defendants to the judicial process. In only 11 percent of the cases was there found to be any action by the bondsman to return the defendant, and in only 6 percent of the cases was the defendant actually located and arrested by a bondsman. In 3 percent of the total cases, the defendant returned voluntarily after a letter or phone call from the bondsman, and in 2 percent of the cases the defendant was arrested by the police after a bondsman had notified them of the defendant's whereabouts. In the remaining 89 percent of the cases, there was no record of any involvement by the bondsman in returning the defendant to the court process.[1]

To be sure, a bondsman will occasionally make an apprehension, and some individual bondsmen probably make quite a few. Generally, however, given the difficulties in tracking down a true fugitive, it is not good economics for the bondsman to pursue the offender. Moreover, even in those few cases where the bondsman does perform this function, his role seems basically undesirable from the point of view of social policy. For the same reasons that society does not have a system of bounty hunters for serious offenses, society should not employ them here.

This is not to say that the bondsman has not often played an honorable and important role in the past. Despite the long history of corruption and improper collusion in the industry, most individual bondsmen have been honest businessmen. As long as the system demanded surety bail, the person who provided that service did the defendants a service. The question now, however, is not the character of the bondsman, but the need for the service. It seems clear that it is not needed.

2. A Cohesive Pretrial Release System

The challenge for the bail reform movement today is to integrate the various pretrial release options which now exist into a cohesive system of pretrial release. From the Manhattan Bail Project to the present, the bail reform movement has moved from innovation to innovation without much effort to rationalize the developments in one jurisdiction with those in others. It has progressed without a concerted effort to capitalize on the experiences of others. To be sure, the Manhattan Bail Project served as a model for a number of the following programs, but each program developed individually and significant differences emerged in the organizational structures and operating procedures of the various programs. With the development of other pretrial release options—such as supervised and conditional

1. Office of the County Counsel, "Survey of County Counsel Case Files of Actions to Exonerate Bail Forfeiture," mimeographed (Los Angeles, Calif.: Office of the County Counsel, 1972).

releases, police citations, and deposit bail—the need for some overall framework has become even greater.

A forward-looking pretrial release system should have two objectives: first, to ensure that each defendant receives the quickest and least restrictive form of release compatible with the smooth administration of criminal justice and the public safety, and second, that the system be one that is reasonably cost-effective. As the quickest and least restrictive methods of release for defendants are also generally the least expensive, these two objectives are largely compatible.

A well-designed system of pretrial release should operate something like a series of filters—each stage screening and releasing the defendants it can handle, while passing the remainder through to the next stage where they can be looked at more closely. The accompanying graph shows how such a system might operate.

A MODEL PRETRIAL RELEASE SYSTEM

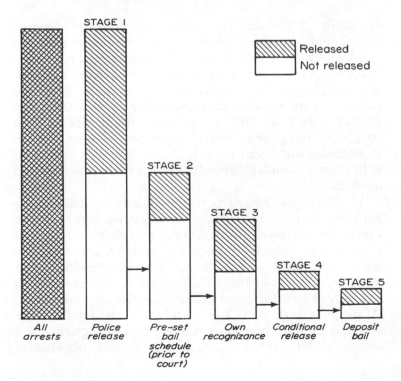

Police Release. One of the most important components of this system is a much greater release authority and responsibility for the police. The police generally create the detention issue by making the arrest. At this stage, they have more information and more rapid information than anyone else about the need for continued detention.

Police release of arrestees on written promises to appear consequently provide the quickest and least restrictive method of release. Since they do not require the employment of additional personnel, police citations are also the least expensive to employ. In addition, field citations reduce police expense in transporting, booking, and jailing arrestees and are, therefore, cost-effective. Because not all arrestees will be suitable for release on the street, the backup use of stationhouse citation releases should also be instituted. Citations should provide for the release of the majority of misdemeanants and many felony defendants as well.

Pre-set Bail Schedules. The second stage of release procedures should be a pre-set schedule of deposit bail amounts which allows the arrestees to know immediately what bail is required and to secure prompt release when they have the necessary funds. This provision is less important when the defendants are immediately presented in court without any waiting period, but it can still be a useful device. The schedules used prior to court should not, however, be the standard by which bail is set in court. Once the defendant is in court, an individualized bail decision is possible and desirable.

An alternative system is to give the police bail-setting authority for cases not released on citations. Either system would operate largely automatically and should require no additional personnel. In promoting early release, they also reduce the detention population and are, therefore, cost-effective. The use of bail schedules in misdemeanor cases has worked well and created few administrative problems. If the police are given the authority to depart from the schedule in individual cases where they feel the scheduled amount is not sufficient to ensure the defendant's appearance in court, pre-set bail schedules should also be usable in felony cases.

Own Recognizance. The next stage in processing is appearance in court. Here two things are necessary. First, there should be a presumption in favor of nonfinancial release. Second, there should be a well-organized pretrial release progam capable of providing rapid, accurate information to the judge.

Fifteen years of experience with own recognizance has demonstrated that, for a sizable percentage of criminal defendants, money bail requirements are not necessary to ensure appearance in court. At this time, however, we simply do not know how far into the defendant population own recognizance can be extended before the rate of nonappearance or the rate of pretrial crime becomes unacceptable. We do not know what personal attributes of defendants make them highly likely to reappear for trial, and therefore acceptable own recognizance release risks, and what attributes make defendants unacceptable. These are important questions to answer because, as a jurisdiction moves to the use of more restrictive forms of release, such as conditional releases, the cost of administering the pretrial release system increases.

Conditional Nonfinancial Release. For those defendants who cannot be released in any of the ways already discussed, releases on nonfinancial conditions should be the next consideration. The experience in the District of Columbia suggests that conditional releases are a viable method for increasing both the number of nonfinancial releases and the overall pretrial release rate.

The danger in conditional release is that the judges may overuse conditions to the neglect of straight own recognizance. Owing to the need to supervise defendants on conditional release, this method of release is considerably more costly than straight own recognizance. The administrative problems of conditional releases used on a large scale are significant, and the benefits in terms of helping the defendant and protecting the community would appear to be minimal. To be effective, conditional releases must be imposed selectively and meaningfully. Used in this manner in the cases of "higher risk" defendants, conditional releases can be an important supplement to the use of straight own recognizance.

Deposit Bail. For those defendants for whom nonfinancial release is deemed inadequate to ensure appearance in court, the court may set money bail. Since surety bail will no longer be permitted, all bail amounts may be met by percentage deposit. This does not affect the judge's capacity to set very high bail where he so chooses. It does mean, however, that where the defendant makes the bail amount and fulfills his commitment to appear in court, he will receive all or most of his deposit back.

It could, of course, be argued that since the defendant receives his deposit back if he appears, deposit bail is as fair as nonfinancial release and should, therefore, be used more widely, rather than simply as a last resort. Strengthening this argument is the possibility that since the defendant has a financial stake in appearing and securing the return of his deposit, he may be more likely to appear than if he were on own recognizance.

To the extent that the defendant is able to meet the deposit bail amount, there may be something to this argument, and some testing of the relative merits of deposit bail and own recognizance in terms of ensuring court appearances would be desirable. The fact that to date there appears to be no difference in the failure to appear rates for defendants on different forms of release does not mean that the present failure to appear rate is acceptable or that it could not be lower. In a sense, every released defendant who fails to appear when his presence is required represents a failure in the pretrial release system, and every avenue should be explored to reduce the number of failures. This should include experimentation with different forms of release, as well as altering the court procedures used in notifying defendants of upcoming court dates. To the extent that deposit bail did come to be considered the preferable form of release, however, it would be necessary for the pretrial release program and the judges to review regularly the amounts set, and to grant some form of nonfinancial release to defendants who should be released but cannot meet the amount set.

The Oregon Plan. No state or local system now in effect is quite like the one described. The Federal Bail Reform Act, which until now has been considered the model for bail reform, comes close. It does not emphasize police release, however, and, more importantly, provides for deposit bail only if the judge specifically authorizes it. The Illinois statute cures the latter point, but does not contain the presumption in favor of nonfinancial release.

The scheme which comes closest to providing the framework needed for bail reform in the decade ahead is the Oregon statute adopted in 1973.[2] This legislation combines the federal act presumption in favor of nonfinancial release with the deposit bail provisions of the Illinois statute. While it does not promote police release, it permits it, and overall it provides a good starting point for the kind of legislation needed for the future.

3. The Future of Pretrial Release Programs

Over the past fifteen years, pretrial release programs have evolved from small, experimental undertakings designed to assist indigents in securing pretrial release into the large, comprehensive pretrial court services agencies which are operating in a number of jurisdictions today. The cost of administering these programs has increased accordingly. Recent figures show that the Brooklyn Pretrial Services Agency operates on two million dollars annually, and the Washington, D.C., Bail Agency and Philadelphia Court Services Agency on approximately one million. Several other programs have annual budgets of $200,000 to $500,000. Without federal support, it is highly doubtful that local jurisdictions can afford to carry such programs for any extended period of time.

It is imperative that these programs not terminate when federal funding is withdrawn. The cohesive pretrial release

2. Oregon Rev. Stats. §§ 135.230-.290 (1973).

system described above demands individualized bail decisions and maximum use of nonfinancial releases. Pretrial
release programs can provide the individualized attention
and also be a powerful force in seeing that the system is
not abused.

To continue as long-term operations, however, the programs will very likely have to reassess their purpose and
redefine their objectives. By doing so, they will probably be
able to reduce the cost of their operation. We believe, for
example, that the programs must reconsider the need for
their involvement in misdemeanor and low-grade felony
offenses. Can the police not perform the same service more
quickly and less expensively than the program? If the police
can assume the responsibility of granting nonfinancial
releases in the less serious cases, the program's time and
money can be more properly focused on those cases where
the release decision is more critical. It is the more serious
felony cases where the intervention of a pretrial release
program would appear to be the most critical.

In focusing upon the more controversial cases, however,
the program may find that its ability to secure releases has
greatly diminished. According to the accepted pretrial
release eligibility criteria, the program may find few defendants who qualify. If those defendants whom the program
was previously releasing are still being released anyway, this
will not be a detriment. If it spurs the program to experiment with its release criteria and standards to promote the
release of more defendants, it will be an advantage. In
addition to preparing background information and release
recommendations for the judge, and supervising defendants
on pretrial release, the programs should play a strong
planning and monitoring role for the entire system. They
should keep track of overall release rates and the proportion
of defendants released by each of the various stages of the
system. They should also be aware of failure to appear rates
and constantly seek to develop a better overall system.

To improve their cost-effectiveness, pretrial release programs must evaluate the efficiency of their current procedures. The question of whether the overall cost of the
program is offset by savings in jail detention costs is

important but very difficult to answer. The more fruitful course would be to assess the cost-efficiency of each area of program activity. For example, are the time and money expended upon verifications and post-release supervision well spent? Are there less expensive but equally effective methods for performing these functions?

In short, pretrial release programs must reassert their innovativeness. They must assess the gains that have already been made in pretrial release practices and redefine their goals accordingly. Quite obviously, the type of pretrial release program which will be most effective will vary from one jurisdiction to another depending upon what the current pretrial release practices are and the attitudes of the local judiciary toward the program and nonfinancial release generally. For example, the suggestion that the programs focus their efforts on felony defendants assumes that the police and the court will undertake the responsibility of granting nonfinancial releases in misdemeanor cases without program intervention. In many jurisdictions, the pretrial release system has not evolved to a point where this is likely to occur. In any case, whether one is concerned with starting a new program or reorganizing an existing one, the dominant concern must be the overall system of pretrial release and defining the program's role within it.

APPENDIX

National Bail Study—
Case Selection Procedures

THE National Bail Study was undertaken in order to gain some understanding of what changes, if any, had occurred in the pretrial release practices of selected jurisdictions between the years 1962 and 1971. The study was designed to select at random 200 felony and 200 misdemeanor cases from each year, which would reflect the bail practices in each of the cities studied.

The sample was drawn from the initial appearance calendar in the lower criminal court servicing the city under study. In most jurisdictions, one or two lower courts handled the bulk of the cases, and thus it was not difficult to identify the court or courts from which to select our sample. In a few jurisdictions, however, several lower courts existed in a single city, and there was no central records office from which to draw a citywide sample. In these cities, our sample was taken from the court which served the central city area. Thus, for example, the Boston sample was drawn totally from the Boston Municipal Court, and the Los Angeles sample was from the central Los Angeles Municipal Court. Kansas City presented a special problem since the city limits encompass parts of three different counties. The bulk of the population, however, resides in Jackson County, and thus our sample was from the Justice of the Peace Courts in that county. Because of the unavailability of court records in several of the Justice Courts, however, the Kansas City sample was limited to the third and fifth district Justice Courts in Jackson County.

In two cities, it was necessary to sample more than 200 cases in 1971. Thus, the 1971 felony sample from Chicago was drawn to include 100 defendants appearing in each of the two felony arraignment courts, 50 defendants appearing in the separate Narcotics Court, and 40 defendants appearing initially in Holiday Court, for a total sample of 290 cases. Also, since the lower court in Chicago includes a number of area courts, our sample was constructed by selecting 40 defendants appearing in each of ten area courts, for a total sample of 400 defendants. The 1971 felony sample in Washington, D.C., also included additional cases to reflect the bail practices in both the Superior Court and the federal District Court. In 1971 most felony defendants appeared in the Superior Court, but those charged with the most serious offenses were handled by the District Court. The Washington, D.C., 1971 felony sample, thus, includes 200 Superior Court cases and 50 District Court cases.

The sample was also constructed to reflect the bail-setting practices of as many different magistrates as possible. In jurisdictions where the magistrates rotated to the initial appearance calendar quarterly—as was most often the case—or less frequently, the samples were drawn by randomly entering the court docket once during each quarter of the year and selecting the next 50 felony and misdemeanor cases. In the Washington, D.C., Superior Court, where the judges rotated monthly, the sample was drawn by selecting 20 consecutive felony and misdemeanor cases from ten different months.

A problem developed in selecting consecutive misdemeanor cases, however, in that a mass police arrest for disorderly conduct, prostitution, or gambling, for example, would result in one offense predominating the sample. For this reason, the misdemeanor cases were taken consecutively, except that where more than three defendants were charged with the same offense in succession, the coder would take only the first three and then skip to the first defendant charged with a different offense. Defendants charged with traffic violations—other than drunk driving or vehicular manslaughter—and public intoxication were not included in the samples unless these charges were included with other offenses.

Each defendant whose case number fell within our sample was traced through the court records from the time of his initial appearance until disposition. For felony defendants, this meant tracking them through two levels of court in most jurisdictions. All facts bearing on pretrial release status were noted. Information recorded included: the number of times bail was set and the amount at which it was set; whether the defendant was released or not and, if released, the date of such release; whether the release was by citation, O.R., or bond and, if by bond, whether the bond was full cash, surety, deposit, or property; the number of days from first court appearance to disposition; the number of days the defendant was on pretrial release; and the number of times the defendant failed to appear and the length of time he was lost to the system, as well as how his failure to appear affected his pretrial release status after his return to court.

NATIONAL BAIL STUDY
DATA COLLECTION SHEET

Name _____

Case No._____   Charge _____

                                       Felony or Misd

Bail Set	Bail Made	Project Rec.	Judge
O.R.	O.R.	Yes No	
Less than $250	Less than $250		
$250-499	$250-499		
$500-999	$500-999		
$1,000-2,999	$1,000-2,999		
$3,000-4,999	$3,000-4,999		
$5,000-9,999	$5,000-9,999		
$10,000-14,999	$10,000-14,999		
$15,000 and over	$15,000 and over		
No Bail	No Bail		
No Data	No Data		

(If bail amount was changed, circle each amount at which bail was set.)

Date Arrested _____   Date Released on Bail_____

                                                       on citation_____

                                                       on O.R._____

                                       No Release _____

Date of first appearance_____ Number of appearances_____

Date of last appearance_____ Time to disposition_____

Failure to Appear
Date Bench Warrant Issued_____   Date Recalled_____

Disposition
LC_____ HC_____

Guilty_____ N/G_____ Jail_____ Prison_____ Prob_____

INDEX